Be My Witness

Be My Witness

The Great Commission for Preachers

Marvin A. McMickle

Be My Witness: The Great Commission for Preachers

Judson Press has made every effort to trace the ownership of all quotes. In the event of a question arising from the use of a quote, we regret any error made and will be pleased to make the necessary correction in future printings and editions of this book.

Cover and Interior design by Wendy Ronga, Hampton Design Group. www.hamptondesigngroup.com.

Library of Congress Cataloging-in-Publication data
Cataloging-in-Publication Data available upon request.
Contact cip@judsonpress.com.

Printed in the U.S.A.
First printing, 2016.

Contents

Acknowledgments

Books are written within a certain period of time, but the formation of the content of certain books is a lifetime in the making. Most writers will agree that the time they spend in the physical writing process is one thing, but the time it took to develop the ideas and to become convicted by and convinced of the content of the book is an entirely different matter. This book was written within a one-year period of time, but it has been in formation for my entire 45-year ministry as a preacher, teacher, and author.

I want to acknowledge the persons whose hands and hearts have helped to shape not only my ministry, but also my life. Martin Luther King Jr., who came to my hometown of Chicago in 1966 for a civil rights demonstration that altered the course of my life as a young man. Kenneth Mull of Aurora College in Illinois, who was my first scholarly model. James A. Sanders and James H. Cone at Union Theological Seminary in New York City, whose lectures and writings continue to inspire and inform me more than 40 years later. William A. Jones Jr., Samuel Dewitt Proctor, and Gardner C. Taylor, who were my preaching models and mentors in New York City. It was from them that I began to discern how to relate preaching to public policy; a central theme of this book.

I also want to acknowledge the schools and church groups before whom the content of this book was shared on the way to final publication. I am grateful for the opportunity to share portions of this material with American Baptist College in Nashville, Tennessee, Ashland Theological Seminary in Ohio, Baldwin Wallace College of Ohio, Boston University, Chicago Theological Seminary, Duke Divinity School in Durham, North Carolina, Houghton College of New York, Howard University School of Divinity, Princeton Theological Seminary in New Jersey, Trinity Evangelical Seminary of Ohio, Virginia Theological Seminary, Virginia Union University Wake Forest Divinity School, and Yale Divinity School in New Haven, Connecticut. I am grateful for my colleagues at American Baptist Churches of the Great Rivers Region, of New Jersey, of New York State, of Ohio, and of the Rocky Mountains. I am also indebted to President James Perkins and the Progressive National Baptist Convention for offering invaluable feedback to the themes raised in this book when I shared with them.

I am grateful for the staff at Judson Press that remains open to and supportive of the ideas I have for new books. What appears in this book is not what was initially presented to them when I turned in my manuscript. Their skillful and sensitive editorial and structural revisions may be invisible to the readers of this book, but they are apparent to me, and I am thankful for their careful work on this project!

Ministry in all of its forms is often a collaborative process with one's family and friends. Therefore, I acknowledge the invaluable support of my life-partner and best friend, Peggy McMickle. She, more than anyone else, has seen what it takes to live out the ministry I have attempted to perform. She is the one who is often left behind when I travel across the country to preach or lecture. Even when I am at home, I am often locked away behind a computer screen or in search of a footnote. I deeply appreciate her sacrifices. It is a true saying and worthy of affirmation that "I am because we are."

Introduction

Certainly much has changed in the two thousand years that separate Peter, James, John, and the other original disciples from those of us who are preaching the gospel today. We are far removed from those disciples both in physical distance and in sociopolitical context. They preached primarily in the context of the Greco-Roman world stretching from Western Europe to the Fertile Crescent and into the Nile Valley. We are preaching with an awareness of a much larger world that includes all of the Americas, the islands of the Caribbean, the nations of Asia and Africa, and lands of the Far East and the Pacific Rim.

Having acknowledged that, I believe there is a timeless quality about the challenge Jesus gives in Acts 1:6-8 to all who feel called to preach. I invite all preachers to consider their work through the lens of this text, which says in part, "Be my witnesses in Jerusalem, and in all Judea and Samaria, and to the ends of the earth."

This passage can and should serve both as the basis for a theology of preaching and as an ongoing challenge for preachers so far as the breadth and depth of their preaching content is concerned. Think about this passage as a combination ordination charge, pastoral installation message, and seminary commencement address. In the final moments of Jesus' time on earth and in his final word to the disciples with whom he had been traveling for the preceding three years, our Savior gave this charge, providing them with an understanding of the *purpose* of the preacher: *Be my witnesses*. He set forth the *parameters* within which he expected their preaching to operate, in terms of both content and context: *Jerusalem*, *Judea*, *Samaria*, *and the ends of the earth*. He then informed them that they should not consider uttering even a word until *the Holy Spirit had come upon them*, for he was the source of their *power*.

This book makes the argument that there is little more that preachers need to know about their role and responsibilities as those who preach the gospel of Jesus Christ than what can be gleaned from this one passage of Scripture. I have long presumed that there is no one acceptable or appropriate model of sermon design and delivery against which all other models must be compared. Great preaching can be heard flowing out of various vocal forms, from men and women, in churches of all ethnic groups, in topical, doctrinal, and exegetical approaches. Moreover, preaching styles will continue to evolve with the times in which the preacher is living. What this book asserts is that while the sound and style of a sermon may change over the years, what does not change is the core of the gospel message and the central mission of the preacher in the world. "The grass withers and the flowers fall, but the word of our God endures forever" (Isaiah 40:8).

Please note that this is not a book about how to preach. The how-to of preaching is about sermon design, modes of sermon delivery, use of vocal techniques, the appropriate degree of passion or enthusiasm to be employed, and the most effective length of a sermon for a twenty-first-century audience. I have written about all of those things in other books.[1]

This book is intended to help preachers not only to think about the content of their sermons from week to week but to plan a schedule of sermon themes and topics that can serve them year in and year out for as long as they are involved in the preaching task. The primary thesis of this book is that preachers in the twenty-first century should pay close attention to what Jesus said about preaching and sermon content to his original disciples in the first century AD.

The central issue here is sermon content and context. What are the themes and topics we are preaching about and where are the places we are willing to go as preachers—in physical geography and in cultural reference? That is what this Acts 1:6-8 passage offers when it becomes the lens through which a theology of preaching is framed. This text contains instructions from Jesus to his first disciples that still remain relevant for present-day preachers on the following five issues:

1. What theme or message should be at the center of our preaching?
2. What should be the hallmarks of our lifestyle as preachers?

3. Where should we be prepared to go in fulfillment of our preaching ministry?

4. What will constitute adequate preparation for our preaching ministry?

5. How can an effective and faithful preaching ministry be sustained over time?

These and other questions lie at the heart of this book that invites everyone who preaches to do so with Jesus' charge in mind: *"Be my witness."*

NOTES

1. Marvin A. McMickle, *Living Water for Thirsty Souls* (Valley Forge, PA: Judson, 2001); *The Star Book on Preaching* (Valley Forge, PA: Judson, 2006); and *Shaping the Claim* (Minneapolis: Fortress, 2008).

CHAPTER 1

Why Do We Need a Theology of Preaching?

"And this good news of the kingdom will be proclaimed throughout the world, as a testimony to all the nations; and then the end will come." —Matthew 24:14

I have spent forty-five years of my life involved in what James Earl Massey calls "the burdensome joy of preaching."[1] I fully understand the challenges associated with preaching over the course of many years. Week after week, month after month, year after year, the preacher stands before a group of people and seeks to say something fresh and impactful. Even if the preacher on any given occasion is not the pastor of that (or any) congregation, he or she still has the challenge of finding a text, shaping an idea, and delivering a sermon to people who may have heard hundreds if not thousands of sermons before, many of them on the very same text the preacher has selected for the upcoming Sunday service.

Those who are invited by God, ordained by the church, and empowered by the Holy Spirit to preach the gospel of Jesus Christ experience great joy. Because there is no nobler vocation to which one can be called and committed, preaching must be approached with rigor and integrity. However, a burden is also attached to the joy of preaching because the preacher needs to prepare not only the sermon, but his or her own mind and heart for the preaching task—over and over again.

How does the preacher avoid the very real risk of becoming too narrow in the selection of themes and topics? How does the preacher find ways to speak to the generational divides confronting the twenty-first century church? How does the preacher find time for the personal spiritual formation that is essential for effective preaching? These burdens must be understood and addressed by those who preach on a regular basis. And in order to accomplish these tasks with consistency and intentionally, the framework of a theology of preaching is needed.

What Are You Going to Preach Next Sunday?

One could easily pair James Earl Massey's observation about "the burdensome joy of preaching" with Gardner Taylor's equally descriptive phrase, "the sweet torture of Sunday morning."[2] For Taylor the sweetness was in the preaching moment itself—in the confluence of a waiting congregation, an anointed message, and a human vessel ready to be used by the Holy Spirit. Anyone who ever heard Gardner Taylor preach observed the "sweet side" of preaching.

What was less obvious was the torture that came, even for a preacher of Dr. Taylor's caliber, in the knowledge that no sooner had he finished preaching on one Sunday, than he had to gear up to begin all over again—the whole process of text and topic selection and sermon design and delivery. Those who have never had the privilege or the responsibility of standing before a congregation or some other worshiping community on a regular basis have little if any appreciation for this challenge. Having just finished the sermon for one week, the preacher is immediately confronted with the awareness that the same process must be repeated starting almost at once.

When children play the game hide-and-seek, the seeker calls out, "Ready or not, here I come!" At that point the search begins for those who are hiding—whether the hiders are fully hidden or not. That same phrase rings true for preachers on a weekly basis as the fast-approaching Sunday morning calls, "Ready or not, here I come!"

This anticipation of Sunday should not be confused with the popular sermon title by Tony Campolo "It's Friday, but Sunday's Coming."[3] When Campolo speaks about Sunday coming, he is encouraging us to recall that the crucified Christ became our risen Savior three days later. His sermon is a resilient reminder that no matter how bleak or hopeless things may seem at any given moment in time, the same power that raised Jesus from the dead can empower Christ's church today to do great things for God. That joyful proclamation should be at the very center of all Christian preaching.

When Taylor used the phrase "the sweet torture of Sunday morning," he was pointing to something very different: the challenging rhythm of weekly preaching and the rigor of preparing both the content of the sermon and the heart and spirit of the preacher. This rigor is required so that when Sunday comes, the preacher will have something substantive to say. Gardner Taylor spoke to this challenge when he observed that "the vision may tarry, but Sunday morning does not."[4]

This tension between the fast approach of Sunday morning and the slow development of the sermon idea, much less the full sermon itself, was powerfully echoed by Reinhold Niebuhr. Before he began his stellar academic career as a Christian ethicist at Union Theological Seminary in New York City, Niebuhr was pastor of a German evangelical congregation in Detroit from 1915 to 1928. It did not take long for Niebuhr to discover the pressures of weekly preaching. Writing in 1915, his first year as a pastor, he said something that has remained true in the intervening one hundred years:

> Now that I have preached about a dozen sermons, I find that I am repeating myself. A different text simply means a different pretext for saying the same thing over again. . . . They say a young preacher must catch his second wind before he can really preach. I'd better catch it pretty soon or the weekly sermon will become a terrible chore. . . . I almost dread the approach of a new Sabbath. I don't know whether I can ever

> accustom myself to the task of bringing light and inspiration in regular weekly installments. . . . The prophet speaks only when he is inspired. The parish preacher must speak whether he is inspired or not.[5]

True enough, there are many ways by which preachers can try to kick-start the vision. As I have set forth in two earlier books, preachers may use a lectionary, follow a liturgical calendar, employ a theological or doctrinal rotation, or seek to match their text and topic to major national holidays or current events.[6] While these devices can help to settle on a biblical passage or on a preaching topic, there remains the sometimes elusive task of actually imagining and designing the structure and content of the sermon. Preachers must learn to deal with the two-sided dimension of their vocation, which is deciding what to say in their sermons and then being prepared to say it by the time Sunday morning rolls around again and again and again!

Two Hazards for Busy Preachers

If the preacher is not careful, one of two things can begin to happen as he or she wrestles with the rigors of weekly preaching. First, there is the chance that the preacher will not begin to look for a sermon text, title, and theme until the last minute. The work of ministry in any of the forms referenced above can be all-consuming of both time and energy. In the midst of pastoral visitations, committee meetings, civic and denominational duties, and time for one's self and one's family, the preparation for preaching seems to get pushed back further and further into the week. Then, seemingly suddenly, Saturday night has rolled around and the only thing between the preacher and a waiting congregation is a blank computer screen or an untouched writing pad. As a pastor in Rochester, New York, recently said when confronted with this situation from time to time, "You end up looking for something you can heat up and serve real fast."

To expand the analogy, in the spirit as in the flesh, fast food is convenient, but it is seldom as nutritious as something that has been seasoned and simmered over time. Part of the sweet torture of Sunday morning is that the preaching moment is a thrilling and exhilarating experience when the preacher is well prepared and when the Holy Spirit has anointed both the sermon and the preacher. The attending torture is not how well the sermon goes on the present Sunday, but how quickly the preacher has to get ready to repeat the process over and over again, no matter where the next preaching assignment may take place.

Some preachers may be able to pull together a quality sermon at the last minute. In the face of certain circumstances, those of us with sufficient experience may find ourselves having to do that from time to time. We may have to or even choose to preach extemporaneously, with a limited time for preparation. That being said, it is far better for the preacher, and for the people who will hear the sermon as well, if adequate time is set aside for sermon preparation each week.

I invite preachers to think about not only their own investment of time in their weekly schedules, but also the time commitment of the people who will gather to hear the sermon. As I observed in my book *Shaping the Claim*, a congregation invests far more time in the sermon than does the preacher. Harry Emerson Fosdick was reported to have spent one hour in preparation for every minute he spent preaching his sermons.[7] That rounded out to between sixteen and twenty hours each week in sermon preparation. That is an impressive number—until you contrast those sixteen to twenty hours over against the number of hours invested collectively by the congregation who gathers to hear that sermon.

> Let us assume that an average American worship service consists of one hundred attendees. Let us also assume that each of those one hundred attendees spends two hours getting dressed and traveling to the church. Let us additionally assume that the worship service lasts for one hour. The preacher may have spent twenty hours in preparation for a twenty-minute sermon, but

> the congregation as a whole will have spent over three hundred hours in order to be in place to hear the sermon that day. That much time dare not be wasted by preachers who have nothing of substance or urgency to say.[8]

Needless to say, the time investment of the congregation goes up significantly as both the size of the congregation and the length of the worship service increase. A two-hour service plus travel time for a two-hundred-person congregation is eight hundred hours invested by the church. A three-hour service plus travel time for a five-hundred-person congregation is twenty-five hundred hours—an investment that dare not be wasted due to a lack of preacher preparation or sermonic depth!

The second danger is that the preacher pressed for time may venture only into texts and themes with which he or she is already familiar, because not enough time has been set aside to study and draw sermons from new biblical sources. This is a special danger in pastoral settings where over the years a congregation experiences lopsided exposure to a preacher's favorite biblical passages, usually drawn from less than half of the books of the Bible.

Here is a question for every preacher who might read this book. When was the last time you read and then preached from Ezra or Nehemiah, Obadiah or Nahum, Titus or 2 and 3 John?

Theoretically, the use of a lectionary should aid those who use that tool to avoid the danger of preaching from too narrow a selection of biblical texts. That strategy is not foolproof, however, first because a great many preachers (perhaps even the majority in Baptist, Pentecostal, charismatic, and independent church settings) make no use of the lectionary. The original danger persists as well because, while the lectionary provides four separate texts per week (Old Testament, Psalm, Gospel, and Epistle), the preacher may still be tempted to select whichever of those four texts seems most familiar. Even worse is what Reinhold Niebuhr pointed to, which is the use of a new text "as a pretext to say the same thing over again."[9]

Take Time to Read and Study the Bible

One of the first casualties of a busy pastoral life may be the time the preacher spends reading and studying the Bible both for personal formation and for sermon material. Here is a nondebatable principle for all preachers: we cannot feed others on Sunday if we have not been feeding ourselves during the week.

Mark 6:31-33 is a glimpse into the pressures of a busy ministry. The disciples had just returned from their first preaching mission in which Jesus had sent them out two by two. On their return they wanted to report to Jesus everything that had happened during their respective ministry involvements. However, they had no time to be alone with Jesus because "so many people were coming and going that they did not even have a chance to eat."

Recognizing the problem and their need for a time for rest and renewal, Jesus said to his disciples, "Come with me by yourselves to a quiet place and get some rest." However, the demands of ministry were not so easily left behind. The text continues: "So they went away by themselves in a boat to a solitary place. But many who saw them leaving recognized them and ran on foot from all the towns and got there ahead of them."

The disciples went from one intense ministry assignment to another with little if any time in between for *reflection* on what had happened in the previous assignments or for *preparation* for the assignments that were awaiting them.

For preachers today the equivalent challenge to spending time alone with Jesus is spending time alone with the Bible in a prayerful and meditative mood. Lack of time spent with Scripture can easily lead to an increasing number of topical sermons on matters of personal interest or current events that are examined through the lens of popular culture rather than biblical authority. In this instance a preacher may feel the need to claim that the sermon is at least based on a biblical text, but very little use is made of that text after it has been read and the sermon begins.

I have made it a matter of personal discipline to make Bible reading the first thing I do in the morning and the last thing I do at night. Thank God for the YouVersion Bible app that pre-selects a passage each day from different sections, genres, and testaments of the Bible. The app allows me to read the passage in as many as ten different versions and translations. Not only do I read the entire chapter in which the selected passage is located, but I read the chapter before and the chapter that follows so as to get a better sense of the context within which the assigned text for the day is located.

Over a period of time, practicing this kind of simple methodology will guide the reader through most of the Bible. Undoubtedly, this discipline will introduce the preacher to sermon possibilities that would otherwise have been missed if regular Bible reading and study were not part of the preacher's regular routine. When a preacher is too busy for daily Bible reading and reflection on those texts, that preacher is *too busy*!

A Theology of Preaching Is Essential

With the pressures of weekly sermon preparation in mind, we come to the consideration of a theological approach to preaching that has the potential of providing a broader and wider approach to the task. While preaching is challenging for even the most gifted of persons, the task becomes more manageable when we take a step back from the focus on weekly preaching and instead focus on an intentional strategy for selecting texts and designing sermons. This strategy should involve a wide range of biblical material and allow the preacher to touch on a broad range of doctrines and topics over an extended period of time.

Acts 1:6-8 can provide the framework for such an approach to the task of preaching. Moreover, this text can also serve to remind preachers of who they are as persons, why they are engaged in the preaching ministry, what God would have them say in their sermons, and how they can be sustained in this work over the course of a long career.

In thinking about a theology of preaching, those of us engaged in this task should be able to answer for ourselves the following questions:

Why Do We Need a Theology of Preaching?

- What charge or mandate informs me when I preach?
- What outcomes am I trying to accomplish through my preaching?
- Who do I understand myself to be as a preacher of the gospel?
- What questions or concerns guide me in my selection of biblical texts?
- What do I believe to be the fundamental purpose of Christian preaching?
- What lengths or limits of context and content inform the focus of my preaching?

Consider these questions from a different angle:

- Why do I have the urge to preach given all the other vocations in the world?
- What long-term impact do I hope my preaching will have on the church and the world?
- What traits and characteristics serve to equip and inform me as a preacher?
- How will I be careful to "proclaim . . . the whole will of God" (Acts 20:27)?
- What do I believe God is attempting to do with and through the task of preaching?
- How far beyond my own local church am I prepared to go to preach the gospel?

Three New Testament Charges to the Preacher

Three places in the New Testament provide instructions for preaching and preachers, and each text features one of the three major leaders of the early church community. When Jesus, Peter, and Paul each take time to discuss both the content of preaching and the personal characteristics of the preacher, those who feel themselves called to this vocation should pay attention to what they are saying. Whether taken together or considered separately, these texts can serve as a biblical basis for a theology of preaching.

What to Preach: 2 Timothy 4:2-5

Paul wrote to his young protégé Timothy about preaching the gospel message in 2 Timothy 4:2-5:

> Preach the word; be prepared in season and out of season; correct, rebuke and encourage—with great patience and careful instruction. For the time will come when people will not put up with sound doctrine. Instead, to suit their own desires, they will gather around them a great number of teachers to say what their itching ears want to hear. They will turn their ears away from the truth and turn aside to myths. But you, keep your head in all situations, endure hardship, do the work of an evangelist, discharge all the duties of your ministry.

In this first text, the issue is the content of sermons and the purposes for Christian preaching. "Preach the gospel" is the message being given to Timothy, and the gospel is also the message that all preachers should deliver to their listeners. Preaching the gospel would certainly include such issues as the nature of Christ, the forgiveness of sins, the duties of discipleship, salvation by faith, the resurrection of Jesus from the dead, and the assurance of resurrection for all those who put their faith in Christ. Preaching that strays too far away from these themes contained in the gospel in favor of more popular notions, such as prosperity theology or theories about the end time, may be attractive to the ears of some people in the twenty-first century just as it was in the first century, but it is not Christian preaching!

In addition, this Scripture warns preachers that preaching may not be as easy as simply standing up and talking. Our preaching may be met with indifference at best and resistance at worst. It may not be received as soon as it is heard, thus requiring patience and persistence on the part of the preacher. While the gospel is the "good news," preaching the gospel does come with some rough edges when the sermon seeks to rebuke or correct. That rough side of the gospel calls to mind the graphic images found in Hebrews 4:12: "The word of God is alive and active. Sharper than any double-edged sword, it penetrates even to dividing soul and spirit, joints and marrow; it judges the thoughts and attitudes of the heart."

In his book *Leaves from the Notebook of a Tamed Cynic*, Reinhold Niebuhr remarks that there was a reason why most of the biblical prophets were itinerant (moving on to another location after having preached a hard prophetic oracle).[10] Preaching that spends as much time on rebuking and correcting as it does on encouraging and comforting may not result in numerical church growth or megachurch status. However, it does result in spiritual maturity on the part of those who hear such sermons.

Preachers, be clear about the kind of growth you are most interested in seeing within your congregation—larger weekly attendance or deeper levels of faith and understanding. This is not to say that both types of growth cannot be achieved, but this text clearly warns preachers about placing numbers in the pews over maturity of the spirit.

Qualifications of the Preacher: Acts 1:21-22

In Acts 1:21-22 Peter was talking about the criteria for whoever would be chosen as an apostle to replace Judas Iscariot, who had committed suicide. This selection occurred before the apostles began the preaching ministry to which they had been called and for which they had been equipped. Peter said to the gathered disciples:

> "Therefore, it is necessary to choose one of the men who have been with us the whole time the Lord Jesus was living among us, beginning from John's baptism to the time when Jesus was taken up from us. For one of these must become a witness with us of his resurrection."

Peter focused first on the length and breadth of the relationship between the candidates for the position and Jesus Christ, whose words and works they were going to declare to the world. Peter warned that the preacher to be chosen had to have known and traveled with Jesus for the entirety of the Lord's earthly ministry, stretching from Jesus' baptism by John three years earlier to the Lord's ascension into heaven just a few verses earlier in Acts 1:9. The passage also focused on the one theological doctrine that seemed paramount in the mind of Peter: the preacher must be "a witness with us" to the resurrection of Jesus.

Preachers in the twenty-first century certainly cannot claim to have traveled with Jesus or to have eyewitness knowledge of his resurrection. On both counts we fall under Jesus' words in John 20:29: "Blessed are those who have not seen and yet have believed." That being said, we are left with two criteria for preachers and for preaching. The first is possession of in-depth knowledge of the words and actions of Jesus during his earthly ministry. Intimate knowledge of the biblical text (in the language of the preacher and congregation) can and should be accomplished over time, as well as some facility with the biblical languages of Hebrew and Greek.

However, just as the first disciples grew in awareness of Jesus over time, so must preachers in the twenty-first century seek constantly to expand on what Luke, writing in Acts 1:1-2, referred to as "all that Jesus began to do and to teach until he was taken up to heaven." Regular study and the discipline of lifelong learning are essential to the life of the preacher, especially when you consider the breadth, depth, and eternality of the subject matter in question. If, as John 21:25 says, there is not enough room in the world to hold all the books that could be written about what Jesus said and did, we should at least make an effort to read as many of the books about Jesus and about matters related to the Christian faith as are available to us.

John 20:29 identifies the resurrection of Jesus from the dead as the centerpiece of our theology—the second criterion for our preaching. As Paul said in 1 Corinthians 15:13-14, "If there is no resurrection of the dead, then not even Christ has been raised. And if Christ has not been raised, our preaching is useless and so is your faith." This is a clear matter of focus, not only of the content of our sermons but also of our personal faith.

Do we think of the resurrection as nothing more than a clever metaphor for new life in Christ? Do we dismiss the resurrection of

Christ as some mythological notion no longer essential for the twenty-first-century church? Or do we view the resurrection of Jesus as a faith claim that points to the power of God generally and the power of God over the finality of death in particular?

Newly called preachers will have to sort this out fairly quickly because sooner or later they will be called on to preside over a funeral service or preach a funeral eulogy in the presence of a dead body and a grieving family. What are they going to say? Does their gospel extend only as far as death having the last word, or will they invite the mourners to rest in the promise of 1 Corinthians 15:19-20: "If only for this life we have hope in Christ, we are of all people most to be pitied. But Christ has indeed been raised from the dead, the first fruits of those who have fallen asleep."

Peter said that whoever replaced Judas must "become a witness with us of [Jesus'] resurrection." As will be discussed throughout this book, a witness is not simply someone who has physically seen something. A witness is someone who is prepared to swear to the truthfulness of his or her testimony and is also prepared to suffer for the sake of that testimony. This is no less true for preachers today than it was two thousand years ago; we are called to be "witnesses of his resurrection."

Acts 1:6-8

This is a perfect segue into the third passage, where the content of preaching and the characteristics of the preacher's life are so powerfully joined together, and this is the primary passage around which this book is organized, Acts 1:6-8. In this text Jesus challenges his disciples concerning the ministry on which they are about to embark by saying, "You will receive power when the Holy Spirit comes on you, and you will be my witnesses in Jerusalem, and in all Judea and Samaria, and to the ends of the earth."

While this passage is at the center of this book as the organizing principle for a theology of preaching, it is appropriate to offer a brief breakdown of the passage to establish it as a framework for a theology of preaching.

This book focuses on three components in this passage that need to be adopted and applied as far as Christian preaching is concerned. The first is found in the promise that power will come to the preacher from the Holy Spirit. Thus our theology of preaching is built on the foundation of dependence on and empowerment from the Holy Spirit. The second component is in the call to be witnesses for the Lord, in all the ways in which that word can be understood. (Chapter 2 will explore the nuances and meanings of the word *witness.*) The third component involves the scope of our commission, which is delineated in ways that are broad and wide: Jerusalem, Judea, Samaria, and to the ends of the earth.

This was the charge that Jesus gave to his disciples in the first century AD. That same charge serves preachers in the twenty-first century just as well, providing us with a theology of preaching that can serve us for all the years we are in ministry. This book is an attempt to build further on these three basic points.

NOTES

1. James Earl Massey, *The Burdensome Joy of Preaching* (Nashville: Abingdon, 1998), 13–14.
2. Gardner Taylor, quoted in Terry Mauck and Paul Robbins, "The Sweet Torture of Sunday Morning: An Interview with Gardner Taylor," *Leadership* 2, no. 3 (July 1, 1981): 16–29.
3. Tony Campolo, "It's Friday, but Sunday's Coming." YouTube has multiple videos of this popular sermon.
4. Gardner C. Taylor, *How Shall They Preach? The Lyman Beecher Lectures and Five Lenten Sermons* (Elgin, IL: Progressive Baptist Publishing House, 1977), 57.
5. Reinhold Niebuhr, *Leaves from the Notebook of a Tamed Cynic* (Louisville: Westminster John Knox, 1957), 12.
6. Marvin A. McMickle, *Living Water for Thirsty Souls* (Valley Forge, PA: Judson, 2001), 24–31; and *The Star Book on Preaching* (Valley Forge, PA: Judson, 2006), 45–54.
7. Robert Moats Miller, *Harry Emerson Fosdick: Preacher, Pastor, Prophet* (New York: Oxford University Press, 1985), 353.
8. Marvin A. McMickle, *Shaping the Claim* (Minneapolis: Fortress, 2008), 34.
9. Niebuhr, *Leaves*, 12.
10. Ibid., 47.

CHAPTER 2

Unpacking the Preaching Theology in Acts 1:6-8

You will receive power when the Holy Spirit comes on you; and you will be my witnesses in Jerusalem, and in all Judea and Samaria, and to the ends of the earth." —Acts 1:8

I began this book by making the claim that everything a preacher in the twenty-first century needs to know about the content and context of preaching can be found in the charge given by Jesus to his first disciples in Acts 1:6-8, with special attention to the words "You will be my witnesses in Jerusalem, and in all Judea and Samaria, and to the ends of the earth." Subsequent chapters give closer attention to what it means to be a witness for Jesus, as well as how to understand and embrace the Lord's challenge to be his witnesses in contexts that stretch from across the street to around the world. This chapter offers a brief, more general analysis of this passage.

"You Will Receive Power"

The first thing Jesus told his disciples, and the first thing we should know as we preach in the twenty-first century, is that sermon content should not be our first concern. The first thing Jesus urged upon his disciples was that they should say and do nothing until they had received the power and anointing of the Holy Spirit.

Note that I am not asserting that this reminder to wait for the anointing of the Holy Spirit was an invitation to the disciples to adopt a style of preaching that has become popular within certain Pentecostal and charismatic church settings. Jesus was not saying in the first century anything about a certain style of preaching in the twenty-first century! As I said in the introduction, I am not arguing for any one style of sermon design or delivery that should be preferred above all others or that should be blindly embraced by all who aspire to the preaching ministry.

Rather, Jesus' promise "You will receive power when the Holy Spirit comes on you" is a much-needed reminder that preaching is not entirely a cerebral or intellectual exercise that can be mastered with courses in exegesis, hermeneutics, and sermon design and delivery. Preaching requires more than our minds; it requires the power that comes from the Holy Spirit.

The Holy Spirit's power will encourage us to preach sermons beyond our natural comfort zone of texts and topics. We will need the Spirit's power to sustain us as we plan our sermons from year to year, seeking always to be fresh and relevant. We will need the Spirit's power to embolden us when we are called on to speak truth to power about matters of human rights and social justice. And we will need the Spirit's power to comfort us when our hopes and plans for our ministry are slow to develop, if they develop at all.

Whether or not you have a theological degree, it is important to understand that preaching is not something that is done by our own human wit and wisdom. It is also not done under our own energy and enthusiasm. Jesus began his instructions to his disciples with these words: "You will receive power when the Holy Spirit comes on you."

"You Will Be My Witnesses"

The second thing Jesus told those first disciples involved the specific work for which the Holy Spirit would equip them: they were to be his witnesses. Being a witness for Jesus involves several things as far as the work of the preacher is concerned.

Unpacking the Preaching Theology in Acts 1:6-8

First, a witness is *someone who sees something* and can offer an accurate eyewitness report. Thus a witness is someone who has been observing, paying attention to, what is going on in the surrounding world. This is reminiscent of the motif of the watchman in Ezekiel 3:17-21 and 33:7-9, where God called on the prophet Ezekiel to pay close attention to what was going on both inside and outside the walls of Jerusalem and to be prepared to announce to the city what he saw.

The work of today's preachers is no different. The first task of effective preachers is to pay attention to what is happening both inside and outside their local churches. In his book *The Preaching of the Gospel*, Karl Barth quotes Paul Tillich, who said, "Preaching must be done with an awareness of the present moment."[1] The witness is someone who sees something.

Second, a witness is *someone who is willing to say something* about what he or she has seen. This second step hints at a witness in a courtroom who promises under oath to tell the truth, the whole truth, and nothing but the truth regarding what he or she has seen. Jesus was inviting his disciples not only to pay attention to what was going on in the world around them, but to be willing to speak openly and publicly about what they had learned from him and about how the world should respond to his message.

On matters dealing with the inadequacy or abandonment of Jewish law, they were being called on to say something. When it came to the role of Gentiles as members of the church without first having to conform to the laws of circumcision, they were being called on to say something. When it came to the most important and the most controversial claim of all, that Jesus was the Son of God and that his resurrection from the dead was confirmation of that fact, the disciples were being called on to say something.

This is a challenge for preachers today: to say something about the things they have seen going on in the world around them. The task of saying something must touch on the broad range of social justice issues, including human rights and equal rights for all persons, including those in the LGBT (lesbian, gay, bisexual, transgender) community; war and peace; mass incarceration; wealth disparity; drug and alcohol dependence; the steady decline of persons identifying as Christian; and the rise of persons self-identifying with hate and terrorist groups. Whenever preachers wonder what they should preach on from week to week, they might want to consider when was the last time they actually said something in a sermon about the things they have seen going on in the world around them. Part of the work of the witness, like the work of the watchman in Ezekiel, is saying something about what has been seen!

Third, a witness is *someone who is prepared to suffer for something*. This third aspect of being a witness is uncovered in the Koine Greek word for witness, which is *marturia*. That Greek word is the basis for our English word *martyr*. As a matter of natural progression, Jesus was challenging his disciples not just to see something, but to say something about what they had seen. Then he challenged them to say something even if it was considered unpopular, controversial, "politically incorrect," or likely to result in both rejection and negative repercussions toward themselves. This is arguably the hardest part of being a witness, because nobody is anxious to do or say something that may result in having to suffer some negative consequences. However, the history of the church is replete with the stories of men and women who were willing to speak even when they knew it would result in some form of suffering. Jesus invites us to join with him, and subsequently with Paul and the other disciples, in preaching that may result in suffering.

Being a witness involves more than worship. This third aspect of being a witness that includes a willingness to suffer for the sake of the gospel and the truth of God is a hard thing to communicate in a generation when so many people want to do nothing more than engage in an emotional time of worship, and when so many preachers are so caught up in the prosperity gospel of health and wealth. Many preachers seem to have ceased any consideration of being a witness for the Lord because they are in hot pursuit of "celebrity preacher" status. Who wants to suffer if they can earn a guest spot on some TV reality show about the preachers of Los Angeles or Detroit, or on *Preach*, a show that focuses on female prophetesses and their protégés? Who wants to suffer if they can get an invitation to appear at some praise fest where the realities of daily life are left safely outside the door?

As Stephen J. Nichols mentioned in his theological analysis of the music genre known as the blues, there are a great many people who want to "celebrate Easter while avoiding Good Friday."[2] Nevertheless, in Acts 1:6-8 Jesus calls his disciples, then and now, to be his witnesses. He calls us to *see something*, to *say something* about what we have seen, and then be prepared to *suffer something* as a result of the truth we are determined to speak.

Broaden the Reach of Your Preaching

We must acknowledge that much preaching today takes place away from the context of a local congregation. Indeed, there are many persons who preach on a regular basis, but they do not deliver their sermons in the same place and to the same people week after week. An increasing number of men and women are now serving as chaplains in colleges, the military, hospitals, prisons, and police and fire departments. In many cases, even those persons who are involved in the traditional model of pastoral preaching still find themselves being called on to preach in other settings as well.

In my own ministry I have been called on to preach on college and private school campuses, inside the walls of maximum security prisons, at fraternal events held in ballrooms in large hotels, before clergy conferences at retreat centers, in open-air settings on campgrounds, under tents in citywide revivals, on an active-duty military base, at a graveside during a memorial service, on the steps of a government building as part of a civil rights protest, and in the locker room of the Cleveland Browns football team prior to kickoff for several of their games. This willingness to preach in settings beyond one's own local church setting is especially important in light of the Pew Research Center report that indicates a steady decline in the number of persons in the United States who self-identify as Christians and who attend any form of church service on a regular basis.[3] If people are less inclined to come into the church for a worship service where they might hear a sermon, then preachers will need to find ways to extend their preaching ministry context beyond the confines of their sanctuaries if they hope to impact the world as witnesses for Jesus Christ.

The Context of Preaching

Increasingly, preachers are not based in local churches on a full-time basis. They may preach on a regular basis but not necessarily in the capacity of being the pastor of a congregation. I run into a great many assistant pastors and staff ministers with responsibilities for visitation, Christian education, and a number of duties assigned by their senior pastors. Though they may have a hundred sermons bubbling up inside their souls, they have few if any opportunities to actually preach in the places where they serve. Some who do serve as pastor of a congregation may be serving in a bivocational capacity in which they must juggle the time needed for sermon preparation with the time committed to the other job on which their financial livelihood depends.

Some preachers may be chaplains on the campuses of secular universities where skepticism and even atheism is as likely a presence as a Christian upbringing complete with some knowledge of biblical teachings. Preaching in that setting on a regular basis is one of the most challenging things a preacher can undertake. The makeup of those congregations can include students, faculty, community members, visiting alumni, parents, trustees of the school, and others. Affiliation to the school rather than a commonly shared faith in Christ might be the main thing binding that group together. Nevertheless, some preachers will find themselves in those settings and should use Acts 1:6-8 as a way to inform them on matters of sermon content as well as the content of their own lives as preachers living in the midst of an academic setting.

Some may be military chaplains like my seminary classmate Ronald Wunsch, who was deployed to Kuwait with an airborne division back in the 1990s with Operation Desert Shield. His spiritual care for the soldiers resulted in a sermon series he entitled Sermons from the Sand!

What do you say to soldiers who are about to go on patrol and may encounter sniper attacks, improvised explosive devices (IEDs), or suicide bombings? What does the chaplain say at the funeral of comrades who have been killed in the line of duty? What does the chaplain say to service members being deployed for the third or fourth time in a ten-year period? The chaplain has seen a lot and can truthfully say a lot. And there is also much that the chaplain could suffer for if he or she chose to say something about the strategy or necessity or legitimacy of the war for which so much money was being sent and so many fatalities and casualties were occurring.

Other preachers may follow the increasingly common decision to enter hospital or hospice chaplaincy, where regular preaching is of less importance than bedside pastoral care for the sick, the suffering, and the dying. Patients are steadily coming and going. Under certain circumstances, professional staff such as doctors and nurses may need a word of encouragement or spiritual counsel. Of course the challenge of this form of ministry comes from the diversity of non-Christian religious traditions present among patients and staff. In some settings the explicit reference to the name of Jesus is discouraged in favor of a spirituality that references God in purely nonsectarian ways. How can one be a witness in a setting where rules and policies about patients' rights can limit what is acceptable to say? (Of course, these restrictions do not apply to visiting clergy who are meeting with members of their own congregation who are hospitalized.)

The Content of Preaching

The context within which preaching occurs is not the only issue to be considered. Just as urgent as the context for our preaching is the methodology by which we determine what will be the content of our sermons as we go about preparing to preach whenever and wherever the next sermon is to be delivered. What themes need to be discussed? What biblical mandates need to be presented?

Whether you are a full-time pastor dealing with all the demands of that vocation or are one of the other types of ministers listed above, you have to deal with the pressures of time and timeliness. You have to find time to prepare a sermon and work hard to be sure that it is relevant and, in the words of Paul Tillich, is mindful "of the present moment."[4] No matter where the sermon is delivered or before which audience, you have the ongoing challenge of finding a way to be ready to preach week after week, month after month, year after year.

That is the burdensome joy of preaching. That is the sweet torture of Sunday morning. And that is why we need the framework of Acts 1:6-8 to develop a working theology for preaching.

NOTES

1. Paul Tillich, quoted in Karl Barth, *The Preaching of the Gospel* (Philadelphia: Westminster, 1960), 54.

2. Stephen J. Nichols, *Getting the Blues: What Blues Music Teaches Us about Suffering and Salvation* (Grand Rapids: Brazos, 2008), 14.

3. "America's Changing Religious Landscape: Christians Decline Sharply as Share of Population; Unaffiliated and Other Faiths Continue to Grow," Pew Research Center, May 12, 2015, http://www.pewforum.org/2015/05/12/americas-changing-religious-landscape/.

4. Paul Tillich, quoted in Barth, *The Preaching of the Gospel*, 54.

CHAPTER 3

The Passing of the Baton

Then [the disciples] gathered around [Jesus] and asked him, "Lord, are you at this time going to restore the kingdom to Israel?"

He said to them: "It is not for you to know the times or dates the Father has set by his own authority. But you will receive power when the Holy Spirit comes on you; and you will be my witnesses in Jerusalem, and in all Judea and Samaria, and to the ends of the earth."
—Acts 1:6-8

Before we undertake a close reading of the words spoken by Jesus to his first-century disciples (Acts 1:7-8), it is important to look first at the words spoken to Jesus by those same disciples (1:6), the words to which he was responding. Notice that the comments from Jesus did not emerge as a piece of unsolicited final advice to those disciples who were about to assume responsibility for carrying out the work and proclaiming the message entrusted to them by Jesus. Rather, Jesus was replying to a specific question asked by his disciples.

And the nature of his response seems to identify a clear disconnect in the understanding between Jesus and his closest followers. Despite three years spent in the intimate company of Jesus, the disciples were entirely unclear as to what was next in their journey as Christ's followers.

Different Expectations

"Lord, are you at this time going to restore the kingdom to Israel?" On first reading, those words may not stand out as inappropriate. To some these words even involve a legitimate question, perhaps reflecting an anxiety to know what was about to happen next in the work that Jesus was doing.

In his book *The Christian Imagination*, theologian Willie James Jennings agrees with those interpreters who find no fault with this question from the disciples. Jennings says that their question "is exactly right."[1] He reads their question wholly within the context of messianic expectation and what the disciples might legitimately expect from Jesus. Surely, now that the Messiah had come (and especially now that Jesus had been raised from the dead), the Roman occupation would be overthrown, and Israel would be restored to its former glory not enjoyed since the days of David and Solomon.

The problem with that reading of the text is that it focuses primarily on what the disciples were expecting from Jesus, when what the text really seeks to disclose is Jesus' expectation of the disciples. One key difference between my view and that of Jennings on this passage revolves around the question of whether the disciples were correct in believing that what Jesus would do was primarily, perhaps exclusively, for the benefit of the nation of Israel. Jennings writes: "They assumed that Jesus' victory over death must mean victory for Israel over the Roman Empire. They rightly sensed in Jesus a new thing emerging in Israel, its rebirth in him. Thus the Spirit of the Father would be given, and Jesus would be glorified as the inauguration of a new age for Israel."[2] Jennings is correct if we were to assume that the expectations of the disciples were synonymous with the intentions of Jesus. So let us consider first what their expectations may have been—and how Jesus' response reflects intentions that stand in marked contrast with those expectations.

There is no doubt that the disciples were operating under a seven-hundred-year-long expectation of what would happen when the promised Messiah did appear. Their question is thoroughly immersed in the theology and the politics of first-century Israel and its longing for deliverance from Roman occupation. Thus, on the matter of the expectations and desires of the disciples themselves, their question did make sense.

A More Inclusive Calling

Most of Jesus' first disciples would have been resistant to the inclusion of Gentiles (non-Jews) into the new community of Jesus' followers. We can make that assumption based on several instances when Jesus did interact with Gentiles. In Matthew 15:23-30 Jesus was approached by a Canaanite woman seeking help for her demon-possessed daughter. The disciples were there to hear him say, "I was sent only to the lost sheep of Israel. . . . It is not right to take the children's bread and toss it to the dogs" (vv. 24, 26).

The same could be said for John 4:9, where a Samaritan woman, who was surprised that Jesus would engage her in conversation, said to him, "'You are a Jew and I am a Samaritan woman. . . .' (Jews do not associate with Samaritans.)" Her shock was matched by that of the disciples who, when they saw Jesus engaged in that conversation, asked him, "Why are you talking with her?" (v. 27).

No passage makes this point more vividly than when Jesus agreed to heal the servant of a Roman centurion in Matthew 8:5-13. That man was not only a Gentile, but he was a representative of the Roman Empire, which had conquered Palestine and was holding the Jews in subjection. It never occurred to the disciples that they might be sharing their kingdom with Canaanites, Samaritans, or Romans.

Even after Jesus made it clear that Gentiles should be included in the disciples' gospel ministry, the early church continued to wrestle with the controversial idea of inclusion. In Acts 6 we see already in the early Jerusalem church complaints about discriminatory treatment of the widows of Palestinian Jews versus the treatment of the widows of Greek-speaking Jews. In Acts 15 a council had to be convened to decide the issue of whether the church would require the circumcision of Gentile converts to Christianity as a condition of their acceptance in the community. The argument by some in the Jerusalem church was, "Unless you are circumcised, according to the custom taught by Moses, you cannot be saved" (Acts 15:1).

That view was typical of those who thought that Jesus' ministry was primarily a continuation of what God was doing in and through Israel. Paul objected, ultimately winning his point that the Jewish Christians in Jerusalem were "putting on the necks of Gentiles a yoke that neither we nor our ancestors have been able to bear[. . . .] We believe it is through the grace of our Lord Jesus that we are saved, just as they are" (Acts 15:10-11).

Thus, while the question from the disciples can be easily understood within the context of first-century Jewish messianic expectation of national renewal, it had nothing in common with the intent of Jesus so far as what he wanted his followers to do after his resurrection. The early church eventually came to consensus that the restoration of Israel's national sovereignty was not the focus for Jesus; rather, his intention was the redemption of all nations and, indeed, the whole of creation.

The problem with Jennings's assessment is that it merely acknowledges the disciples' continuing misunderstanding of the nature of God's reign. Jennings seems to overlook that the disciples are still fixated on their own expectations of a triumphant military or political messiah. The cross and tomb were unexpected but temporary detours. Surely *now* Jesus intended to assert his messianic sovereignty and restore Israel to its former glory!

In chapter 4 we will analyze the multiple flaws in the disciples' apparently simple and reasonable question. But first it is critical to consider how the question as a whole reflects the disciples' lack of understanding of the moment in which they found themselves. It is my conviction that Acts 1:6-8 is not just about the end of the earthly ministry of Jesus; it is also, perhaps primarily, about the work that the disciples were about to undertake.

A Momentous Transition

The interaction between Jesus and his disciples in Acts 1:6-8 was a pivotal one at a significant transition moment in the life of the fledgling

Christian community. Jesus' earthly ministry had drawn to an end while his disciples' ministry was poised to begin.

This moment was similar to the most crucial time in a relay race in an athletic contest. The most important thing in a relay race is not the speed of the runners, although speed does have great bearing on the outcome. Rather, the most important aspect comes with the passing of the baton from one runner to the next runner who is set to enter the race. The efficiency with which the baton is passed three separate times is the most crucial part of the relay race. A relay race is won or lost primarily on the successful passing of the baton. If the baton is dropped by any one runner, the time lost in picking it up and then trying to gather full speed again will almost certainly keep that entire team out of the winner's circle.

This passing of the baton analogy is at the heart of the events described in Acts 1:6-8. Jesus had finished his portion of the race. The work of redemption and justification had been accomplished, signified by two separate moments in his life. First, there was his own anguished cry from the cross: "*Tetelestai!*" "It is finished!" (John 19:30). Of course, it was not primarily his own life to which he was referring with those words. What was finished was the work he had entered the world to accomplish. The debt of sin had been paid in full. The estrangement between God and humanity had been ended.

The second defining moment, after his atoning death, was Jesus' victorious resurrection from the dead. The power of death was broken. The fear of the grave in the lives of those who put their faith in Christ was snatched away. Paul pointed to this triumphant finale in the life of Christ when he wrote in 1 Corinthians 15:55, "Where, O death, is your victory? Where, O death, is your sting?"

The death, burial, and resurrection of Jesus from the dead are the central proclamations of the Christian gospel. After the work of Jesus had been accomplished, all that remained was for this message about his life and work to be preached throughout the world. In Acts 1:6-8 the time had come for Jesus to pass the baton to the disciples. This was the moment for which they had been in training for the preceding three years.

From "Follow Me" to "Go into All the World"

Acts 1:6-8 takes us inside that critical moment of transition from the earthly ministry of Jesus to the evangelistic ministry of the church. The focus was shifting from what Jesus had done up to that point to what Jesus now expected the disciples would do going forward. That was always the plan that Jesus had in mind. In Matthew 4:19 Jesus began the work of gathering around him those who would be his disciples. It began with Simon Peter and his brother Andrew who were fishermen. His invitation was, "Come, follow me, and I will send you out to fish for people." In Matthew 9:9 Jesus issued the same invitation to Matthew: "Follow me."

Matthew 10, which lists the original twelve disciples, also offers a hint at what their mission was to be. Jesus told them to go and preach that the kingdom of God was near. He told them to display his power through miraculous work. He also told them what to do whenever their work and their words were not received by the people to whom they were being sent. Note that he also expressly told them, "Do not go among the Gentiles or enter any town of the Samaritans. Go rather to the lost sheep of Israel" (vv. 5-6). (It is, perhaps, no wonder the early church struggled with how they were called to relate to Gentiles!)

The disciples should have had little doubt that this moment would come when the baton would be passed from Jesus to them. Most of what Jesus talked about in the extended account of the Last Supper in John 13–17 concerned what he expected from them after he was removed from their midst. After washing the feet of his disciples, he told them, "No servant is greater than his master, nor is a messenger greater than the one who sent him" (John 13:16). He told them that the Advocate would be sent, who would teach them and remind them of the things Jesus had taught them (John 14:26). He told them, "You did not choose me, but I chose you and appointed you so that you might go and bear fruit" (John 15:16). He told them that they would face danger and possibly even death when they went out to preach (John 16:2-3). In his prayer to the Father concerning the disciples, he said, "As you have sent me into the world, I have sent them into the world" (John 17:18).

The time had come for the disciples to begin the work for which they had been preparing since Jesus had said to them three years earlier, "Come and follow me."

From Follower to Leader

Perhaps the reason the disciples were not prepared to receive the baton from Jesus was because they were not prepared, or at least not eager, to engage in ministry without having him around. There were very few times during their three years with Jesus that the disciples were either not all together with one another or not in Jesus' presence.

Matthew 10 records one of those rare intervals when Jesus and the disciples seemed to be in ministry on separate tracks. They had gone forth in pairs to do what he had instructed, and while they were away from him, Jesus conducted his own ministry in the regions of northern Galilee. He also interacted with the disciples of John the Baptist concerning who he (Jesus) really was and what he was doing.

However, by the beginning of Matthew 12, the disciples had once again come back into Jesus' presence. This same sequence of events is described in parallel texts in the other Synoptic Gospels (Mark and Luke), but the interval during which the disciples operated apart from Jesus' presence only got shorter—at least in terms of the space allotted by the Gospel writers.

In Mark 6 the disciples were sent away to do ministry, but they were away from Jesus for only eighteen verses in that same chapter. In Luke this same story is repeated, but the narrative separation from Jesus when they were on their own lasted only five verses (9:6-10). Just eighteen and five verses, respectively, in contrast with Matthew's two chapters' worth of separate-ministry narratives.

These passages reflect for us that over a period of three years, the disciples of Jesus had been away from Jesus (and apart from one another) for only very short periods of time. No matter what happened during any given day, they knew that by evening—or at most, within a very few days, they would be back with Jesus to seek his counsel, his companionship, and his comfort.

When the parables Jesus spoke to the crowds seemed confusing even to them, they were able to speak to him privately and gain greater clarity concerning his teachings, as in Matthew 13:10-23; Luke 12:35-48; and John 16:16-30. In Mark 9, as they descended from the Mount of Transfiguration, Peter, James, and John were able to ask clarifying questions about messianic prophecies about Elijah (vv. 9-13), and then after Jesus drove out a demon from the body of a young man, something which his other disciples had collectively been unable to do, they immediately turned to him to inquire about what had just happened and why (vv. 28-29).

This larger context is vital in order to appreciate the importance of what was at stake in Acts 1:6-8. It is important for today's readers to grasp the fact that nearly every day for a period of three years the disciples of Jesus had constantly been in his presence. All of that was so they could be equipped and prepared for the day depicted in Acts 1:6-8 when Jesus would leave them forever and they would be on their own.

Now we turn to the language in Acts 1:6-8 spoken on the day for which Jesus had been preparing them: "Be my witnesses in Jerusalem, and in all Judea and Samaria, and to the ends of the earth." This message is similar to those spoken by Jesus in the closing verses of each of the Synoptic Gospels where Jesus challenged those disciples with the work that was about to be set before them: "Go and make disciples of all nations . . . teaching them to obey everything I have commanded you" (Matthew 28:19-20). "Go into all the world and preach the gospel to all creation" (Mark 16:15). And "Repentance for the forgiveness of sins will be preached in [the Messiah's] name to all nations, beginning at Jerusalem. You are witnesses of these things. I am going to send you what my Father has promised; but stay in the city until you have been clothed with power from on high" (Luke 24:47-49).

This was the relay race that Jesus had envisioned. His own earthly, incarnate ministry was now over, and the ministry for which the disciples had been in training for three years was about to begin. Those who had been invited to follow were now directed to go forth and serve. The planned exchange of the baton was about to happen.

Unfortunately, based on the question the disciples asked on the eve of Jesus' ascension, they were still unprepared for the race that was being set before them.

NOTES

1. Willie James Jennings, *The Christian Imagination: Theology and the Origins of Race* (New Haven, CT: Yale University Press, 2010), 266.

2. Ibid.

CHAPTER 4

The Disciples Drop the Baton

"Lord, are you at this time going to restore the kingdom to Israel?"
—Acts 1:6

Having established the disciples' three years of intensive preparation and training as a backdrop for our focus Scripture, we can only imagine how shocked and disappointed Jesus must have been when, moments before he would ascend to the heavenly realm, his disciples asked this question of him. Surely he was tempted to repeat familiar refrains from earlier in his ministry: "How long must I put up with you?" "Do you still not understand?" (see Matthew 17:17; Mark 8:17-21; 9:19; Luke 9:41).

When we recall the disciples' three-year training and preparation for leadership, it is easier to perceive just how far off the mark those disciples actually were with their question. The problems with their question can be broken down section by section, examining each phrase in Acts 1:6 to observe where the baton was dropped.

"Lord, Are You . . . ?"

Consider this first phrase in verse 6: *"Lord, are you . . . ?"* After three years with Jesus, knowing that they had been preparing for just this moment, the disciples were fully aware that this would be their final time in his earthly presence. In that final encounter with Jesus, all the disciples could think to ask was what he was going to do next before he left. They did not ask him what he wanted them to do next. They were not trying to get any final clarity on the mission that was awaiting them. They were certainly not volunteering for any assignments. All that was on their mind was what else Jesus was going to do. What a colossal failure in the exchange of the baton. Instead of being prepared to run their leg of the relay race, these disciples seemed content to invite Jesus to take one more lap around the track. *"Lord, are you . . . ?"*

What Jesus Had Already Done

This question from the disciples about what Jesus might do next must be considered in light of how much Jesus had already done during his earthly ministry. He had already walked on the water. He had already fed five thousand people with two fish and five loaves of bread. He had already raised from the dead both Lazarus and the daughter of Jairus. He had already preached so powerfully that even one of the temple guards in Jerusalem in reporting to the Pharisees had to say, "No one ever spoke the way this man does" (John 7:46). He had already calmed a raging sea. He had already restored sight to the blind and restored strength to withered limbs. The disciples had seen miracle after miracle and had heard parable after parable, but they wanted to know what more he was prepared to do.

Jesus had already endured the anguish of the Garden of Gethsemane followed by the brutal beating and cruel mocking at the hands of Roman soldiers. He had already been handed over to be crucified by Pontius Pilate, who thought that by washing his hands he could wash away his complicity in the mockery of a trial that Jesus had been through. Once nailed to the cross, Jesus had already accomplished the wonderful work of redemption by offering up his own body as atonement for the sins of the world. He had already spoken words of forgiveness to his executioners and the promise of paradise to a thief hanging from a nearby cross.

Not only that, but Jesus had already been raised from the dead on the third day and become the promise of eternal life for all who put their faith in him. He had already robbed the grave of its victory and robbed his enemies of their victim. Death could not hold him. The grave could not keep him. Once and for all the church can sing, "I serve a living Savior!"[1] Now Jesus was only moments away from ascending back into heaven, and all the disciples could ask him was what more he was prepared to do before he left.

Not a Spectator Sport

Perhaps the disciples had become too comfortable with their role as spectators who simply looked on while Jesus spoke and acted. They had certainly been spectators at some truly remarkable moments. Three of them had seen the glory of Jesus displayed during his transfiguration in Matthew 17:1-9. All of them had probably seen the drama unfold when a woman caught in adultery was brought before Jesus by the Pharisees and Jesus told the crowd that whoever had no sin should cast the first stone (John 8:3-11). They were there, looking on, when Jesus had ridden into Jerusalem amid shouts of "Hosanna!"

Every church has people who have this same mentality. They have an uncanny habit of knowing exactly what other members of the congregation should be doing. "You should do this," you can hear them say. "Why don't you sign up for that task?" they will inquire of someone else. What they frequently seem to lack is the Isaiah 6:8 impulse of saying, "Here am I. Send me!" They are reminiscent of the following story:

> This is a story about four people named Everybody, Somebody, Anybody, and Nobody. There was an important job to be done, and Everybody was sure that Somebody would do it. Anybody could have done it, but Nobody did it. Somebody got angry about that, because it was Everybody's job. Everybody thought that Anybody could do it, but Nobody realized that Everybody wouldn't do it. It ended up that Everybody blamed Somebody when Nobody did what Anybody could have done.

We've already used the athletic analogy of a relay race to consider the ministry of Jesus and the disciples. Let's consider another sporting metaphor for the ministry of the church. Have you ever heard a football game described as an event where 45,000 people who badly need some exercise are observing 22 people who badly need some rest? How often are our congregations functioning more as a crowd of spectators rather than as a team on the field? Being a spectator may be an acceptable role when one is attending a sporting event. But it is an altogether inappropriate role to play when the work of the church is what is being considered.

In Acts 1:6 the disciples knew there was an important job to be done, and they knew precisely who should do it: "Lord, are you . . . ?" This was certainly not the passing of the baton that Jesus had been preparing them for the previous three years.

The Tales of Two Forts

This business of people preferring the role of a spectator over the active engagement of a participant calls to mind two historical events of great significance in American history; namely, the events that occurred at Fort Wagner in South Carolina during the American Civil War, and at Fort McHenry in Baltimore, Maryland, during the War of 1812.

On July 18, 1863, the all-black 54th Massachusetts regiment of the Union Army assaulted Fort Wagner, a Confederate fort that protected the approach to the harbor of Charleston, South Carolina. As dramatically retold in the 1989 film *Glory*, this heroic and ultimately unsuccessful charge on a nearly impregnable military fortress was one of the most memorable acts of heroism during the entire US Civil War. It resulted in Sergeant William H. Carney becoming one of the first African Americans to be awarded the Congressional Medal of Honor.[2]

That struggle at Fort Wagner was a firsthand act of engagement and personal commitment. Contrast it with events recorded about another fort in another battle.

In September 1814, during the War of 1812, at the Battle of Baltimore, Fort McHenry was bombarded by the British Navy. An American lawyer and poet by the name of Francis Scott Key was being held as a prisoner on board one of the British ships. From the deck of that ship, he observed the horrific bombardment that the British hurled at Fort McHenry, but he was also able to observe the fact that the American flag continued to fly over that fort at the end of the battle. Francis Scott Key was moved to write a poem called "The Defense of Fort McHenry," a poem that was later set to music and subsequently named "The Star Spangled Banner." In 1931, more than a century after its words were written, Congress declared that song to be the national anthem of the United States.[3]

As significant as Francis Scott Key was in creating the lyrics that ultimately became our national anthem, his role in the actual battle was merely that of an observer. He was not responding to the fury of that naval bombardment. He was not personally acting in defense of Baltimore or of the national sovereignty of the United States. He watched from a distance while others ran the risks and fought the battle. He was a spectator.

The fundamental difference between Key and the soldiers in the 54th Massachusetts regiment was not their race or ethnicity; it was their relationship to the task at hand. At Fort Wagner one group acted while at Fort McHenry another person observed the actions being taken by others.

Participants and Observers

The sharp distinction between participant and observer, reflected in the question of the disciples, haunts the church to this day: *"Lord, are you . . . ?"* How do preachers motivate and energize members of their congregations to become actively involved in the work of the church? How do passive preachers themselves, those who are perfectly content to remain safely locked up inside the walls of their pastor's study and their church sanctuary, find the motivation to get involved in the problems and struggles that are going on just outside the doors of their church building?

The preacher Robert McCracken, who had the unenviable task of succeeding Harry Emerson Fosdick at Riverside Church in New York City, said that there are four desirable outcomes to the sermons we preach: "kindle the mind, energize the will, disturb the conscience, and stir the heart."[4] In my book *Living Water for Thirsty Souls*, I reference these ideas from McCracken, and I argue for the careful and regular use of all four of these sermon outcomes in our preaching today.

When you *kindle the mind*, you are provoking thought around some controversial issue concerning which neither the local church nor the church universal is of one common mind. The issues related to abortion or to human sexuality may fall within this area.

When you *disturb the conscience*, you are intentionally focusing on harmful forms of human behavior that are very likely at work within the listening congregation of which the preacher is urging people to repent. Such human behavior can range from racism and sexism, to homophobia and domestic violence, to various forms of greed.

When you *stir the heart*, you are equipping people with those spiritual resources of faith and hope and patience that can enable them to endure the times of grief and suffering that inevitably arise in their lives. "Weeping may stay for the night, but rejoicing comes in the morning" (Psalm 30:5).

When you *energize the will,* you motivate people to move from observers to participants, not only in the life of the church but in the community at large. This movement might include an increase in laborers for the church workday, additional volunteers for ministries of Christian education, or a substantial presence of church members engaged in community service or activism in local government. This is perhaps the outcome most needed so that more and more church members will choose to get involved in the work of their church both inside and beyond the walls of their local church.[5]

When preachers are wondering what to preach from week to week, these four sermon outcomes provide a lot of possibilities. To put it plainly: preaching should not be done as an end in itself. Rather, the sermon should be viewed as a means to an end that has been carefully contemplated by the preacher in terms of what he or she is going to urge the congregation to do as a result of having heard that sermon: kindle the mind, energize the will, disturb the conscience, stir the heart.

As I have observed previously, other communicators in various professions seek to achieve real outcomes from their listeners all the time.

> Athletic coaches appeal to the players' pride and their desire for glory for themselves and for their team. Salespersons appeal to how affordable their products are and how much time and effort they will save us if we buy and use what they are selling. Military leaders appeal to patriotism and point to the tyranny that needs to be driven from the land. Investment bankers assure us that we can make more money for ourselves if we take the risk and invest in what they are offering. Political candidates paint a picture of how much better off the voters will be if they choose to vote for them.[6]

The task of preaching is no different when it comes to energizing the will. There are hot meals to be served in the soup kitchen. Who is willing to go? There are scout troops that need adult leaders. Who is willing to serve? There are persons who need tutoring in reading or computer science or parenting. Who is willing to help? There is a need for child care for persons who have come to the church for an HIV/AIDS test and consultation or for an Alcoholics Anonymous meeting. People should practice the spiritual disciplines of tithing, regular Bible study, and visiting the sick and shut-in members of their own local church. Who is willing to make that commitment?

All of these things and more can be addressed in sermons designed to achieve an outcome that brings the kingdom of God nearer to the people of God, in the church and in the world. That is the best way to combat the problem raised by the disciples when they asked Jesus, "Lord, are you . . . ?"

"At This Time"

Now we turn to the second phrase in verse 6 of our focus Scripture: "Lord, are you *at this time* going to restore the kingdom to Israel?" (emphasis added). The issue here was not just a matter of *who* would be doing something but of *when* something was going to be done. At the heart of those words "at this time" was the anguish of people who had been waiting for seven hundred years for a Messiah who would come to deliver them from the oppression they had continually felt from the time of the Assyrian conquest of their country in the eighth century BC, to their captivity by the Babylonians in the seventh century BC, to their subjugation to the Persians in the fifth century BC, to the domination by the Greeks that began in the fourth century BC, and to their current subjugation to the Romans that had been in force since the first century BC.

We begin to understand the urgency that was attached to the disciples' question about timing in Acts 1:6. If you were to add on the four hundred years the Hebrews spent enslaved in Egypt, you could readily understand that for the vast majority of their history, the people of Israel were not a sovereign and self-governing nation. They were a subjugated and colonized nation for centuries and generations. The disciples were hoping that all of that would end once the Messiah came, and in their mind Jesus was that Messiah.

Probably from the moment they started walking with Jesus, these disciples had it in their minds that he was the one for whom Israel had been waiting all those years. He was the one who would finally end their centuries of oppression. Surely he was the one! Peter made that expectation explicit with his confession about Jesus in Matthew 16:16 when he said, "You are the Messiah, the Son of the living God."

With every miracle Jesus performed and with every verbal assault he launched on the rulers in the country, the disciples became more and more convinced that he was the one. They would not have been alone in this speculation. From his prison cell inside of Herod's palace, John the Baptist dispatched his disciples to seek confirmation from Jesus of the same question: "Are you the one who is to come, or should we expect someone else?" (Matthew 11:3). With the memory of those Palm Sunday crowds still fresh in their minds with their shouts of "Hallelujah!" and "Blessed is he who comes in the name of the Lord," the disciples who had walked alongside Jesus that day could not help but believe that the people of Jerusalem held the same view: Jesus was the one.

Palm Sunday Was a Clue

When Jesus rode into Jerusalem on that Palm Sunday he seemed to be fulfilling the prophetic expectation found in Zechariah 9:9 which says: "Rejoice greatly, Daughter Zion! Shout, Daughter Jerusalem. See, your king comes to you, righteous and victorious, lowly and riding on a donkey, on a colt, the foal of a donkey."

Surely when Jesus rode into Jerusalem in just this manner there were many in that crowd who saw that event through the lens of that Old Testament text. Scripture was being fulfilled. The long-awaited Messiah was finally here. The Romans would soon be overthrown. The reign of God on the earth would soon be established. Undoubtedly, it was not only the disciples of Jesus and the people in that crowd who were filled with this sense of euphoria that the Messiah had at last arrived. It was also the Romans and the Jewish religious and political leaders who sensed the euphoria in that crowd, though their feelings were based on an entirely different issue.

While few if any of the Roman and Jewish leaders actually believed that Jesus was the Messiah, they were undoubtedly concerned about what Jesus had stirred up within those who did believe him to be the fulfillment of messianic expectation. Little wonder that after Jesus began teaching in the temple, "the chief priests and the teachers of the law heard this and began looking for a way to kill him, for they feared him, because the whole crowd was amazed at his teaching" (Mark 11:18). Something had to be done about Jesus!

From Triumphant Entry to Death on a Tree

What came next was something for which none of the disciples was prepared: within a few days' time their triumphant Messiah would become the Suffering Savior or crucified Christ.

True enough, Isaiah 53:5 had long ago declared that salvation would come from a suffering servant who would be "pierced for our transgressions . . . crushed for our iniquities." Jesus himself had also made it clear to them on more than one occasion that he understood his ministry in precisely these terms of suffering and death. What he said is recorded in all three Synoptic Gospels: "The Son of Man must suffer many things and be rejected by the elders, chief priests and the teachers of the law, and he must be killed" (Luke 9:22; cf. Matthew 16:21; Mark 10:33). This was not what the disciples had in mind when they abandoned their livelihoods and families three years earlier.

Equally clear was that none of the disciples was expecting the resurrection that would occur three days later. Depending on which of the Gospel narratives you read, after the crucifixion of Jesus, the disciples either went into hiding in Jerusalem or abandoned their ministry altogether and returned to their homes and to their former vocations back in Galilee. It must have seemed to them that the powers of Rome and Jerusalem had prevailed now that the dead body of Jesus was sealed inside of a guarded tomb. This was the case even though in every instance mentioned above in which Jesus had foretold them of his death, he had also foretold that he would be raised from the dead. None of that seemed to occur to them. All they knew was that Jesus was dead and that once again they seem to have been waiting in vain.

We can hear the shock and sadness that must have gripped all of the disciples and followers of Jesus in the voice of a man named Cleopas when he and another follower of Jesus walked on the road from Jerusalem back to Emmaus in the aftermath of the crucifixion. Not initially aware that they were in the presence of the resurrected Lord, those two disciples were trying to make sense of the dashed hopes they had harbored about Jesus. We can feel the pain and disappointment of an expectant people who were reduced to saying, "Jesus of Nazareth . . . was a prophet, powerful in word and deed before God and all the people. The chief priests and our rulers handed him over to be sentenced to death, and they crucified him; but we had hoped that he was the one who was going to redeem Israel" (Luke 24:19-21).

Then their deep shock and sadness were just as suddenly turned into joy. One by one the disciples of Jesus discovered that he had been raised from the dead. "He is risen" was the good news that altered their lives forever. Whether it was these men on the road to Emmaus, the disciples still hiding in the upper room or having returned to

Galilee, or the courageous women who had returned to the tomb to further anoint the body of Jesus, all of them encountered Jesus after his resurrection. Their hope was rekindled because the possibility still existed that their dream of a glorious restoration of Israel could yet occur.

However, things would have to happen quickly. The risen Christ was about to return to the realms of glory, leaving his followers to carry on without him. Time was running out for what they expected their Messiah would accomplish on the earth. Time was running out for the conquered and subjugated people of Israel to be restored to the glory Israel had not known since the time of King David and King Solomon almost one thousand years earlier. Time was running out, because Jesus was about to ascend back into heaven. Whatever he was going to do, and whatever they had hoped he was going to do, he would have to do now. All of that anxiety about their expectations and their sense of Christ's unfinished work is what must be heard when we hear them say in Acts 1:6, "Lord, are you *at this time* going to restore the kingdom to Israel?" (emphasis added).

How Long, O Lord?

We can easily identify with the desire of the disciples to have the reign of God begin "at this time." We have many examples of people in more recent years who have been left to wonder how long it would take for the God in whom they had placed their faith to act on their behalf. Elie Wiesel, the Jewish Nobel laureate who survived the Auschwitz concentration camp, reported on the night when several rabbis in that camp put God on trial for not doing anything to prevent the horrors of the Holocaust.[7] One can only imagine how many African, Caribbean, and African American slaves wondered how long it would be before their captivity and misery came to an end. Prisoners of war looking forward to their release and the right to return home have undoubtedly asked how much longer their hopes would go unfulfilled.

Looking at this question of "How long, O Lord?" through the lens of twenty-first-century America, one wonders how long it will be before there is an end to the repeated instances of unarmed black people being stopped by the police for minor offenses and ending up shot and killed or dying after being taken into custody. That is what happened in Ferguson, Missouri, in Cleveland and Cincinnati, Ohio, in Charleston, South Carolina, in Smyrna, Georgia, and in Waller County, Texas, all within one year. One could also wonder how long the even greater carnage caused by black-on-black crime or intracommunal violence will last before some needed remedies can be introduced.

Persons battling diseases that seem to resist all existing treatments, ranging from certain cancers to HIV/AIDS, are all too familiar with the wish that something good would happen for them "at this time." Whether you are an unemployed person looking for a job, a devout single Christian looking for godly companionship, or a person who believes that society has gotten so bad that these must be signs of the end-time, the feeling may well be the same: "Lord, are you going to do it *at this time*?"

Regrettably, the long wait for healing, for justice, for deliverance, or for an equal opportunity often goes on and on. It does not mean that God cannot do what we are asking. It only means that we cannot speed God up in accomplishing whatever the divine plan or purpose might be. Jesus told his disciples, "It is not for you to know the times or dates the Father has set by his own authority" (Acts 1:7). The same is true for us modern-day disciples as well. God is worth waiting for no matter how long that wait might be. In the meantime, we draw hope from the words of Isaiah 40:31-32, spoken at the very time Israel was finally being delivered from her Babylonian captivity after seventy years of exile: "Those who hope in the LORD will renew their strength. They will soar on wings like eagles; they will run and not grow weary, they will walk and not be faint."

"Restore the Kingdom"

The third problem with the disciples' question as far as Jesus must have been concerned involved this same urgent expectation that what Christ had come into the world to accomplish had more to do with Israel's glorious past than it did with the world's uncertain future. Their question was "Lord, are you at this time going to *restore the kingdom* to Israel?" (Acts 1:6, emphasis added). They imagined that brief moment in time during the successive reigns of King David and King Solomon in the tenth century BC when Israel was a powerful, prosperous, and sovereign nation. Given the horrors Israel had experienced in the years prior to David and Solomon, and in the years that came after Solomon's death, it is little wonder that an oppressed people dreamed about a day when they could reclaim their former glory.

Like many other nations I have read about, and like many churches I have known all too well, there is the pervasive sense of nostalgia for some golden past. "If only we could get back to the way things were before. If only we could recapture the status and stature we enjoyed when so-and-so was the pastor. If only we could get back to the way things were before those people showed up." Some among the first followers of Jesus thought that his entire mission was to result in the return of Israel to its "good old days." Likewise, some among Jesus' modern-day disciples cling to the desire to go back to a time when things were better.

Many in our country today are preoccupied with a longing for a glorious past. Senator Trent Lott of Mississippi confirmed this truth when he lamented in 2002 that the arch-segregationist Strom Thurmond had not been elected president of the United States when he ran back in 1948. Lott said, "When Strom Thurmond ran for president, we in Mississippi voted for him. We are proud of it. And if the rest of the country had followed our lead we wouldn't have had all these problems over the years, either."[8] (The "problems" he was referring to were the events of the civil rights movement of the 1950s and '60s.) Trent Lott and Strom Thurmond both wanted to restore America to a time when white supremacy prevailed and black people knew their place and stayed in it.

A few years ago I heard a woman on a C-Span broadcast that was covering a Tea Party Convention in Arkansas. She too expressed her desire for a return to America's golden past. She could be heard repeating over and over again, "I want my America back." I could guess at once what it was that she wanted back. That broadcast occurred not long after President Barack Obama had nominated Sonia Sotomayor to become an associate justice of the United States Supreme Court. What that Tea Party attendee wanted back was an America where there was no African American president who could nominate a Puerto Rican woman to the nation's highest court.

Like ancient Israel, many people in contemporary America are hoping that their golden past can be restored. Like ancient Israel, there are many contemporary Americans for whom their golden past was someone else's nightmare.

Those Were the Days

My years in seminary happened to coincide with the airing of the TV series *All in the Family*. It was a weekly situation comedy that revolved around a character named Archie Bunker. He was a bigot of the first order who seemed to have grievances with or contempt for every racial and ethnic group in the country with the exception of white Protestant males. He didn't like African Americans. He didn't like Jews. He did not like the Chinese. He didn't like intellectuals. He didn't like Hispanics. He didn't like anybody who was very much different from himself. The whole tone of the show was captured by the lyrics of the song Archie and Edith Bunker sang together at the beginning of each weekly program: "Those were the days!"

That is the language of a person whose only interest was to recall a time that worked to his advantage. The song speaks about knowing one's place in society and not doing anything to challenge or rearrange that social order. Needless to say, in the worldview of Archie Bunker, anyone other than another equally bigoted white male need not apply. "Those were the days." *"Lord, are you . . . going to restore . . . ?"*

Nostalgia over some long-past bygone era is one of the biggest obstacles to societal advancement. While one group that has long been locked out of the mainstream is making strides toward equal opportunity and expanded access to the benefits of the nation, there always seems to be another group trying to prevent change from occurring lest they lose some of their personal privilege and power. Hence, one group's sense of nostalgia over a preferred past often results in attempts to deny another group's desire to move from the margins of society where they have been intentionally and systematically confined toward a brighter future for themselves and for their children and grandchildren.

Consider Voting Rights in the United States

The clearest example of this struggle between restoring a preferred past and laying claim to a brighter future can be seen with the debates and struggles that have attended the fight for the expanded voting rights of African Americans. This struggle has been ongoing for the last 145 years since the passage of the Fifteenth Amendment in 1870 guaranteeing voting rights without regard "to previous condition of servitude." As examined in a *New York Times* article dealing with the fiftieth anniversary of the signing of the Voting Rights Act, every step forward in terms of voting rights for blacks was met with stiff and even violent resistance by whites who wanted to hang on to a world where only they had the power of the ballot box.[9]

The article's author, Jim Rutenberg, pointed out that the effects of the Fifteenth Amendment came quickly as black voters sent hundreds of their own people into offices at every level of government. Eric Foner, in his study of the era known as Reconstruction, the years between 1865–1877, estimated that more than two thousand black people were elected to office, most of them in the states that constituted the former Confederacy.[10] Rutenberg also reported that the reaction to those political advances by blacks, who in many instances were former slaves who now had political authority over former slave owners, came just as quickly and with devastating force.

> Democrats throughout the South responded to the growing influence of black legislators with a brutal effort to suppress the black vote, enforced by the Ku Klux Klan and its many paramilitary imitators, who kept blacks from election polls at gunpoint and

> whipped and lynched many who resisted. The Southern Democrats ran on an open message of white supremacy and quickly retook statehouses, city halls and courthouses throughout the South. Within 15 years Reconstruction was just a memory.[11]

You could almost hear white Southern Democrats singing their own version of "Those Were the Days" as they did everything they could, legally and illegally, to restore the South to the political power structure that had existed prior to the end of the Civil War. "And you knew where you were then."

That song has reemerged all across the former Confederacy as a result of the 2013 case of *Shelby County v. Holder* argued before the US Supreme Court. The court ruled as unconstitutional certain provisions in Section 5 of the Voting Rights Act, and thus no longer required those requiring nine Southern states with a long history of voter suppression to get approval from the federal government or a federal district court judge before any changes in their voting laws could be made. Since that time there has been an endless string of efforts to go back to a time before there were such things as early voting, same-day registration, the use of provisional ballots when names do not appear on the voter rolls, and voting on Sunday, which in many black churches had come to be known as "souls to the polls."

On the very next day after that ruling from the court, North Carolina, Texas, Alabama, and Mississippi began implementing rules that essentially had the effect of tightening voting laws to the disadvantage of blacks and other minorities.[12] Requiring government-issued IDs as a prerequisite for voting in many states was called a safeguard against voter fraud, except that those same states could not point to a single instance of voter fraud going back many years. The issue was not voter fraud; the issue was who was being limited in their right to vote.[13]

There are still people in this country who stand with the Lord's first disciples with their eyes fixed squarely on the past, hoping that the world will be restored to a time when things worked solely to their advantage. They still sing, "Those were the days!"

"Restore the Kingdom to Israel"

The final fault with the question from the disciples flows straight out of the sentiments of the Lotts and Thurmonds and Archie Bunkers of the world: "Lord, are you at this time going to restore the kingdom *to Israel*?" (Acts 1:6, emphasis added). Those first-century disciples of Jesus knew there were Romans, Greeks, Egyptians, and Ethiopians in the world, but they did not seem eager to include any of them in their kingdom. They had no doubt encountered people from many different countries as caravans passed through Israel and as sailing ships docked in Caesarea and Joppa, bringing diversity of goods, cultures, and ethnicities from faraway places.

Exposure to diversity was one thing; inclusion of that diversity in their long-awaited kingdom was apparently another matter altogether. There have always been people who stumble over the difference between "justice" and "just us." They want justice, but only for "just us." They want health care, but only for "just us." They want the police to protect and serve, but only for "just us." They want upward economic mobility, access to the fullest dimensions of the American dream, and the promise that the world they pass on to their children will be a better world than they themselves inherited. They speak the words of the Pledge of Allegiance regarding "liberty and justice for all." But from a political and economic point of view, what they really prefer is "liberty and justice for just us."

Racial and Ethnic Divides

The problem of racial and ethnic division has haunted the world for centuries and millennia. It showed up during the pogroms against Jews in Eastern Europe and in the Holocaust during the Nazi era in Germany. It is showing up in full force today in Israel/Palestine and in the ideologies of ISIS and Boko Haram. It is also showing up in the streets of Ferguson, Missouri; Staten Island, New York; Cleveland and Cincinnati, Ohio; Madison, Wisconsin; Charleston, South Carolina; Harrell County, Texas; and other big cities and small towns across this country where police encounters with black citizens seem so often to result in the death of those civilians.

Gender Politics in the Church

Divisions are not limited to matters of race or ethnicity. A great many males still acknowledge God's prerogative to call people into the ministry, but they would prefer from a gender point of view that God would limit the selection to "just us." Would male clergy who privately support women in ministry run the risk of speaking publicly in favor of women in ministry if doing so might result in the loss of the friendship of male colleagues who do not agree with them on the issue? The silence about the role of women in ministry is deafening in many American churches. The tortured exegesis employed by those who oppose women in ministry often goes unchallenged by other preachers who are not opposed to women in ministry; they just choose silence over the possibility of suffering some consequence for their convictions.

The argument that women should not be allowed to exercise leadership gifts in the church is based primarily on two texts from the first century AD, 1 Corinthians 14:34-35 and 1 Timothy 2:11-12. Of course, these two texts are a perfect reflection of the low social status assigned to women in that patriarchal, first-century society. Why would women who were not important enough at that time to be counted in the census, and whose status in society was always in relation to some male family member, be considered as deserving of a leadership role in the synagogue or the early church? The essential question for the church in the twenty-first century is whether we can and should attempt to maintain a first-century view of the role of women.

As Martin Luther King Jr. observed, the church is more often the taillight of society than the headlight. The church is always trying to catch up to changes that have already occurred throughout society. Hillary Clinton is seeking the nomination of the Democratic Party to run for the office of president of the United States. Prior to seeking that political office Clinton had been a United States senator from New York and US Secretary of State under President Barack Obama. Needless to say, she also served as First Lady of the United States from 1992–2000. Nevertheless, if she expressed a call to ministry some would object and insist that she should not be ordained or allowed to serve in a pastoral leadership role. "Just us" say the male clergy.

Homophobia: The Last Allowable Form of Discrimination

Because some people are absolutely certain that God's love is limited to "just us," they have no hesitation in condemning their LGBT (lesbian, gay, bisexual, transgender) neighbors to hell. The late preacher and theologian Peter Gomes pointed out that hatred of and bigotry toward persons in this group is "the last allowable form of discrimination that will not result in broad societal condemnation."[14] A national uproar was raised by a small but vocal group of black Baptist pastors who objected to the presence of a certain preacher on the campus of one of the historically black colleges solely because she was in a same-sex marriage.

None of those pastors sought to rally the nation around the issue of adultery within the ranks of the clergy or in the pews of their own churches. No such restrictions were being suggested for high-profile black preachers who had been publicly exposed for improper sexual activities with women and children who were members of the very congregations where those male pastors were serving as spiritual leaders! Such an attack might come closer to home.

Those black Baptist pastors came to the conclusion, based on their reading of Leviticus 18:22 and Romans 1:26-27, that LGBT persons and especially those who have entered into a same-gender marriage cannot and should not be allowed to serve in the ministry of the church. I wonder how much more of Leviticus they are willing to live by. Leviticus 11 prohibits the eating of rabbit, pork, shellfish, and many other foods that are a regular part of our twenty-first-century diet. What about Leviticus 12, which requires women to perform ritual bathing after childbirth? That chapter also requires circumcision of the newborn male on the eighth day after birth. Not only that, but when the mother of a newborn child returns to the place of worship after giving birth, she must first offer a lamb as a burnt offering. Leviticus

17:10-14 outlaws eating rare steaks because some blood remains in the meat. Leviticus 18:19 instructs husbands not to have intimate relations with their wives during their menstrual cycle. Leviticus 25:10 calls for the observance of a Jubilee year during which all debts are forgiven and all prisoners are released. Leviticus 21 prohibits persons with any physical handicap or defect such as a limp or blindness from serving at the altar of the tabernacle or temple.

No one seriously believes that twenty-first-century Christians are going to govern their lives by these tenth-century BC religious laws. Yet Leviticus 18:22 continues to be invoked as if time has stood still! The fact is those black Baptist preachers and thousands like them across the country do not want the church to conform to Levitical law. They are simply hopelessly engaged in selective biblical analysis that only focuses on those verses and prohibitions that support their own bigotry and bias. They have fallen into the problem of "justice" for "just us." *"Lord, are you at this time going to restore the kingdom to Israel?"*

There is a lot of preaching material at this point for those with the courage to wade in, not just to the twenty-first-century issues being considered, but also into what constitutes faithful and authentic biblical exegesis. A great many issues are confronting the church and the broader society that are fueled more by prejudice and fear than by any careful biblical or theological analysis.

Jesus Left No Group Behind

This narrow view of the kingdom of God longed for by the disciples must have been especially disappointing to Jesus because over the preceding three years they had witnessed him operating in an entirely different way. Jesus' disciples had seen the Lord ignore multiple social barriers when he interacted with a Samaritan woman (John 4:4-29). They had seen him cross cultural and political boundaries when he agreed to heal the servant of a Roman centurion (Matthew 8:5-13). They had heard him tell the parable of the Good Samaritan, which would have been the ultimate contradiction in first-century Israel (Luke 10:25-37), because no Samaritans were ever considered to be good. In short, they had repeatedly seen Jesus open his heart to persons who were not Jewish. But all they were interested in was the restoration of their own country.

They were even aware of the one occasion when Jesus at first refused to open his heart to a Canaanite woman because he said he been sent only to the children of Israel (Matthew 15:24). He told her, "It is not right to take the children's bread and toss it to the dogs" (v. 26). But she would not be deterred. She responded by saying, "Yes it is, Lord. Even the dogs eat the crumbs that fall from their master's table" (v. 27). With that show of faith in Jesus, the woman's request was honored and her daughter was healed.

Nevertheless, at the end of three years with Jesus, the disciples had not learned to include anyone but other Jews in their kingdom. *"Lord, are you at this time going to restore the kingdom to Israel?"*

A Lesson from the Synagogue in Nazareth

One of the most revealing moments in Jesus' life as far as his worldview was concerned is recorded in Luke 4:16-30 and occurred in Nazareth, his boyhood home. He went to the synagogue, and on entering he was given the honor of reading a portion of Scripture, Isaiah 61:1-3. The actual text from Isaiah says:

> The Spirit of the Sovereign LORD is on me,
> because the LORD has anointed me
> to proclaim good news to the poor.
> He has sent me to bind up the brokenhearted,
> to proclaim freedom for the captives
> and release from darkness for the prisoners,
> to proclaim the year of the LORD's favor
> and the day of vengeance of our God,
> to comfort all who mourn
> and provide for those who grieve in Zion.

After reading that text dealing with what Israel expected when the Messiah came, Jesus said, "Today this scripture is fulfilled in your hearing" (Matthew 4:21). Jesus declared himself to be the long-awaited Messiah. In response to that startling proclamation, Luke 4:22 says, "All spoke well of him and were amazed at the gracious words that came from his lips. 'Isn't this Joseph's son?' they asked." A young man whom they all had watched grow up in Nazareth announced to them that he was the Messiah they had been waiting for over the last seven hundred years, and the people in that synagogue did not accuse him of blasphemy, which would have been the normal reaction for anyone who claimed to be the Messiah. Instead, they just sat there amazed at the gracious words that fell from his lips.

However, a few verses later, we find Jesus saying:

> "Truly I tell you, no prophet is accepted in his hometown. I assure you that there were many widows in Israel in Elijah's time, when the sky was shut for three and a half years and there was a severe famine throughout the land. Yet Elijah was not sent to any of them, but to a widow in Zarephath in the region of Sidon. And there were many in Israel with leprosy in the time of Elisha the prophet, yet not one of them was cleansed—only Naaman the Syrian." (John 4:24-27)

When Jesus suggested that non-Jews could possibly be a part of God's divine actions, the response he got was immediate and visceral: "All the people in that synagogue were furious when they heard this. They got up, drove him out of the town, and took him to the brow of the hill on which the town was built, in order to throw him off the cliff" (Luke 4:28-29).

It is astounding to think that Jesus could claim to be the Messiah while standing inside the synagogue in Nazareth, the town in which he had grown up, and no one spoke a single word of censure, shock, or disapproval. However, when he spoke favorably about two people, both of whom were not Jewish, and suggested that the love of God could possibly be extended to them, the people in his hometown sought to kill him. These people had been waiting a long time for their Messiah to appear, and it seemed to matter less to them that Jesus had just claimed to be that Messiah than that he had suggested that their Messiah could possibly be sympathetic to Phoenicians and Syrians. *"Lord, are you at this time going to restore the kingdom to Israel?"*

Time for a Last-Minute Lesson

The remainder of this book must be read and understood against the background of the disciples' question in Acts 1:6. Jesus did not seek to answer the narrow and self-centered inquiry of his disciples. Instead, he used his last minutes on earth to refocus their attention on the work he had really come into the world to accomplish. Instead of assuring them of a swift return to a glorious past, he was about to challenge them to embrace the risks and challenges of an uncertain future: "Be my witnesses in Jerusalem, and in all Judea and Samaria, and to the ends of the earth." This was not a "just us" mission; this was the beginning of establishing God's justice and reign throughout the world.

Modern-day disciples of Jesus must also give shape to their preaching and their character formation against the backdrop of Acts 1:6-8. The work that Jesus assigned to his disciples in the moments before his final departure from the earth in physical form remains the work of preachers and churches today: "Be my witnesses in Jerusalem, and in all Judea and Samaria, and to the ends of the earth."

Preaching becomes one of the ways our common faults and flaws can be lifted up and discussed. Thus this question raised by these first disciples is beneficial to the church today only to the degree that we learn from their mistakes, seek to discern more clearly what Jesus was and is actually saying, and respond appropriately to those teachings. For those looking for themes, texts, and topics for upcoming Sunday sermons, this single question from the disciples in Acts 1:6 provides an almost unlimited supply of possibilities.

Times Have Changed, but People's Hearts Have Not

To be sure, today's world is separated from the world of the early church and those first twelve disciples by two thousand years of history, culture, politics, religious practice, and language. As a result of that fact, there are many aspects of church life and practice that while true in the first century in Palestine or Asia Minor or southern Europe are not embraced or observed in twenty-first-century American church life. For instance, the quiet acceptance of slavery as a fact of life ordained by God and to be accepted by those being held in bondage is no longer argued or accepted. The fervent expectation of the imminent return of Christ to the earth during their lifetime, undoubtedly in a blaze of apocalyptic glory, has long since been replaced by the realization that the true mission of the church is to work in the world and not worry about when we might be leaving it for the fairer confines of some New Jerusalem.

That being said, some remarkable and time-resistant realities link our two worlds together and make the challenges of preaching now very similar to preaching then. Karl Barth referenced a phrase from Paul Tillich about preaching. Tillich said that preaching must be done with "an awareness of the present moment."[15] In the first century and no less in the twenty-first century, the challenge and the opportunity of the preacher was and is to declare the gospel of Jesus Christ in a way that shows an awareness of the present moment.

The first disciples were being sent out to preach in a world dominated by the military and political power of the Roman Empire, as well as by the rival claims and practices of competing religious groups, each of which offered an alternative vision of what religious polity and piety should involve. Within that world, the task of the preacher was to declare the lordship of Christ, knowing full well that such a claim was an affront to Rome, which ascribed lordship and divinity to Caesar (Romans 10:9). It was an equal affront to both Jews and Gentiles who would resist and even ridicule the idea that believing in Jesus of Nazareth who had died on a cross was the sole way to God (1 Corinthians 1:23). Those first disciples also had to preach in the face of those who argued that a confession of faith in Christ was not sufficient for salvation, that converts would still need to be circumcised, adhere to Jewish dietary laws, or pursue the secret knowledge known only through adherence to Gnosticism.

Preachers today face similar challenges. Our world is dominated by the military and economic power of the United States, even though that reality is currently being challenged by the military power of China and Russia and by the growing economic clout of nations like Brazil, India, China, and others.[16]

Rival religious claims are no less present now than they were for the first disciples. A wide variety of expression exists even within the three Abrahamic religious traditions. Christianity, Judaism, and Islam defy any singular description, whether in theological or sociopolitical terms. Then there are the various other religious groups, to say nothing about those persons who self-describe as agnostic, atheist, spiritual, or "none." And some people still argue that confession of faith in Christ is not sufficient for salvation and that some other action, such as speaking in tongues, is required.

In the remainder of this book, I set forth an approach to biblical and topical text selection for preachers that flows out of the challenge Jesus set before his disciples in response to their misinformed question. We will look closely at what Jesus said to those first disciples about *what* they should be prepared to preach, *where* they should be prepared to go to do that preaching, and *how* they should expect to be sustained and empowered once their preaching ministry was under way.

I will make the case that despite the passing of two thousand years of history, and despite the fact that this book is written from a social and cultural location far different from the world where Christian preaching first occurred, Acts 1:6-8 remains instructive for today's preachers. The words Jesus spoke when he sent forth his original disciples to preach the gospel can and should serve as a challenge for all who undertake the preaching task in the twenty-first century.

What does preaching in today's culture need to involve? How do today's preachers declare the gospel in ways that reveal an awareness of the present moment? The answer to those questions is essentially the same as the answer given by Jesus two thousand years ago in Acts 1:6-8: *"Be my witnesses."*

NOTES

1. Alfred H. Ackley, "He Lives," in *African American Heritage Hymnal* (Chicago: GIA, 2001), 275.

2. Benjamin Quarles, *The Negro in the Civil War* (New York: DaCapo, 1953), 210; Harry Ploski and Ernest Kaiser, *The Negro Almanac* (New York: Bellwether, 1971), 596.

3. "This Day in History, September 13, 1814, Key Pens Star-Spangled Banner," history.com, http://www.history.com/this-day-in-history/key-pens-star-spangled-banner/print.

4. Robert McCracken, *The Making of the Sermon* (New York: Harper and Brothers, 1956), 18.

5. Marvin A. McMickle, *Living Water for Thirsty Souls* (Valley Forge, PA: Judson, 2001), 177–84.

6. Ibid., 180.

7. Jenni Frazer, "Wiesel: Yes, We Really Did Put God on Trial," *The Jewish Chronicle Online*, September 19, 2008, http://www.thejc.com/news/uk-news/wiesel-yes-we-really-did-put-god-trial.

8. "Lott Apologizes for Remark," FoxNews.com, December 12, 2002, http://www.foxnews.com/story/ 2002/12/12/lott-apologizes-for-remark.html.

9. Jim Rutenberg, "A Dream Undone: Inside the 50-Year Campaign to Roll Back the Voting Rights Act," *New York Times Magazine*, July 29, 2015, http://www.nytimes.com/2015/07/29/magazine/voting-rights-act-dream-undone.html?_r=0.

10. Eric Foner, *A Short History of Reconstruction* (New York: Harper Perennial, 1990).

11. Rutenberg, "A Dream Undone."

12. Myrna Perez, "After 'Shelby County', Ruling Are Voting Rights Endangered?," Brennan Center for Justice, www.brennancenter.org, September 23, 2013, p. 3.

13. Of more than 21 million U.S. citizens who don't possess government-issued identification, a disproportionate number are found among racial and ethnic minorities, low-income individuals, and the elderly. https://www.aclu.org /oppose-voter-id-legislation-fact-sheet.

14. Peter Gomes, *The Good Book: Reading the Bible with Mind and Heart* (New York: Avon, 1996), 144ff.; and "Black Christians and Homosexuality: The Pathology of a Permitted Prejudice," *African American Pulpit*, Summer 2001, 30–33.

15. Karl Barth, *The Preaching of the Gospel* (Philadelphia: Westminster, 1961), 54.

16. See Thomas Friedman, *The World Is Flat: A Brief History of the 21st Century* (New York: Farrar, Strauss and Giroux, 2005); and Fareed Zacharia, *The Post-American World* (New York: W. W. Norton, 2009).

CHAPTER 5

Be My Witnesses

"Be my witnesses in Jerusalem, and in all Judea and Samaria, and to the ends of the earth." —Acts 1:7-8

Let's now give attention to Jesus' exact language in his challenge in Acts 1:7-8. What, precisely, did he say to his first disciples in the moments before he ascended into heaven, leaving to them the responsibility of carrying on the work he had begun three years earlier? Because the premise of this book is that the challenge set before those first-century disciples forms the basis for a theology of preaching in the twenty-first century, we need more than a simple recounting of what Jesus said to those gathered around him on his last day on earth. Our primary objective is to reflect on what Jesus is saying to us today through this text as far as our preaching ministry is concerned. Any preacher wondering what he or she should be preaching from week to week and from year to year should regularly reflect on the lessons set forth in Acts 1:6-8.

Remember, this was the moment for which Jesus had been training and equipping the disciples all along. They had followed him, listened to him, observed his actions, and hopefully absorbed his message. Now was the time for them to go and preach the gospel throughout the whole world (Matthew 28:18-20). However, as demonstrated in Acts 1:6 and discussed in detail in the preceding chapters, those disciples were not at all clear about what it was that they should do next. Rather than seek clarity about their assignment, they turned to Jesus and asked, "Lord, are you at this time going to restore the kingdom to Israel?" The disciples were about to drop the baton so far as understanding what was expected of them once Jesus was physically gone from the earth.

What Does It Mean to Be a Witness?

It was in response to the disciples' apparent lack of clarity concerning their assignment that Jesus stated his expectations as plainly as possible. Jesus told them that their job was not to ask what he was going to do next. Their job was not to speculate about when God might usher in the messianic era. Their job was quite specific: "Be my witnesses in Jerusalem, and in all Judea and Samaria, and to the ends of the earth."

The question for us today is, what does it mean to be a witness? As I noted in the introduction, the word itself is open to various levels of understanding and interpretation. Therefore, we must glean as many insights as possible into the meaning of this word and the imperative "Be my witnesses." As we gain greater clarity about the word, we can better see how the first generation of disciples went about the task of being witnesses to Christ. Having done that, we can then make some suggestions about how today's preachers can use that word and that imperative as the primary lens through which to approach our own preaching ministries.

Jesus at the Center of Our Preaching

On the most basic level, being a witness for Jesus means that the gospel story must be at the center of our preaching all the time. Preachers are not sent out to determine for themselves what the content of their preaching should be; they are to bear witness to the message of Jesus Christ. The work of Christ's disciples then and now is to focus on "all that Jesus began to do and to teach until the day he was taken up to heaven, after giving instructions through the Holy Spirit to the apostles he had chosen" (Acts 1:1-2). The first challenge for preachers today is to be sure that Jesus is at the center of what we are preaching and not some other topic or theme.

The advice of Karl Barth on the connection between preaching and Scripture is useful at this point. To paraphrase him lightly, Barth stated:

> The purpose of preaching is to explain the Scriptures. . . . There is, therefore, nothing to be said which is not already to be found in the Scriptures. No doubt preachers will be conscious of the weight of their own ideas which they drag after them; but ultimately they must decide whether they will allow themselves to compromise or whether, in spite of all notions at the back of their mind, they will accept the necessity of expounding the Book and nothing else.[1]

What God expects from every faithful preacher, and what all faithful preachers must demand of themselves is that their sermons as well as their lives bear witness to the things that Jesus has said and done. In seeing and hearing us, people should be able to catch a glimpse of the spirit and values of Jesus. At this point preachers are joined together with all the followers of Jesus under the obligation to "let your light shine before others, that they may see your good deeds and glorify your Father in heaven" (Matthew 5:16).

However, when it comes to those who preach the gospel, the expectation set before us extends beyond the matter of personal piety and daily discipleship. The expectation of the preacher is that the sermon will serve primarily to point people to Christ, who is the source of their deliverance from sin. The gospel offers them spiritual sustenance throughout the journey of life, exhorting them in their daily duties as disciples and grounding them in the hope that at the end of their days there awaits them a house not made with hands. Faithful preaching that centers on this gospel helps people cope with what may have been a shameful past, a present that may be marked by challenges and setbacks, and possible uncertainty about what awaits them in the future.

Balancing the Personal and Public in Preaching

Let us note that the gospel is not mainly or even primarily about matters of personal salvation and individual spiritual formation. As important as it is to place "the plan of salvation" on the minds of those who hear our sermons, it is just as important if not more so to place the mandate of Matthew 25:31-44 before them as well: "I was hungry . . . thirsty . . . a stranger . . . [in need of] clothes . . . sick . . . in prison and you. . . ." If we preach as witnesses for Jesus, then we must regularly challenge people with a message that echoes Jesus' concern for the poor, the marginalized, and the powerless.

We are not fulfilling our role as witnesses for Jesus in this world if we continually favor the ease and safety of sermons about individual sin while failing to talk about the corporate and societal sin that we see every night on the evening news, every morning in the newspaper headlines, and virtually every hour as news alerts appear on our mobile phones and electronic tablets.

Here is a good way for busy preachers to think about sermon materials and about the sources of new ideas, all the while keeping Jesus at the center of their sermons. A rotation between matters of the individual soul and matters of the broader society can result in a rich array of sermon materials. That is the major lesson offered by Cleophus LaRue in his book *The Heart of Black Preaching*. He argues that black preachers have sought to direct their sermons to what he refers to as "domains of experience"[2]:

- *personal piety*, or spiritual formation and daily devotions;
- *care of the soul*, or ministry in times of crisis for individuals or families;
- *social justice*, or matters calling for and helping to bring about societal reform;
- *corporate concerns*, or the self-help needed to overcome problems within one's own racial or ethnic group; and
- *maintenance of the institutional church*, or the constant search for the human and financial resources needed to fund, staff and operate all the programs of the local church.[3]

This notion of preachers being a witness by keeping Jesus at the center of our sermons is a good point of departure for this chapter, but it does not exhaust the possible ways by which the idea of being a witness can be understood or enacted. Jesus' challenge to "be my witnesses" supplies a key phrase that can and should be understood in three distinct ways. When considered together, those three facets of *witness* bring into clearer focus the mission of those first disciples and our own mission as preachers.

As observed briefly in the introduction, a *witness* is someone who *sees something*, *says something* about what he or she has seen, and understands that he or she may end up *suffering something* as a result of saying something. This chapter offers an overview of these three aspects of what it means to be a witness, and subsequent chapters will follow with a more thorough analysis of each one.

See Something

First and fundamentally, a witness is someone who, by paying close attention to the surrounding world, is able to *see something*. This is clearly the most basic aspect of being a witness; it implies that the person is an observer of events unfolding around him or her. This is being a witness in the sense of being an *eye*witness and, more importantly, being the kind of eyewitness who not only sees with the physical eye in a superficial way but perceives the importance of what he or she observes.

Preachers must be good witnesses; that is, we must pay attention to what is happening in the lives of the people in our congregations and communities. Our witness does not end at the front doors of our sanctuaries. To be a witness for Jesus is to extend our focus to areas of advocacy and even activism on behalf of the community in which we live and serve, continuing Christ's redemptive and prophetic ministry by expanding the reign of God in the world.

The work of witnessing, or paying attention, does not stop within our neighborhoods; it must extend as far as the sovereignty of God extends over creation—namely, to the country in which the preacher lives and beyond that to events unfolding in the global community. To quote the song by Motown artist Marvin Gaye, a witness is someone who can answer the question of "What's going on?"[4]

The preacher must seek to know "what's going on" in the neighborhood and in the nation, across the street and across the country, around the corner and around the world. This cannot be done solely by visual observation. Seeing things this broadly requires that preachers pay attention to various news media, whether print, online, or broadcast on TV and radio. Preachers need to follow trends in the arts and entertainment, resolutions and statements of concern from denominational gatherings, and issues that inspire local street demonstrations. We need to observe what is going on with police and community relations and with the ever-widening political, cultural, and wealth gap throughout this country.

Preachers need to develop the daily discipline of taking time to *see something*. Reading and studying the Bible should always be the center of preachers' devotional and professional lives. However, as we seek to be witnesses who are able to *see something* through close observation of daily events both at home and abroad, we will be more effective in relating the truths of Scripture to the needs and challenges of daily life for people in the twenty-first century.

Say Something

The second part of being a witness for Christ involves a person's willingness and determination to *say something* about what he or she has seen. The best way to think about witnessing at this point is to think about an oath in a court of law in which an individual swears to tell the truth, the whole truth, and nothing but the truth concerning the event that has been seen.

Preachers need to speak the whole truth about what they have seen and about what we as Christians should do about what we have seen. When we see human suffering, spiritual decline, political corruption, impending ecological and environmental disaster, or a steady buildup toward another war that will cause as much damage as leaders claim it will prevent, what are we prepared to say about those things as preachers? Better yet, what does the gospel and the whole of the biblical story have to say about those things?

This is not an invitation for a preacher to make up something to say on whatever topic is trending. A sermon is not the appropriate occasion for hearing the preacher's personal opinions on one matter or another. As humbling as it may be for us to accept this fact, nobody gets up on Sunday morning eager to hear what we think or have to say about current events. And even if that is what some people are expecting from the preacher, that is certainly not what God is expecting from us. God did not entrust us with the gospel so we can expound our personal views. The point of the sermon is for the preacher to echo the words of the biblical prophets whose authority to speak was cloaked in the phrase "thus says the Lord." Or as Karl Barth observed, we must "expound the Book and nothing else."[5]

I learned this lesson about what people come to church to hear in a very memorable way during my pastoral assignment at St. Paul Baptist Church in Montclair, New Jersey, from 1976 to 1986. Every Sunday morning before the worship service, I was visited by the chair of the board of deacons, who asked the same question each week: "Rev, is there any word from the Lord?" This question, borrowed from King Zedekiah's question to the prophet Jeremiah (Jeremiah 37:17), was a weekly reminder to me of what the congregation was expecting—"a word from the Lord" and not an op-ed statement from me.

We must keep Jesus at the center of our preaching. People in our churches are hearing messages of one type or another all the time. They are bombarded with information from emails, text messages, and voice mail at home, work, and on mobile phones. They hear messages on a wide variety of topics from political advertising, financial planners, talk radio and TV hosts, and even their own family and friends. In the midst of this information overload, people are still willing to grant authority and legitimacy to the preacher who stands up to *say something* in the name of the Lord—something that will help them face the challenges of daily life.

What might help people decide whether to pay more attention to one message than another? People are more likely to pay attention to a message that deals with a subject *relevant* in their lives and with a source and substance *rooted* in the teachings of Scripture.

This is a good time to consider another point paraphrased from Karl Barth, himself a skilled preacher before he became one of the defining theologians of the twentieth century: "Preaching should be an explanation of Scripture. Preachers do not have to speak 'on' but 'from,' drawing from the Scriptures whatever they say. They do not have to invent, but rather to repeat something. No thesis, no purpose derived from their own resources must be allowed to intervene; God alone must speak."[6] If preaching is going to have any chance of being heard and heeded, the preacher will have to *say something* that is not his or her opinion but is God's will and God's word. "Rev, is there any word from the Lord?"

Suffer Something

The third dimension of being a witness may be less obvious to those of us who read Acts 1:7-8 in the English Bible, for it emerges from the Greek word *marturia*, translated as "witness," but from which we also derive our word *martyr.* The meaning becomes clear, but it is one that will always prove to be the most difficult to embrace. It defines a witness as someone who may have to *suffer something* for the sake of what he or she has seen and said.

Jesus challenges his disciples in every generation to speak the truth about what they see going on around them, even if they face the possibility of some form of suffering as a consequence of their speaking. That suffering may take many forms, ranging from ridicule to rejection to reprisal to removal—whether that removal is from the pulpit or from this earth.

Consider Peter and John in Jerusalem in Acts 4:20 after they had been told to stop preaching about Jesus. After having just been released from prison and knowing that any further preaching could return them to prison, they replied, "We cannot help speaking about what we have seen and heard." They faced ridicule by the religious leaders in Jerusalem, especially on the claims that Jesus was the Messiah and that after Jesus' crucifixion God had raised him from the dead. They faced imprisonment and physical abuse. Both of them would eventually suffer martyrdom.

That is what being a witness in the first century often looked like, and that is what Jesus' words in Acts 1:7-9 challenge every preacher in the twenty-first century to consider. How much suffering are we prepared to face in response to the things we have seen and spoken about?

You might not have expected to encounter this subject in a book on preaching. You might be more interested in learning about the mechanics of preaching—introductions, illustrations, applications, vocalization, and conclusions. You might want to learn about the ways preaching can aid in church growth and how skill as a preacher can broaden your opportunities to preach in ever-widening circles of prestige and influence. Such thinking points to the unmistakable problem confronting the twenty-first-century pulpit in too many places: the focus is more on numbers of people in the pews and the fame and popular appeal of the person in the pulpit than it is on the content of the biblical message. Under such a scenario, everything Jesus said to his first disciples and everything we should learn from them is lost in a mad quest for fame and broad popular appeal.

The call to be prepared to *suffer something* implies that the preacher may need to say some things that will not result in increased popularity, packed pews, and megachurch status. The preacher may need to say some things that will not speed up his rise in the convention or the denomination, will not result in younger preachers mimicking her style, and will not guarantee an appearance on Trinity Broadcasting Network. The preacher may have to speak an unpleasant truth, and if and when that happens, he may encounter an audience whose verbal response is not "Amen!" but "How dare you?"

The idea that God's people should expect to *suffer something* for the sake of their faith actually runs throughout the whole Bible. From Moses to the prophets to John the Baptist to the apostles of the early church, this principle proves to be true. (We will explore this biblical and early church history further in chapter 9.)

The Greek word for witness, *marturia*, means someone who is willing to face martyrdom or some lesser form of suffering as a direct result of having faithfully declared "Thus says the Lord" regarding the things she or he has seen. Thus we who preach from week to week need to ask ourselves when the last time was that our faithful preaching of the gospel resulted in some form of ridicule, rejection, reprisal, or removal from office. If the answer is that you have never met with any negative reactions of any kind after a faithful presentation of the teachings of Scripture, then you may need to reconsider the content of your sermons in light of the challenge found in Acts 1:7-8: "Be my *marturia*."

NOTES

1. Paraphrased from Karl Barth, *The Preaching of the Gospel* (Philadelphia: Westminster, 1963), 42–43.
2. Cleophus LaRue, *The Heart of Black Preaching* (Louisville: Westminster John Knox, 2000), 20.
3. Ibid., 21–25.
4. Marvin Gaye, Al Cleveland, and Renaldo Benson, "What's Going On?" Tamla Records, January 21, 1971.
5. Barth, *The Preaching of the Gospel*, 42.
6. Ibid., 15.

CHAPTER 6

See Something

The central assertion of this book is that what was true for the preachers of the first century AD is no less true for those of us who preach today. Witnesses for the Lord are the ones who have *seen something* that troubled them, *said something* that troubled those in power or who benefited from the status quo, and *suffered something* as a result of their faithful witness. We are called on to be witnesses for Jesus in all of these forms, so in this and the following two chapters, we will look at each in more depth.

An eyewitness is someone who *sees something* for himself and does not need to rely on second-hand information, whether rumors or reports. More precisely for our purposes here, a witness is a preacher who is paying attention to what is going on in the world and in the lives of those to whom that modern-day disciple is called to preach.

A witness is a preacher who has noticed both the rise in shootings of black men by police officers and the even steeper rise in black-on-black or intra-communal violence. A witness is a preacher who is paying attention to the steady decline of church attendance in most Protestant denominations, as well as the steady rise of perfectly good people who are deciding to self-identify their religious affiliation as "none." A witness is someone who sees the staggering wealth disparity in the United States and how that impacts everything from politics to education and from housing to health care.

The first step to being a witness is being someone who sees what is going on in the surrounding world. In the context of preaching, a witness is someone who is paying attention to what is happening to people inside the church, within the community, across the country, and around the world. When Jesus called the apostles to be his witnesses, he was calling them to be those who *see something*.

The words of theologian Paul Tillich quoted in chapter 2, "Preaching must be done with an awareness of the present moment,"[1] will run like a thread throughout this book. Karl Barth built on Tillich's observation by saying, "What demands does the contemporary situation make on the preacher and the congregation? Together they are sharing a historical experience; the words of the preacher must be relevant to immediate preoccupations of the hearers."[2]

How can such preaching take place if the preacher is unfamiliar with or out of step with the "immediate preoccupations" of the congregation? How can the preacher say anything of benefit or relevance to the congregation without working every day to *see something* that impacts the lives of those who will hear the sermon?

See the Social Environment

Seeing something must involve paying attention to everything from the physical neighborhoods in which people live to the social and cultural biases that place limits on the hopes and dreams they are seeking to live out day by day. This means paying attention to matters of age, economic status, any existing physical disabilities or mental illnesses, any anxieties over their own sexual orientation or that of someone in their family, or any broad disagreement within the congregation over matters that are being discussed and even acted on by the denominational body with which that local church might be affiliated.

Seeing something means taking note of what is happening in the lives of the most vulnerable and needy in our society. Consider the following things currently going on in the United States, and ask whether we preachers have been paying attention.

Immigration Reform

Have we paid attention to some of the hateful language employed as our nation thinks about immigration policy, especially as it involves our southern border with Mexico? Consider the anti-immigrant tone with which Republican Donald Trump began his quest for the 2016 presidential nomination, suggesting that "Mexico is sending rapists and murderers into the United States," and that 11.5 million undocumented immigrants must be arrested and removed from this country.[3] That mass deportation would include the children of those immigrants who were born in this country and thus, under the 14th Amendment to the US Constitution, are legal citizens of the United States. (Other candidates campaigning for their party's 2016 presidential nomination described those children as "anchor babies,"[4] implying that their birth in this country anchors or cements their status as US citizens.) This is especially odd considering that one of the persons using that term was himself born in Canada![5]

Following the forced removal of these immigrants, Trump said, a wall would be built to keep others from entering the country illegally. All of this at a time when illegal immigration into this country is actually at its lowest level in more than twenty years, and when the same is true about crimes committed by undocumented immigrants.[6]

All lives matter, it seems, unless they are Hispanic lives seeking greater economic opportunity outside of war-torn places like Guatemala or El Salvador or crime-ridden sections of Mexico.

A case can and should be made for reforming the process for legal immigration into the United States, but it should be made without criminalizing or dehumanizing those undocumented workers who are already in this country. A case should be made with integrity so that we do not on the one hand seek to profit from the hard labor provided by undocumented workers, especially in the agricultural sector of our society, while on the other hand demonizing their presence in the country.

How many farms and fields across the United States are worked from one agricultural cycle to another by persons who are undocumented with the full knowledge of those who own those fields and farms? Under what conditions do they work? For what wage do they work? With what worker's rights do they work? With what fear of being deported do they live on a daily basis if they complain about their working conditions?

I remember the first time I heard the racial slur "damn wetbacks." It was used in the same tone and context as persons at that and at earlier times in US history might have used the *N* word. "Wetback" crudely described migrant workers whose backs became wet when they entered the country illegally by hanging on to a truck that brought them across some river from Mexico to the United States. They became "damn wetbacks" when they did not provide their labor at a rate that satisfied the owners of the fields where they worked. The incentive of those men, women, and children to work harder was not a wage increase or improved living conditions. Rather, they worked hard to please the landowners so that they would not be reported to the Immigration and Naturalization Agency and end up being deported.

Homelessness

Preachers, have we seen the steady rise in the number of homeless persons sleeping on the streets of our great cities? I remember attending a professional conference meeting near the campus of the University of California at Berkeley. Every day as we walked back and forth from the hotel to the site of the conference, we passed a public park that was home to dozens of homeless people under makeshift tents, in sleeping bags, or simply on pieces of cardboard. And this was going on in the shadow of one of the most prestigious universities in the world.

It reminded me of Luke 16:19-31, where Jesus talked about a rich man who lived in luxury and a sick and impoverished beggar who was laid just outside that rich man's door. For the sake of the local church, for the good of society, and for the integrity of the gospel, we who preach must take the time to *see something* going on in the social environment in which those to whom we preach are living every day.

Human Sexuality

How does the Bible help to inform people concerning gender identity, sexual orientation, and controversies about same-sex marriage? What should people of faith make of Bruce Jenner/Caitlyn Jenner and the issue of being a transgender person? Why are 50 percent of heterosexual marriages ending in divorce? Why is there an online service called Ashley Madison that is used by 32 million people who are looking for ways to engage in extramarital affairs?[7] Why are more than 70 percent of babies born in the African American community born out of wedlock?

When we are looking for something to preach on from week to week, we should begin by taking the time to *see something* that is being debated and discussed in the news media, in the marketplace of public dialogue, and in the minds of the very people to whom we preach.

See the Spiritual Environment

Preachers must also be aware of any other religious messages or spiritual influences that may be directly competing with the gospel message that is being set before the congregation. The first-century disciples had to preach in an environment in which some people were already deeply committed to a radical form of monotheism (the belief in the existence of only one God who alone should be worshiped and honored) and to a faith informed and shaped by the law of Moses and its insistence on circumcision and strict adherence to certain dietary codes. Others were hearing the gospel after years of exposure to the teachings of Greek and Roman religious philosophy and in a society characterized by easy acceptance of polytheism (belief in the existence of and the need to honor and respect many different gods).

In addition to these first-century religious traditions, there were hedonists who talked about living a life marked by the enjoyment of all human pleasures, and there were Stoics who taught the exact opposite, preferring a life devoid of any excesses in self-indulgence and self-expression. There were Epicureans who advocated the enjoyment of food and drink, and there were ascetics who taught and practiced a severe form of self-denial of anything that might bring physical pleasure or enjoyment. There were Gnostics and followers of mystery cults that taught of hidden truth that could be accessed only through adherence to their teachings. There were fertility cults whose practice of ritual prostitution as a way to curry favor with certain gods was commonplace.

The early disciples clearly understood that they would have to present the gospel message in this environment of conflicting religious and philosophical teachings. Some of the first disciples, such as Peter and James, initially clung to the idea that a convert to Christianity could not be fully accepted without first conforming to all of the requirements of the Mosaic law, beginning with circumcision. A great deal of the book of Acts is devoted to this struggle, and it was not resolved until the Jerusalem Council was called and the participants agreed that any Gentile converts to Christianity would only have to "abstain from food polluted by idols, from sexual immorality, from the meat of strangled animals and from blood" (Acts 15:20).

While the church in Jerusalem addressed the controversy around Jewish versus Gentile identity in the Christian community, Paul's message in Acts 17 dealt with the question of monotheism versus polytheism in the city of Athens, the center of ancient polytheism. In verse 16 Paul attempted to exalt the person and the message of Jesus above all of the various gods of the Greco-Roman world. That text explicitly refers to Epicureans and Stoics who were gathered in the city. When Paul saw all the idols they reverenced, including one idol erected "TO AN UNKNOWN GOD" (Acts 17:23), he challenged them about being "very religious" ("superstitious" might have been his real meaning), using the reference to the unknown god to introduce them to the gospel of Jesus Christ.

At the end of Paul's sermon in Athens, some people believed and began to follow Christ. Others were at least interested enough to say, "We want to hear you again on this subject" (Acts 17:32). Paul's ministry in that moment was effective because he was a witness for Jesus Christ who was able to *see something* that was going on in the world around him that became a bridge to better communicating with his listeners.

The Postmodern Religious Landscape

Our day is a lot like Paul's. Preachers need to see that an increasing number of people are abandoning organized religion and church attendance.

They are substituting a claim of their "spirituality" for adherence to Christianity. The allure of being an agnostic who doubts and demurs on the existence of God or an atheist who openly denies the very existence of God is becoming increasingly popular in American society. We also have a growing number of persons who self-identify as "nones," who may claim to be "spiritual but not religious" or who decline to identify with any particular religious group.

The popularity of the book *God Is Not Great: How Religion Spoils Everything* by Christopher Hitchens[8] is an indication of the spiritual and theological climate in which we must do our preaching. The same is true with the television and public appearances of Bill Maher, who openly challenges religious faith on a nightly basis.

A recent *New York Times* story described the rise of what is called "new atheists" in America, which the article defined as people "who have scornful contempt for those with whom they differ—that includes religious believers, agnostics and other atheists who do not share their vehement brand of non-belief."[9] At the same time, the Pew Research Center reported a steady increase in religious nonbelief among younger Americans. Those born after 1980 are much more likely not to be religious than older Americans. "A remarkable 25 percent of Americans born after 1980, the group often known as millennials, are not religious, compared with 11 percent of baby boomers and 7 percent of the generation born between 1928 and 1945."[10]

These numbers must inform every preacher in this country. We are called on to preach at a time when the trend line for self-declared religious believers is gradually going down and the trend line for self-declared nonbelievers is steadily going up. If we are not paying attention, if we are not observing these cultural shifts, if we do not take the time to *see something* that has taken root all around the nation, then our preaching will be less able to present the gospel relevantly to people who are becoming increasingly familiar with other religions and philosophies, as well as to people who have rejected religious language and practice entirely.

Even in my present capacity as the leader of a theological seminary, I have been forced to take note of this change in the spiritual environment in which both local churches and seminaries operate. There was a time when a certain symmetry or symbiosis existed between the church and the seminary campus—a cycling of people from the church to the seminary and then back to the church as pastors and church leaders. The church would identify persons who showed gifts for ministry and urge them to attend seminary so as to discern and develop those gifts. The seminary would train those persons for careers in the church and send them out to serve local churches. Those graduates of the seminary would then direct another wave of students to the seminary along with monetary support for current operations, which included estate plans or planned giving to the school's endowment to provide for long-term financial stability.

Today that relational reciprocity has been disrupted, perhaps permanently. Fewer people are self-identifying as Christians, fewer people are attending and supporting churches, fewer churches are able to hire and support a pastor on a full-time basis, fewer people are seeking careers in pastoral ministry, and thus fewer students are entering seminary. That shift also results in substantially less support from churches being directed to seminaries.

How will the church in all of its forms react to these changes? What will be our missions and outreach efforts? What will be our facilities and maintenance challenges? What will we be able to do to sustain the church through these uncertain times? Preachers who are not already thinking about how to respond to these signs of the times will likely not last very long in the ministries to which they have been called.

Prosperity Theology

Not only have large numbers of persons in the United States left "organized religion" in terms of an open affiliation with Christianity, but just as many may have detoured to pursue an affiliation with a quasi-Christian message where something other than the gospel of Jesus Christ sits at the center. For more than seventy-five years, a movement that began as "name it and claim it" or "Word faith" has offered a message that does not center around the traditional themes of the sinfulness of humanity, the atoning death of Christ, and the forgiveness of sins through the act of repentance and redemption. Instead, an alternative theological formulation first proposed by Kenneth Hagin of Tulsa, Oklahoma, emerged "with a primary emphasis on money and wealth as signs of the blessings of God in the lives of true believers."[11]

Better known today as "prosperity theology," this distortion of the message entrusted to the apostles in Acts 1:6-8 (which is now entrusted to today's preachers) is an absolute distortion and perversion of the gospel, possible only through the most twisted and tortured interpretation of a select number of biblical texts. As I point out in my book *Where Have All the Prophets Gone?*, such preachers have moved from being prophets to being profiteers. Proponents of this prosperity gospel use their own personal prosperity as validation of the message they are offering to others. The more extravagant their lifestyle the more people can see what level of prosperity awaits them if they take to heart what this prosperity message is setting forth. William Martin of Rice University said that "the preacher's wealth is confirmation of what they are saying."[12] That leads to the obvious conclusion that you can share in this wealth as well "if you just sow a seed into this ministry."

This prosperity gospel has taken root within the twenty-first century church largely as a result of the efforts of preachers ranging from "Rev. Ike" (Frederick Eikenrotter) in the 1970s and '80s to Creflo Dollar over the past twenty years. The biggest problem with this approach to preaching is that it takes the focus of the church away from the issues laid out by Jesus in Matthew 25:31-46, in which he urges his followers to care for "the least of these." Instead, in the language of Rev. Ike, "The most important thing you can do for the poor is not be one of them."[13]

The preacher who seeks to be a witness for Jesus and the gospel message must *see something* and then *say something* about the heavy emphasis on possessions and the accumulation of wealth that bombards people in virtually every venue of popular culture and also within the confines of the church itself. What does it mean to "seek first

[God's] kingdom and his righteousness" (Matthew 6:33) in a country and a culture that value human lives based on their annual income, their tax bracket, their zip code, and the color of their American Express card? What does it say about churches in which members have to present their W-2 forms each year so the amount of their tithe to the church can be determined and imposed?

Preaching must be done with a keen awareness of the power of consumerism and material prosperity and the ways in which the pursuit of those things can corrupt both the individuals and the society that allow those values to occupy the center of their concern. There is a reason why Jesus warned his followers about storing up treasures on earth where robbers can break in and steal and where moths and vermin can destroy (Matthew 6:19). It is because "where your treasure is, there your heart will be also" (v. 21).

One challenge of preaching in this environment is that so many preachers have been drawn into this culture of consumerism themselves. They have exchanged the abundant life of Jesus Christ for the good life of the American dream. They have confused the teachings of John Locke with the teachings of Jesus Christ. It was Locke whose Second Treatise of Government influenced Thomas Jefferson to write in the Declaration of Independence about the "inherent and inalienable rights" of life, liberty, and the pursuit of happiness.[14] Sermons on their TV ministry broadcasts are interrupted so they can peddle their products, which range from books to CDs and DVDs to ocean cruises and family festivals. The sermon becomes a pretext for their real agenda, which is to push their products and pad their personal wealth. If preachers are to be witnesses for Jesus, then we need to see what is masquerading as the gospel these days and call those false teachers to the attention of the people who will hear their sermons.

The level of audacity of these prosperity preachers reached an all-time high with the 2015 appeal from Creflo Dollar for donations from "friends of the ministry" toward the purchase of a $65 million jet that was deemed "necessary to spread God's word."[15] I wonder what earlier evangelists would think about the claim that private luxury jet travel was necessary for the spread of the gospel. I think about Jesus roaming Palestine on foot, Paul and Barnabas traveling in small boats throughout the Mediterranean region, and John Wesley riding an estimated 250,000 miles on horseback in the United States and England during the eighteenth century. Creflo Dollar may prefer private air travel to operate his megachurch activities, but he should be cautious about suggesting that such a luxury is required to spread the gospel!

Despite the absurdity of their message and the audacity of their lifestyles, prosperity preachers continue to attract huge audiences. Preachers need to be careful to *see something* regarding the core message of the prosperity gospel. The problem is not solely with what *is* being said, but also with what *is not* being said. "Nothing is said about justice or injustice, nor is anything said about the responsibility of Christians to care about or respond to such issues."[16]

While much is said about wealth and health, nothing is said about the grinding poverty that grips the lives of millions of people in this country and billions of people around the world. Nothing is said about the mass incarceration of persons of color, even though many of the people listening to a prosperity preacher may have been personally impacted by the prison system in one way or another at the city, state, or federal level.

While people are teased with the possibility of personal wealth, they are not challenged by the genuine call to discipleship based on Matthew 6:33, which says, "Seek first [God's] kingdom and his righteousness, and all these things will be given to you as well." People are also not challenged by the even more explicit description of discipleship as found in Matthew 25:31-46, which references the appropriate faithful response to persons who are hungry, thirsty, naked, strangers (foreigners or immigrants), sick, or in prison.

This is what it means to be a witness for Jesus in the twenty-first century. Just as Jesus' first disciples had to preach the gospel amid many other messages that offered one false claim after another, the same remains true for those who are determined to be witnesses for Jesus in the twenty-first century.

Women in Ministry

Why are some denominations and local churches still resisting the presence of women in ordained ministry? Although many denominations have long since moved beyond their earlier restrictions regarding an all-male clergy, we still have people trying to make the biblical case for excluding 50 percent of the global population and 75 to 80 percent of their own church membership from the roles of preacher and pastor. They say their views are rooted in the instructions from Paul in 1 Timothy 2:11-12 and in 1 Corinthians 14:33-35, and also in the fact that Jesus' original disciples were males. But these passages have been used as if the world in which they were written two thousand years ago has remained unchanged. As I wrote in *Challenging Gender Discrimination in the Church*:

> Paul was writing within the context of a patriarchal world in general and within the context of the patriarchal structure of ancient Israel in particular. There was a time when women were excluded from leadership roles within most ancient societies. There was a time within the history of ancient Israel when women were not even counted as members of the community. Only males could form a synagogue. Only males could serve as rabbis, scribes, Pharisees, or members of the Sanhedrin. It was within the context of that male-dominant, patriarchal culture that Paul wrote those words. The first rule of biblical exegesis is to read and understand a passage within the context in which it was written, but then to faithfully interpret that passage in the context in which it is now being read and applied. Were the words of Paul meant to remain in place as a permanent obstacle to women serving in leadership in the church? Or are we obligated to read those words within a first-century context, but ask ourselves how those words should be understood today?[17]

Preachers who continue to object to women in ministry, based on the social practices of ancient Israel and first-century Judaism, need to recall that if the role of women as defined in the first century AD was still in force in the state of Israel, then Golda Meir would not have been eligible to serve in public office. However, because the nation of Israel did not feel constrained by ancient Jewish law, she was elected to be the prime minister of Israel, the Jewish state, from 1969 to 1974. How odd that twenty-first-century Christians are trying to cling to practices that both Judaism and the state of Israel that introduced that policy have long since abandoned!

Today women serve competently in the highest levels of education, industry, the military, government, journalism, and entertainment. Recently two women completed training to become US Army Rangers. And at the time of this writing, two women are running for their party's nomination for the office of president of the United States. One has already been the US secretary of state as well as a United States senator from New York. The other one served as CEO of Hewlett-Packard, a multibillion dollar international corporation.

Given how much the social status of women has changed since Paul first wrote those two passages, and given what can be learned about Paul's actual meaning and purpose when he wrote them, what should today's preachers do? Is it reasonable to tell the woman in your community who is the police chief, the superintendent of schools, the editor of the local newspaper, or an NBA or NFL team coach that she cannot be trusted with work of the ministry or the preaching of the gospel?

See the Political Environment

There is no way we can be faithful witnesses for Jesus without taking heed of the tangled and contentious political environment in which this country finds itself. Preachers need to notice the debates about health care and who will have access to it at an affordable price. Members of our churches are suffering with every imaginable ailment—from high blood pressure to HIV/AIDS to Alzheimer's and dementia to cancers of many different kinds. Female members of our churches may be turning to Planned Parenthood, not for abortion services but for mammograms and other health care needs. All of these have become highly charged political debates over which many people campaign for elected office. They will only become more charged as one election cycle after another rolls around.

These issues also contribute to the personal concerns that people carry with them when they come into the house of the Lord. Not having health insurance is not something people are likely to forget about when they go to church on Sunday. More likely, they are going to church in the hope that something will be said that will strengthen them to face the harsh realities that confront them every day, and also in the hope that some moral argument will be put forth that allows them to see that involvement in addressing and rectifying these social ills is part of the church's responsibility.

What does it say about our nation that more effort is being invested in the issue of abortion and the rights of the unborn than is being spent on school reform, prison reform, repair of the nation's infrastructure, rational gun control legislation, preservation of the global environment, control of the spread of nuclear weapons, and rectification of the staggering wealth gap between the top 1 percent of people in this country and the rest of the population?

All of these things directly impact the lives of the people to whom we preach on a regular basis. All of these things are political in their cause, their affect, and their eventual resolution. More importantly, all of these things are matters that can and should be considered through the lens of Scripture and in relationship to the church's claim about the sovereignty of God.

One cannot help but think about the recent water crisis in Flint, Michigan, where political decisions were made about how to provide water to that beleaguered city at a cheaper cost. Dangerously high levels of lead were found in the water in that city once the source of the water was shifted from Lake Huron, one of the five Great Lakes, with an ample supply of fresh water, to the Flint River, which had been a dumping ground for industrial waste for decades. It is impossible to calculate the health damages done to that population as a result of drinking and bathing in that water. It is even harder to grasp the frustration of the homeowners in Flint who cannot sell their homes and move away because nobody will buy those houses at any price until this water crisis is resolved. Given the fact that the water has corroded the pipes going into every home in Flint, and that, as of the date of this writing, the pipes have not been replaced in all of the impacted homes because the state deemed the price to be too high, this politically induced crisis may linger for many years to come.[18] (What is worse is that the corrosion that occurred could have easily and inexpensively been avoided. The water from the Flint River could have been treated with a corrosion inhibitor that could have reduced the amount of lead in the water.[19])

Michigan voters should ask themselves what they would do if such a thing had happened in the city or town where they live. Every preacher in Michigan and across this country should ask themselves how they would interpret the text "I was thirsty" as found in Matthew 25:31-46 with the people of Flint in mind. Sadly, outrageous political conduct is not limited to the state of Michigan. It is present in every nationally televised debate involving persons seeking the office of president of the United States.

It is difficult to know which outlandish statement by 2016 presidential candidates should first demand our witness, our call as preachers to *see something* and then *say something*. Before he dropped out of the race, Scott Walker supported the idea that, even in cases of rape, a woman should not be allowed to have an abortion, thus requiring her to bring to term a child conceived under the most horrific of circumstances. In an interview aired on CNN, another early candidate, Mike Huckabee, said that he agreed with those who said that a ten-year old girl from Paraguay who had been raped by her stepfather should be required to carry that child to term.[20] Huckabee concluded his statement by saying, "If life matters, and that's a person, then every life matters."[21]

That comment about "every life matters" undoubtedly comes easy to male politicians who seek to legislate on matters that affect neither their bodies nor their psyches. Rape is a horrific act, and when done to a ten-year-old girl, it leaves a scar that can last for decades to come. Yet Walker and Huckabee were on record as insisting that life in the womb in every instance supersedes the impact of that birth on the mother who became pregnant, not through casual sexual activity that resulted in an unintended outcome, but through a forced, brutal assault on the body of an adolescent. It seems in this instance that one life (the unborn) matters far more than the other life (the victim of rape).

Huckabee's offhanded comment about "every life matters" also flies in the face of another pronouncement made by others seeking the nomination for president of the United States. If every life matters, then does that principle apply once that life has left the womb and been born into the world? The policies and pronouncements being made by many throughout our society but especially by many of those seeking to become our nation's next president take on a decidedly antilife tone concerning those who are living in poverty, living without health insurance, or living with the burden of being ex-offenders long after they have served their prison sentences and paid their debt to society.

All lives matter except for those lives in states where their governors have worked to deny Medicare coverage to senior citizens, including the states where former presidential candidates Rick Perry and Bobby Jindal serve as governors. Preachers need to *see something*—namely, that their opposition to the Affordable Care Act (which was approved by Congress and signed into law in 2009, essentially voted on in the 2012 presidential election, and then upheld as constitutional by the US Supreme Court in 2013) has resulted in denying federal funds that could improve access to health care for the most impoverished citizens in their respective states. It is worth seeing that they oppose a plan that is presently in effect without them having any alternative plan of their own that could meet the needs of the persons who now enjoy health care coverage as a result of enrolling in one of the many forms of the Affordable Care Act. Do all lives matter when people campaign for elective office by promising to take away health care coverage?

Have preachers noticed the attack on voting rights in this country? Have we seen the US Supreme Court throw out the most important provision of the 1965 Voting Rights Act? Have we seen the new restrictions on voting rights that popped up as soon as the court made that ruling? Just as troubling is the self-imposed decline in black voter participation. This troubling trend is not because of any external forms of suppression. Rather, it must be viewed either as a loss of faith in the political process or perhaps as a loss of interest in something that earlier generations of black people were once willing to risk death in order to attain.

Whether the issue is the election of the US president or any other public official, the approval of a public works ballot issue for water treatment or the rezoning of property for a new use, the passage of a funding formula for a local school district or the use of public funds to support those struggling with mental illness or learning disabilities, all of these are political issues that impact the lives of our parishioners and the world in which they live. Preachers need to pay attention to the things going on around them so we can better apply the gospel to the lives of those to whom we are preaching. Preachers who want to be witnesses must first of all *see something*.

NOTES

1. Paul Tillich, quoted in Karl Barth, *The Preaching of the Gospel* (Philadelphia: Westminster, 1963), 54.

2. Barth, *The Preaching of the Gospel*, 54, paraphrased.

3. Michelle Ye Hee Lee, "Donald Trump's False Comments Connecting Mexican Immigrants and Crime," *Washington Post*, July 8, 2015, https://www.washingtonpost.com/news/fact-checker/wp/2015/07/08/donald-trumps-false-comments-connecting-mexican-immigrants-and-crime/.

4. Jeremy Diamond "Donald Trump: Ted Cruz is an anchor baby," cnn.com, January 29, 2016, p. 1.

5. Josh Barro "Just What Do You Mean by Anchor Baby?," *The New York Times*, www.nytimes.com, August 28, 2015, p., Pamela Constable, "For illegal immigrants with babies, the anchor pulls in many directions," www.washingtonpost.com, September 20, 2015, p. 1.

6. Raul A. Reyes, "Donald Trump's Clueless Immigration Plan," CNN, August 18, 2015, http://www.cnn.com/ 2015/08/17/opinions/reyes-trump-immigration/index.html.

7. Dana Ford, "Josh Duggar after Ashley Madison Hack: 'I Have Been the Biggest Hypocrite Ever,'" CNN, August 21, 2015, http://www.cnn.com/2015/08/20/us/josh-duggar-ashley-madison/index.html.

8. Christopher Hitchens, *God Is Not Great: How Religion Poisons Everything* (New York: Hatchette, 2007).

9. Michael Ruse, "Why God Is a Moral Issue," *New York Times*, March 23, 2015, http://opinionator.blogs.nytimes.com/2015/03/23/why-god-is-a-moral-issue/.

10. David Leonhardt, "The Rise of Young Americans Who Don't Believe in God," *New York Times*, May 12, 2015, http://www.nytimes.com/2015/05/13/upshot/the-rise-of-young-americans-who-dont-believe-in-god.html?ad-keywords=MAYAUD-DEV.

11. Marvin A. McMickle, *Where Have All the Prophets Gone?* (Cleveland, OH: Pilgrim, 2006), 106.

12. Bill Smith and Carolyn Tuft, "The Prosperity Gospel: The End of the 1980s Was a Bad Time for Preachers," *St. Louis Post-Dispatch*, November 18, 2003, Cult Education Institute, http://www.culteducation.com/group/1205-tv-and-radio-preachers/21032-the-prosperity-gospels.html.

13. Dennis McClellan, "Rev. Ike Dies at 74: Minister Preached Gospel of Prosperity," *Los Angeles Times*, July 31, 2009, http://www.latimes.com/local/obituaries/la-me-reverend-ike31-2009jul31-story.html.

14. John Locke, *The Two Treatises of Civil Government* (Hollis ed.; 1689), http://oll.libertyfund.org/titles/222.

15. Abby Ohlheiser, "Pastor Creflo Dollar Might Get His $65 Million Private Jet After All," *Washington Post*, June 3, 2015, https://www.washingtonpost.com/news/acts-of-faith/wp/2015/06/03/pastor-creflo-dollar-might-get-his-65-million-private-jet-after-all/.

16. McMickle, *Where Have All the Prophets Gone?*, 117.

17. Marvin A. McMickle, *Challenging Gender Discrimination in the Church* (Valley Forge, PA: The Ministers Council of American Baptist Churches USA, 2011), 1.

18. Josh Sanburn, "The Toxic Tap," *TIME*, February 1, 2016, 34.

19. Ibid., 37.

20. Justin Worland, "Mike Huckabee Supports Denying Abortion to 10-Year Old Rape Victim," *TIME*, August 16, 2015, http://time.com/3999799/mike-huckabee-abortion-rape/.

21. Ibid.

CHAPTER 7

Say Something

If the first challenge for being witnesses for Jesus is to *see something*, the second dimension is the willingness to *say something* about what we have seen. These two aspects of the work of a witness go hand in hand. You cannot say something if you have not first seen something. In the courtroom, if you have not seen or heard something related to the matter under trial, your testimony will have no value. This has a direct link to the work of a preacher seeking to be a witness for Jesus. Of course, it must be reiterated that, as preachers, what we choose to say must be scripturally based and theologically informed.

Preachers cannot speak prophetically about what is happening in the world if they have not been paying attention. In fact, the heart of prophetic preaching is to challenge other people to pay attention to what the prophet has already noticed. Preaching cannot speak to the deepest needs in the lives of people if the preacher has not been paying attention to the problems and pressures being felt by those people. However, once we have seen what is going on and can discern those events through the lens of the gospel, preachers are obligated to *say something* about what we have seen and to do so no matter how unpopular or unpleasant our message might be. (More on that in chapter 8.) So a witness for the Lord is first of all someone who *sees something* and then someone who *says something* about what she or he has seen.

Consider what Mark Greenlee, a practicing attorney and active churchgoer, wrote about being a witness: "Looking first to the Bible, the word *witness* calls for testimony to God's saving acts. For instance, the prophet Isaiah speaks for God, making the case for his redemptive acts: 'I have revealed and saved and proclaimed—I, and not some foreign god among you. You are my witnesses, declares the Lord, that I am God.'" Greenlee continued by saying that Isaiah used the word *witnesses* in a legal manner, calling on witnesses to prove that God was the Savior of the people. In a courtroom, witnesses may speak truthfully or falsely. Faithful witnesses speak the truth as they have seen, heard, and experienced it.[1]

I think almost immediately of Peter and John in Acts 4:20 being told not to preach about Jesus as a condition for being released from jail in Jerusalem. Their response should be that of every preacher today: "As for us, we cannot help speaking about what we have seen and heard." When preachers begin to wonder what to preach on next Sunday, we should ask ourselves what we have noticed going on in the world around us. How does what we see square up with what God desires from the church and for the world? It will not be long before that preacher who has paid attention will be able to *say something* about what he or she has seen.

The responsibility of a courtroom witness is to tell the truth, the whole truth, and nothing but the truth, and that responsibility belongs to those of us who respond to Jesus' challenge to be his witnesses as well. To do anything less as preachers would make us guilty of homiletic perjury—for failing to tell the truth of God's will, the whole truth of God's will, and nothing but the truth of God's will.

Speak Up!

So much of what is wrong in our society is not because people have not *seen* things going on around them that they believe to be wrong. In many instances they cannot help but see the evils around them. The problem is that those people are not willing to speak up and *say something* about what they have seen. We could list countless examples of things that people around the world and across this country certainly have seen but concerning which they chose to say nothing. Here is only a short list of such instances.

Indian Removal Act of 1830

In 1830 the United States Congress instituted the Indian Removal Act. This act essentially signaled the government's intent to separate Native Americans and not attempt to assimilate them into majority society. It authorized the US president (then Andrew Jackson) to forcibly remove Native American tribes from the southern United States to resettle them in federal lands west of the Mississippi River. In exchange the government would gain immediate access to the ancestral lands being abandoned. In 1838 the Cherokee Nation was forced to move from their lands in Georgia to the Oklahoma Territory. That mass relocation became known as the Trail of Tears because more than nineteen thousand Cherokee died during that journey.

John Quincy Adams was personally opposed to any forced removal of Native Americans, but he said nothing about it while he was serving as the nation's sixth president from 1825 to 1829, nor for many years after he left that office and served in the House of Representatives. "Adams' principles did not trump political expediency. He feared that a frank declaration of his views would prevent him from being elected president. Adams chose silence until he was elected to Congress in 1831, which allowed him to play the role of the prophet rather than the statesman."[2] Adams *saw something*, but he failed to *say something* about it.

The Holocaust

In 1995 I accompanied a Holocaust survivor back to the Mauthausen concentration camp in Austria where he had been confined from March 1944 until the liberation of that camp in April 1945. Mauthausen was the center of a cluster of smaller slave labor camps where Jews, Communists, homosexuals, gypsies, trade unionists, and any other group despised by the Nazis were confined. My friend reported that when he was sent to that camp from Hungary he was fifteen years old and weighed 135 pounds. When he was released from that camp just thirteen months later at age sixteen, he weighed just 85 pounds. Starvation and hard manual labor were the order of the day in a Nazi slave labor camp.

One of the smaller camps around Mauthausen where workers were occasionally sent was in the Austrian town of Melk. The prisoners were marched into that camp in their striped uniforms with a diamond-shaped badge attached. The color of that badge indicated the reason that person was being held in the camp: pink for being homosexual, red for Communist, green for trade union membership, and blue for Jewish. These emaciated persons marching in groups were paraded on foot from Mauthausen to the camp in Melk, a distance of four miles. The people who lived in Melk saw these prisoners being marched into that camp on a daily basis.

Melk's labor camp was equipped with cremation facilities to dispose of the bodies of those who were either worked to death or killed for not working hard enough. A towering chimney belched out the ashes of the bodies that were regularly being burned. Unlike the much larger concentration camps of Auschwitz in Poland or Dachau in Germany, which were set up in remote and somewhat concealed locations where civilians could claim not to have seen what was going on, the camp in Melk was well within view of the local population. Residents saw the camp. They saw the prisoners. They saw the chimney. They saw the smoke and ash. However, during the war none of the residents of Melk said anything about what was going on in that camp, and after the war when they were questioned by the Allies, none of the residents acknowledged having seen anything going on there.

On a hill overlooking that camp is a Roman Catholic monastery. As I stood on the grounds of that peaceful monastic retreat, I had a clear view not only of the camp itself, but more importantly of the chimney that remains to this day. During the time when that camp was in use, those monks had a clear view of the camp and that chimney with its constant flow of smoke and ash and the smell of burning human flesh. The religious community gathered on that hill saw what was happening in that camp just as clearly as the citizens who resided in the little Austrian town beneath them. When I visited this concentration camp in 1995 along with

Andrew Sternberg who was a survivor of imprisonment in Melk, the tour guides reported that like the residents in the village, the monks on the hill overlooking the camp never said a word during the war, and when the war was over they testified that they had never seen anything that might suggest the horror that occurred in Mauthausen or Melk.

The sin surrounding human suffering is too often made worse by good people who see the evils going on around them but decide that silence is the safer course. That is true when the sin in question rises to the level of the Holocaust, the transatlantic slave trade, or the wholesale extermination or forced removal of Native Americans. It is also true when it comes to acts of cruelty and injustice occurring throughout this country every day. There is no doubt that most of the urban violence in America's streets has been seen by citizens who, perhaps out of fear of retaliation, decide to say nothing. Their silence allows the cycle of violence to go on unabated.

Excessive Force and Police Brutality

Having spent twenty-four years as a pastor in Cleveland, Ohio, I know the exact spot where Tamir Rice, a twelve-year-old black boy, was shot and killed by a white police officer within two seconds of that officer arriving on the scene. That horrific incident in November 2014 did not even result in a trial and indictment of that police officer. Our judicial system *saw something* but *said nothing*.

The rage of the Black Lives Matter movement is not only over the shootings of black people but over the apparent disregard of the shootings by the criminal justice system. The rage is fueled not only by the August 2014 shooting of Michael Brown in Ferguson, Missouri, but also by the four hours his body was left lying in the street after he was shot and killed.

The anger is fueled not only by the July 2014 choking death of Eric Garner in Staten Island, New York, at the hands of police, but by the fact that Garner was swarmed by six police officers for a misdemeanor offense (selling individual cigarettes), for which any one of the officers simply could have issued him a summons that would have resulted in a monetary fine. Instead, it culminated in a choke hold that had been declared illegal by the New York Police Department. Despite all that, no indictment was brought against the officer who initiated that arrest and who also applied the choke hold.

One could add to this litany of offenses the take down and arrest of tennis star James Blake in September 2015, who was tackled to the ground and handcuffed by a person who never identified himself as a New York City police officer. It was a case of mistaken identity and Blake was quickly released—but without comment or apology from the arresting officer. Had it not been for surveillance video, the aggressive nature of the arrest would never have come to light. The mayor of New York City and the police commissioner both apologized to James Blake, but not the police officer in question. Worse, the New York City police union called attention to the professional manner in which the "take down" occurred but never said a word about why the officer failed to identify himself or show his badge, or why he had tried to arrest someone who was simply standing alone in front of a hotel in midtown Manhattan.

Did people pay attention to what happened during the one-year anniversary of the death of Michael Brown? Unarmed black people involved in peaceful protests outside the federal courthouse in St. Louis County, Missouri, were handcuffed, arrested, and subjected to DNA swabs that will be sent to the FBI, all on the charge of creating a disturbance on federal property. Meanwhile, members of a white paramilitary group called the Oath Keepers, all carrying automatic weapons and wearing flak jackets, were allowed to walk among those protesters without being stopped, questioned, or turned away by local law enforcement agencies. Given that the stated purpose of the Oath Keepers is to "defend the Constitution against all enemies foreign and domestic,"[3] one is left to wonder what they were doing at a rally where unarmed and peaceful citizens were exercising their First Amendment constitutional right of free speech and the freedom of assembly.

Did people *see something* when this militia group was allowed to roam the streets fully armed and unaccompanied by official on-duty law enforcement officers? More importantly at this point, did any preacher across the country *say something* about that obvious disparity in justice?

In truth, the armed presence of the Oath Keepers (who happened to be an all-white group of former military, police, fire, and other first-responder groups) was even more outrageous than the militarized response employed by local and state law enforcement officers in Ferguson in the immediate aftermath of the shooting death of Michael Brown. Since when does the job of patrolling the streets of our cities fall to retired firefighters and medics? Why was there no public outcry from every level of government and the legitimate members of the nation's armed forces over an unsolicited and highly provocative action on the part of an undeputized posse whose presence may continue to haunt this country if it is not curtailed now?

I hate to think what would have happened if the African American protesters in Ferguson and St. Louis County had shown up outside the federal court house openly carrying automatic weapons. Would they have been allowed to walk around in the ways allowed for the Oath Keepers? Would Fox News, CNN, MSNBC, and other news channels have said nothing about that matter as they have said nothing about the presence of the Oath Keepers whose presence in the streets of Ferguson was the equivalent of pouring gasoline on an already inflamed situation?

On the Sunday following the Ferguson protests held to mark the one-year anniversary of the death of Michael Brown, none of the morning news programs (*Face the Nation*, *Meet the Press*, *Fareed Zakaria GPS*, etc.) said a word about the protests or the precedent they may have set for future public demonstrations. There was some discussion about the protests, which were lawful even if they were raucous, and also about the state of emergency resulting from a gunfire exchange between police and one black person in that massive crowd. However, journalists never referenced the danger inherent in the role of the Oath Keepers, a group of private citizens taking it upon themselves to carry automatic weapons as they walked through a crowd of peaceful protesters. People saw what was going on, but apparently nobody in the police department, at City Hall, in county government, or in the national news media was prepared to *say something* about that nationally televised display of intimidation.

This pattern of focusing on the behavior of black people while totally ignoring the far more provocative conduct of white law enforcement (much less the intimidating presence of civilian paramilitary groups) fuels the need for people to disrupt the campaign events of political candidates as a way to gain a platform from which to cry out that black lives matter. The question is who else will *see something* and *say something* about what has happened in Ferguson, Baltimore, Staten Island, Cleveland, Cincinnati, North Charleston, Charlotte, Minneapolis, and a dozen other cities and towns that were sites of black people being killed at the hands of or while in the custody of white police officers?

Failure to pay attention to these events, to *see something* and then to *say something*, fuels the argument by the Black Lives Matter movement that there is a separate and unequal standard of justice for blacks and whites and rich and poor in the United States. Just as importantly, insisting that all lives matter in response to the Black Lives Matter movement robs society of any credibility. This was the mistake made by Martin O'Malley, former Maryland governor and Baltimore mayor, by former Secretary of State Hillary Clinton, and by Senator Bernie Sanders during their campaigns for the Democratic Party presidential nomination. Trying to insist that all lives matter without working to create a system of justice within which all lives are treated equally is dismissive of the claim that angry black protesters are attempting to make about what they see going on in their country.

All Lives Matter

All this being said, preachers still need to find the courage to move toward the view that all lives *do* matter and that all lives should be valued and protected. What preachers in general, but black preachers in particular, have to be willing to acknowledge is that black lives matter just as much when the cause of death for a black person is not excessive force by a white police officer but homicide at the hands of another black person.

It is no secret in the African American communities of this nation that the vast majority of deaths by gunshot occur when no police officer is even present. The black community and the rest of the nation must face up to this one inescapable fact. It is true that in Ferguson, Baltimore, Cleveland and Cincinnati, Staten Island, Charleston, Charlotte, and many other places around the country one white person killed or led to the death of unarmed black people. However, in those same towns and cities, unarmed black people—men, women and children—continue to be killed in record numbers on a nearly daily basis by other black people.

They are being killed over drugs, in turf wars and gang feuds, over imagined slights and insults, and by random acts of absolutely senseless violence. Seldom if ever do those incidents result in mass marches, public outcries, media attention, or Sunday morning pulpit commentary. I have seen clergy show up and call press conferences over these events, but more often than not the interest of many clergy seems to end as soon as the TV cameras are gone. Do black lives matter less when they are ended by black people?

This black-on-black or intra-communal violence happens every day in black communities across this country. Here in Rochester, New York, where I now reside, black-on-black homicides take place throughout the year. While I was working on this book, a drive-by shooting by a black male here in Rochester resulted in seven people being shot, three of them fatally. This happened on one of the main streets in the black community just outside a popular gathering place for teens who had come together that evening to play basketball. Another black person was shot and killed here in Rochester by a black person five days later. Two weeks later another mass shooting, black on black, resulted in four injuries and two fatalities. Then, in the first week of February 2016, a black-on-black shooting incident occurred every day, with seven persons shot and one person killed.[4]

Say Something

A report in the *Democrat and Chronicle* newspaper in Rochester recently reported a tragic spike in gun violence among the cities along Route 90 in western New York—Buffalo, Rochester, and Syracuse. Nearly one thousand shootings have occurred in these three cities alone. Most of them have involved black-on-black violence, and not one of them involved a shooting of a black person by a white police officer.[5] For all our talk about "state sanctioned violence" by white America, the African American community here in Rochester cannot make a moral argument against it when black people have shot and killed more black people in our city alone than in all the tragic shootings of blacks by white police officers throughout the entire country since the death of Michael Brown in Ferguson, Missouri. And my city is not alone with such statistics.

Many have tried to argue that this black-on-black homicide rate is somehow the result of racism, poverty, unemployment, bad schools, gang-related activity, and a feeling of marginalization within the broader American society. The problem with that argument is that none of those conditions are new to the black community, and things were considerably worse even during the years of 1948–1970 when I resided in my hometown of Chicago and across the country. This is to say nothing about what earlier generations of black people endured in this country over the last four hundred years. Yet at no time was there this rampant epidemic of black-on-black homicide. Perhaps the cause is the increasing presence of guns, or drugs, or a gradual devaluation of human life. Whatever the root causes may be, there can be no integrity in declaring that black lives matter if they only seem to matter when they have been ended at the hands of white police officers.

I appreciate the impassioned voices of the Black Lives Matter movement that I have heard on TV. Preachers must be the ones who challenge the black communities of this country to embrace this flip side of the issue. We need to challenge preachers and protesters alike to *see something* and *say something* when black-on-black homicides occur every weekend in cities and towns across America.

In 2013–14, after a series of shootings in Rochester, I took part in a citywide effort by social service and not-for-profit groups to reduce black-on-black gun violence in our city. Multiple attempts were made to meet with most of the clergy within a particular ward in Rochester where gun violence has been highest for the last thirty years. Despite repeated attempts to secure the involvement of those clergy whose churches were located within that impacted area, we were not able to gain their interest, much less their support. However, when a white police officer Tasered a black male who subsequently died from the aftereffects of that event, most of the clergy we had been unable to reach for black-on-black gun violence gathered in City Hall ready for a fight with the mayor and the chief of police.

I have often reflected on the experiences of my own mother in my hometown of Chicago, where I lived from 1948–1970. She was the victim of six separate home break-ins, and on three other occasions she was assaulted while walking down the street in broad daylight. In each instance the attackers were young black males. To protect whatever household and personal items that had not already been stolen during those break-ins, she had to install steel bars over the windows of her house and a steel door outside the front entrance. If a fire had ever erupted inside her house, she would likely have died inside because it took her so long to unlock her front door. She often said that she felt like a prisoner within her own home. Her fear was not of the police. Like millions of black people who live behind steel bars and doors inside their own homes, her fear was of the next break-in or street assault by the African Americans who are terrorizing the people in the very community where they live.

Many black preachers have rightly criticized their white colleagues for failing to speak out against instances of excessive force by white police officers against unarmed black citizens. They rightly wondered what white preachers focused on in their sermons in the weeks after unarmed black citizens were shot and killed by white law enforcement in Ferguson, Baltimore, Cleveland, North Charleston, Cincinnati, and elsewhere.

Nothing I am saying here should be construed to minimize the breadth of the problem between police departments and black communities across this country. Nothing I am saying here should be viewed as a criticism of what I believe to be the legitimate expression of rage by black protestors over the repeated abuses of police power in black communities dating back more than 150 years when police power joined by white militia groups (very much like the Oath Keepers) did everything in their power to frustrate the lives of black people after the end of slavery and the end of the Civil War. I support and affirm those who go on stage at a Bernie Sanders event to shout out to America that *back lives matter*!

That being said, it is still disingenuous and wholly unworthy of the gospel for preachers not to *say something* about the fact that the overwhelming instances of crime in black communities across this country are black on black. I make these observations as an African American preacher only to say to other preachers that we will have no credibility when we chant "Black lives matter" unless we also make the case that black lives matter *whether the injury is done to us or done by us.*

Do Black Transgender Lives Matter?

Of even greater importance in this discussion about "All Lives Matter" is the fact that the Black Lives Matter movement was begun by persons who were initially objecting to the treatment of black transgender women who were being killed as a result of their lifestyle choice.[6] Sadly, that part of the story is often overlooked and left unaddressed, because even in the black community there is a sense that not all black lives matter. It matters a great deal when Jamar Clark is shot and killed by white police officers in Minneapolis. It seems to matter much less when 18 transgender women of color have been murdered in this country just in 2015.[7] Most people in the black community have said nothing about this reality, and needless to say most preachers and pulpits have remained silent. A Victorian Age sense of morality has reduced so many forms of human sexual activity to unpardonable sins that often carry with it the strange notion that the victim is somehow responsible for the treatment they receive. I say again, All Lives Matter, including the lives of transgender persons who should not have to face vigilante justice for their lifestyle.

Somebody Say *Something*

As one of my Cleveland friends regularly says on her Facebook page after another black-on-black homicide has occurred: "Will somebody please say something?" This is a clear instance when the words of Paul Tillich must be heard and adopted: "Preaching must be done with an awareness of the present moment."[8] For preachers, being witnesses for Jesus is both a challenge and an opportunity to *see something* and then find the courage and conviction to *say something* about crucial issues that directly affect the lives of the people listening to their sermons.

Despite the challenges we see around us, we have no reason for despair. We are not the first generation of preachers to face these challenges. We can learn how to preach the gospel in an unfriendly world by observing the disciples of Jesus who went forth to preach in a world where their message was both unpopular and unwelcome. But we will not know how or when or why to face these challenges if we have not been paying attention to the spiritual environment in which we and those to whom we preach are living every day.

Why Do Some Preachers Choose Not to Be a Witness?

In endless instances people have seen something that they believed to be wrong, unfair, illegal, or immoral but chose to say nothing. Sadly, we who preach the gospel are not free of this problem. We too have seen things or heard things that made our hearts break and made our anger rise, but then something took place that caused us to preach on a different subject and not respond in any way to what we saw. The absence of righteous indignation flowing from the pulpits of churches across this country is astounding. Their silence in the face of all the things taking place both in this country and around the world is deafening.

What might be the reason why those called on to speak the truth about what they have seen end up saying nothing? The answer may reside within the third dimension of what it means to be a witness.

NOTES

1. Mark B. Greenlee, *Witnesses: Cleveland's Storefront Churches* (Oregon, IL: Quality, 2015), 5.

2. Gary Scott Smith, *Religion in the Oval Office* (New York: Oxford University Press, 2015), 113.

3. See the Oath Keepers website at www.oathkeepers.org.

4. Patti Singer, "No arrests after 1 dead, 7 hurt at State St. Club," democratandchronicle.com, February 8, 2016.

5. John Hand and Will Cleveland, "Rochester tops upstate NY in mass shootings," democratandchronicle.com, February 7, 2016.

6. Perry Stein, "Black Lives Matter organizers hold rally in D.C. for black trans women," Washingtonpost.com, August 25, 2015, p. 1.

7. Rebecca Ruiz, "Black Lives Matter rallies for transgender women after multiple murders so far this year," Mashable.com, August 25, 2015.

8. Paul Tillich, quoted in Karl Barth, *The Preaching of the Gospel* (Philadelphia: Westminster, 1963), 54.

CHAPTER 8

Suffer Something

The third understanding of the word *witness* becomes evident only in light of the original Greek word in Acts 1:7-8 (noted in chapter 5). This Greek word, *marturia*, is the basis for our English word *martyr*, which carries the sense of someone who suffers for the cause to which she or he is committed. Thus, in the context of Jesus' challenge to his disciples, witnesses are those who are aware of the very real possibility that if what they say is too controversial in the eyes of some of their hearers, they may end up having to *suffer something* as a result of what they have said.

Needless to say, most preachers have never considered this third dimension of being a witness, being willing to *suffer something* as a result of *saying something* in a sermon as an occupational hazard for faithful preaching. Nevertheless, this word *marturia* points to what God expects from our preaching. There must come a time when our preaching and our public ministry in all forms moves us away from popular themes and timid topics that are crowd-pleasing and reputation-building but never challenge the status quo of our community or our nation. At some point we must move toward matters that are more controversial, more contentious, and even more confrontational.

In the imagery and language of the Old Testament scholar Walter Brueggemann, we must adopt what he has called a "prophetic consciousness" or God's way of viewing the world so as to challenge "royal consciousness," which is the dominant culture's way of viewing the world.[1] The major problem with "prophetic consciousness" was clearly set forth by Brueggemann when he said, "Hope is the refusal to accept the reading of reality which is the majority opinion; and one does that only at great personal risk."[2] This is what lies at the very heart of being a *marturia*: what, if anything, are we prepared to do or say if we know that our actions may result in "great personal risk"?

History has shown us that when courageous and committed people are determined to *say something* that may go against the views held by those with power and influence in society, they can face swift and sometimes harsh consequences. When courageous and committed preachers dare to say something that goes against the widely held assumptions and prejudices operating within their own racial and/or ethnic group, they do so "at great personal risk."

A Lesson from Socrates

Writing in *Black Prophetic Fire* and while describing that trait of prophetic fire in Malcolm X, Cornel West referred to the Greek word *parrhesia*, which means speaking the truth boldly and freely without any regard for the speaker's safety or security.[3] *Parrhesia* is a good way to consider the intersections of *seeing something*, *saying something*, and *suffering something* for what you have said. Socrates had seen certain practices and noticed certain beliefs in Athens with which he did not agree. He spoke openly about his disagreements, believing it was his right and his duty to do so. As a result of what he said (*parrhesia*) that was contrary to popular opinion, he was forced to drink the cup of poison known as hemlock. In this sequence of events, Socrates became a perfect example of what it means to be a witness in all three steps or stages of that process.

That word *parrhesia* was how Socrates described his speech when he offered his defense before the people of Athens, as recorded in Plato's *Apology*: "And this, O men of Athens, is the truth and the whole truth; I have concealed nothing, I have dissembled nothing. And yet I know that this plainness of speech makes them hate me, and what is their hatred but proof that I am speaking the truth? This is the occasion and reason of their slander of me, as you will find out either in this or in any future inquiry."[4]

This is the work of the preacher who would fulfill the call from Jesus to be his witness. We are to be attentive to the practices and policies, the people and problems that are present in the world around us. When those things do not conform to the teachings of Christ regarding justice and righteousness and mercy, we are called on to say something as boldly and as truthfully as we can.

When we do speak with *parrhesia*, we fully understand that we may be subjected to some form of suffering—for going against popular opinion at the least, and even more so for going against the preferences of those who are in positions of power who benefit from the status quo that we are now condemning. Then, as Brueggemann noted, when we refuse to accept the majority view of reality, we do so at great personal risk. The degree to which we are ever prepared to take this third step in our preaching and in our living will determine whether we are truly witnesses for Jesus!

Reinhold Niebuhr on Prophetic Preaching

Reinhold Niebuhr rightly observed, "I am not surprised that most prophets are itinerant."[5] He gave two reasons why so few pastors behave like prophets. The first is the pastor's economic dependence on those to whom he preaches. How harsh will you be in critiquing the conduct of those who provide your salary? The second is the tendency of pastors to establish friendships within the congregation so that "there is difficulty in telling unpleasant truths to people whom one has learned to love."[6] For these two reasons, perhaps among many others, Niebuhr finally concluded that "most budding prophets are tamed in time to become harmless parish priests."[7] Whether because of finances, friendships, or fear, there are factors that prevent a great many preachers from *saying something* that might result in "great personal risk."

Jesus did not send his first disciples out into the world so they could become "harmless parish priests." He sent them forth with a very clear expectation: "Be my witnesses." In fulfilling that role in the twenty-first century just as in the first century, preachers must be willing to *see something*, *say something*, and then be prepared to *suffer something* as a result of what we have said. In the social, spiritual, and political spheres of today's culture, any number of matters should capture our attention and generate concern in our hearts. Once those matters have captured our attention, the issue becomes how we work them into our preaching schedule, for as Paul Tillich said, "Preaching should be done with an awareness of the present moment."[8]

Suffering: A Central Biblical Theme

What may be surprising to many preachers and parishioners in this era of the prosperity gospel and "feel good" theology, such as what Joel Osteen and many other TV evangelists pump out on a regular basis, is just how often the Bible refers to suffering as an expected part of life for Jesus' followers. Sometimes the word used for suffering is *marturia*. Other times the Greek word meaning "suffering" may be *pathetos*, *path ma*, or *sugkakopatheo*, each of which carries the sense of undergoing or enduring hardship or pain.

Whether the English translation of the idea is "suffering," "persecution," or "afflictions," we find a thread running through the New Testament. It teaches those of us who seek to live out the Christian life to its fullest dimensions that we will likely encounter some hardship along the way. Here is a sampling of New Testament texts that make explicit reference to suffering in one form or another:

> "Blessed are you when people insult you, persecute you and falsely say all kinds of evil against you because of me. . . . For in the same way they persecuted the prophets who were before you." (Matthew 5:11-12)

> "'A servant is not greater than his master.' If they persecuted me, they will persecute you also." (John 15:20)

Now if we are children . . . of God . . . we share in [Christ's] suffering in order that we may also share in his glory. . . . I consider that our present sufferings are not worth comparing with the glory that will be revealed in us. (Romans 8:17-18)

Who shall separate us from the love of Christ? Shall trouble or hardship or persecution or famine or nakedness or danger or sword? . . . "For your sake we face death all day long." (Romans 8:35)

When we are cursed, we bless; when we are persecuted, we endure it; when we are slandered, we answer kindly. We have become the scum of the earth, the garbage of the world—right up to this moment. (1 Corinthians 4:12-13)

We are hard pressed on every side . . . persecuted, but not abandoned. (2 Corinthians 4:8-9)

I want to know Christ—yes, to know the power of his resurrection and participation in his sufferings. (Philippians 3:10)

Now I rejoice in what I am suffering for you, and I fill up in my flesh what is still lacking in regard to Christ's afflictions. (Colossians 1:24)

Among God's churches we boast about your perseverance and faith in all the persecutions and trials you are enduring. . . . As a result you will be counted worthy of the kingdom of God, for which you are suffering. (2 Thessalonians 1:4-5)

Do not be ashamed of the testimony about our Lord or of me his prisoner. Rather, join with me in suffering for the gospel. (2 Timothy 1:8)

> Everyone who wants to live a godly life in Christ Jesus will be persecuted. (2 Timothy 3:12)

> You were publicly exposed to insult and persecution. . . . You suffered alongside those in prison. (Hebrews 10:33-34)

> Some faced jeers and flogging, and even chains and imprisonment. They were put to death by stoning; they were sawed in two; they were killed by the sword. (Hebrews 11:36-37)

> If you suffer for doing good and you endure it, this is commendable before God. (1 Peter 2:20)

> Even if you should suffer for what is right, you are blessed. (1 Peter 3:14)

> Dear friends, do not be surprised at the fiery ordeal that has come on you to test you. . . . Rejoice inasmuch as you participate in the sufferings of Christ. (1 Peter 4:12-13)

> "These are they who have come out of the great tribulation; they have washed their robes and made them white in the blood of the Lamb." (Revelation 7:14)

Suffering in the First Century

The challenge of being a *marturia* is enough to frighten most people away from a twenty-first-century ministry that would be informed by Jesus' commission in Acts 1:7-8. However, remember that for many people in the early Christian church, suffering for Christ was the norm. And by suffering, we are talking about physical torture and death. Jesus himself was crucified. Stephen was stoned. John was imprisoned on Patmos. James was killed by order of Herod Antipas. Tradition holds that Peter was crucified upside down in Rome during the persecution of the church under Emperor Nero.

On multiple occasions in his second letter to the Corinthian church, the apostle Paul reflects on his sufferings in the service of Christ. The best known passage is probably 2 Corinthians 11:23-27, where Paul speaks about being flogged, stoned, shipwrecked, and imprisoned, as well as being hungry, thirsty, weary, cold, naked, hated, and much more. An earlier passage, 2 Corinthians 6:4-10, speaks about Paul's endurance, troubles, hardships, distresses, beatings, imprisonments, riots, hard work, sleepless nights, hunger, and dishonor. And in 2 Corinthians 4:8-9 Paul describes being hard pressed, perplexed, persecuted, and struck down. These are the extremes to which many first-century preachers of the gospel were led because of their obedience to the call to become a *marturia*.

Peter and John

Many of the original eleven disciples took to heart Jesus' call to be his witnesses. Consider the example of Peter and John in Acts 3:14-15, where their behavior reflects the pattern of *seeing something*, *saying something*, and later *suffering something* for the sake of their witness. While standing in the temple in Jerusalem, Peter and John offered a forceful testimony about Jesus and about how the people of Jerusalem, who had earlier hailed Jesus as their Messiah, turned against him and handed him over to Pilate to be crucified. Then, in the presence of those who had conspired to have Jesus killed, the disciples declared, "We are witnesses of this" (v. 15). Their witness began with what they had seen in Jerusalem when Jesus was arrested, tried, and then crucified. Their witness continued when they spoke boldly about what they had seen, which resulted in their being brought before the leaders of the Jewish faith in Jerusalem (the Sanhedrin), who had them arrested and placed in jail.

The same pattern occurred in Acts 5:31-32 after Peter and John had been released from jail and had been warned not to preach any longer in Jerusalem about Jesus. Their response was first to say, "We must obey God rather than human beings" (v. 29). Then they once again recounted the events that resulted in the crucifixion of Jesus, events in which those to whom they were preaching were chiefly responsible. They concluded their sermon with these words: "We are witnesses of these things" (v. 32).

Here is the perfect example of what this book is about: preachers who act on the charge given to them by Jesus to be his witnesses. Here is the exact point of origin for my three-part emphasis on the meaning of being a witness. This is not some clever and imaginative wordplay; this is the precise behavior of Peter and John in the days after they had been challenged by Jesus to be his witnesses. They *saw something*, they *said something*, and they *suffered something* for their ministry.

Stephen in Jerusalem

The second first-century example that comes to mind when I consider accepting the role of a *marturia* is Acts 7, where the Sanhedrin in Jerusalem responds to what they have just heard from a disciple named Stephen. Based on what he had come to know about the rejection of Jesus by that very council, Stephen preached a sermon in which he said, among other things, "You stiff-necked people! Your hearts and ears are still uncircumcised. . . . You . . . have received the law that was given through angels but have not obeyed it" (Acts 7:51-53).

Rather than responding with a love offering after his sermon in appreciation for his message, the text says, "When the members of the Sanhedrin heard this, they were furious and gnashed their teeth at him. . . . They all rushed at him, dragged him out of the city and began to stone him" (Acts 7:54, 57-58).

This example of Stephen being a *marturia* is significant because it illustrates movement of the responsibility beyond Jesus' original disciples and involves someone who was numbered among the first group of deacons (*diakanoi)* as established in Acts 6. Stephen was not one of the Twelve. He was one of the seven persons presented to the Twelve who would carry out much of the daily administration of the early church while the apostles devoted themselves to the ministry of the Word.

Nevertheless, it seems that Stephen was drawn into a more active role as a preacher or evangelist. The language of Acts 6:3 that calls for "seven men from among you who are known to be full of the Spirit and wisdom" is actually our word *martureo*. Thus, the essential qualification for being a disciple, an apostle, or a deacon was that one be a witness for Jesus.

That is precisely what Stephen was doing in Acts 6 and 7. He saw what the leaders of the temple had been doing, not only with the practical aspect of the Jewish religion, but more precisely with what they had done regarding Jesus. It seems painfully ironic that part of the truth spoken by Stephen in Acts 7 was related to the inevitability of having to *suffer something* for the sake of *saying something* on behalf of the Lord to God's people: "Was there ever a prophet your ancestors did not persecute? They even killed those who predicted the coming of the Righteous One. And now you have betrayed and murdered him—you who have received the law that was given through angels but have not obeyed it" (vv. 52-53). So it was that, in commenting on the suffering that Jesus had to endure as a result of what he had said and taught, the same fate then fell on Stephen.

Stephen linked the suffering experienced by Christ's witnesses in the first century AD to the experience of Israel's prophets in earlier generations. A brief discussion of the experiences of one prophet in particular will help to make Stephen's point even clearer. That prophet is Amos.

Amos

The prophet Amos *saw something* (corruption in Israel), he *spoke* forcefully about what he had seen, and he *suffered* the consequences of preaching an unpopular message that targeted the rich and powerful in his nation. Of course, Amos was speaking in the eighth century BC, long before the time of Jesus or the ministry of the Lord's disciples, but the prophet's themes were consistent with the gospel message Jesus himself proclaimed. Perhaps what Jesus was urging, then, in speaking to his disciples about being his witnesses, was a return to the form and focus of the preaching of the biblical prophets.

The eighth-century BC prophets Amos, Micah, Hosea, and Isaiah railed against economic injustice and the abuse of the poor, which were rampant in their society. They also preached against the bland religious ritualism that constituted temple worship at that time. They were appalled by the notion that the nation or any individual within the nation could please God solely by emphasizing animal sacrifice and other temple duties while neglecting the works of justice that God had commanded, beginning with care for the widows, orphans, and strangers in the land.

When Amos brought his prophetic message to Bethel, he was confronted by the local temple priest Amaziah, who was allied with King Jeroboam. Amaziah had already reported to the king that Amos's preaching was so powerful that "the land cannot bear all his words" (Amos 7:10). Amaziah then ordered Amos to leave town and do his preaching elsewhere.

The words of Amaziah were as revealing about his true loyalties to King Jeroboam as the words of Amos were in revealing his ultimate allegiance to God: "Get out, you seer. Go back to the land of Judah. Earn your bread there and do your prophesying there. Don't prophesy anymore at Bethel, because this is the king's sanctuary and the temple of the kingdom" (Amos 7:13).

What is interesting to note about Amos is that the full length of his prophetic career may have been no longer than one season in the agricultural cycle. His main career was as a shepherd and a caretaker for sycamore fig-trees (Amos 7:14). He reported to Amaziah that "the LORD took me from tending the flock and said to me 'Go prophesy to my people Israel'" (v. 15). And while, as Donald Gowan pointed out, little is known of the actual lives of the prophets, it does seem that Amos was an outsider to the established temple hierarchy, and as such, he seemed to bypass the institutional order of the northern kingdom of which Amaziah was the defender.[9] Thus Amaziah's rebuke was not simply over what Amos said, but just as importantly about whether the prophet had the right to say it in the place where he had no institutional standing.

Recognizing that God had sent Amos to that precise location, Gowan offered the following observation: "When God chooses to bypass our institutions, it is inevitable that those who maintain them and benefit from them will resist, as Amaziah did. So the prophets always faced opposition, some of it severe."[10] Gowan continued, "Speaking the truth by no means guarantees acceptance, for the truth will be uncomfortable to someone, and if it disturbs the comfort of those in power it will produce serious opposition."[11]

Being a witness will not always happen in the safety and security of the local church where the preacher has standing and authority. A witness for the Lord must inevitably venture outside the bounds of safety into places where he or she has no institutional support and is only able to speak after saying, "Hear the word of the Lord."

Gowan offered one more caution so far as prophetic preaching is concerned: "Opposition is no proof that one has spoken the truth, and that needs to be reemphasized when one thinks about the prophets. More than a few people have succumbed to the temptation of thinking that they are in trouble because they are being 'prophetic,' when on occasion it is just because they have been undiplomatic, stupid, or wrong."[12] I sincerely hope that twenty-first-century preachers can navigate the thin line between being prophetic and being stupid!

That being said, there ought to be those Sundays when there is no long line to shake the preacher's hand or tell the preacher how great the sermon was. There ought to be those Hebrews 4:12 sermons where "the word of God is alive and active. Sharper than any double-edged sword, it penetrates even to dividing soul and spirit, joints and marrow." There ought to be those sermons when some in the congregation may actually want to ask, urge, or even demand that the preacher leave town—or least leave their local church. In short, there ought to be some occasions in the course of our ministry when the congregation may not say, "Amen," but God will say, "Well done," to a faithful witness who has seen something, said something, and then suffered something as a result of what she or he has seen.

As I wrote some years ago in *The African American Pulpit*:

> We must not reserve our harshest critique for the Wall Street traders and the Main Street corporate executives, though they are not without fault in the creation of many of society's problems. Rather, we must be willing to direct much of our preaching to those persons within the community of faith who are unmoved and unresponsive in the face of the misery they see all around them. They are going through the motions of religion, but, like Israel in the days of Amos, they have drawn a distinction between the observance of rituals and the practice of righteousness.[13]

Billy Graham: A Contemporary Amos or Amaziah?

Perhaps no other preacher in American history has had a better opportunity to serve as a witness for Jesus and his message than the evangelist Billy Graham. For more than sixty years of public ministry, Graham preached to massive crowds in indoor arenas and outdoor stadiums all over the world. It would be well within the bounds of truth to say that Billy Graham preached to more people than any other person in the history of the Christian church, including John Wesley and George Whitefield combined. Even more unique than his long-term, global ministry is that Billy Graham had regular access to every US president from Harry S. Truman in 1947 to Barack Obama in 2010, either at the White House or at Graham's home in Montreat, North Carolina.[14]

The question here is whether Billy Graham was a witness in the ways discussed in this book. Was he more like Amos or more like Amaziah? I'm not holding up Graham for scrutiny solely on the basis of his celebrity. His unparalleled access to and association with persons who sat at the pinnacle of power makes him the object of interest here. Graham undoubtedly passes the test if the concept of being a witness is limited to the first and most basic understanding of the term mentioned in chapter 5. I quote again from Karl Barth:

> The purpose of preaching is to explain the Scriptures. . . . There is, therefore, nothing to be said which is not already to be found in the Scriptures. No doubt preachers will be conscious of the weight of their own ideas which they drag after them; but ultimately they must decide whether they will allow themselves to compromise or whether, in spite of all notions at the back of their mind, they will accept the necessity of expounding the Book and nothing else.[15]

While one could argue over Graham's interpretation of biblical passages from time to time, there is no denying that the contents of the Bible served as the center of his preaching ministry.

That brings us to the other ways the term *witness* has been discussed in this book; namely, to *see something*, *say something* about what you have seen, and be prepared to *suffer something* as a result of what you have said. On those accounts, I argue that Graham falls woefully short and reveals himself to be far more like Amaziah than like Amos.

Billy Graham lived through some of the most tumultuous times in American history: the Korean War; the Cold War; the civil rights movement; the Vietnam War and the demonstrations that protested it; the Watergate cover-up and subsequent impeachment of Richard Nixon; the US military interventions in Nicaragua, El Salvador, and Granada; and more. But did the most widely traveled and politically connected preacher in the world ever say anything about those events that might have called into account any US president?

Graham's contemporary for most of that period in history was the theologian Reinhold Niebuhr, who had this to say about Graham's work as a witness, especially during the presidency of Richard Nixon and what Niebuhr referred to as "the Nixon-Graham doctrine":

> The Nixon-Graham doctrine contravened the Bible's subjecting of all historical reality (including economic, social and radical injustice) to God's absolute standards of justice. . . . Graham abandoned his responsibility to promote justice in order to gain the president's favor. America did not need Amaziah who colluded with the king to maintain the status quo, but rather an Amos who prophetically criticized the defective and unjust social order.[16]

Niebuhr continued:

> Nixon relied on the views of Graham and Peale (Norman Vincent Peale) and other popularizers of the Christian message. Ignoring its prophetic function, Nixon used religion primarily to sanctify the status quo and justify his policies. . . . Nixon seemed impervious to the radical distinction between conventional religion that sanctified contemporary public policy, even if it was morally inferior or outrageously unjust, and prophetic religion that censured all government policies that violated transcendent biblical standards.[17]

Graham's ministry is a keen example of what can happen when the preacher-prophet becomes too closely identified not only with the politician, but more importantly with the policies of the politician. Playing golf with President Kennedy in Palm Springs, California, or swimming with President Johnson in the White House pool, or leading dozens of worship services and Bible studies at the various vacation homes of US presidents spoke to Graham's access to twelve presidents.[18] A near total absence of any *parrhesia* (bold speech) by Graham directed to any of those presidents or their public policies speaks to the very limited way in which Billy Graham understood his role as a witness.

Graham certainly embraced the idea of keeping the Scriptures and Jesus at the center of his preaching so far as the issue of personal salvation was concerned. But he never ventured into the more challenging prophetic tasks of *seeing something*, *saying something*, and being prepared to *suffer something* as a result of what he said.

To be informed by Acts 1:6-8 is to understand that we cannot spend an entire career in the preaching ministry without *seeing something* that is displeasing to God in the world around us, *saying something* about what we have seen, and then *suffering something* as a consequence of what we have said.

NOTES

1. Walter Brueggemann, *The Prophetic Imagination* (Philadelphia: Fortress, 1978), 44–45.
2. Ibid., 67.
3. Cornel West and Christa Buschdorf, *Black Prophetic Fire* (Boston: Beacon, 2014), 112.
4. Socrates, quoted in Plato, *Apology*, trans. Benjamin Jowett, http://classics.mit.edu/Plato/apology.html, para. 11.
5. Reinhold Niebuhr, *Leaves from the Notebook of a Tamed Cynic* (Louisville: Westminster John Knox, 1957), 47.
6. Ibid.
7. Ibid.
8. Paul Tillich, quoted in Karl Barth, *The Preaching of the Gospel* (Philadelphia: Westminster, 1963), 54.
9. Donald Gowan, *Amos*, The New Interpreter's Bible, vol. 7 (Nashville: Abingdon, 1996), 341.
10. Ibid., 412.
11. Ibid.
12. Ibid.
13. Marvin A. McMickle, "The Prophet Amos as a Model for Preaching on Issues of Social Justice," *African American Pulpit*, Spring 2001, 8–9; cf. "Preaching in the Face of Economic Justice" in *Just Preaching*, ed. Andre Resner Jr. (St. Louis: Chalice, 2003), 3–10.
14. Nancy Gibbs and Michael Duffy, "President Obama Meets Billy Graham," *TIME*, April 25, 2010, http://content.time.com/time/nation/article/0,8599,1984421,00.html.
15. Paraphrased from Barth, *Preaching of the Gospel*, 42–43.
16. Reinhold Niebuhr, "The King's Chapel and the King's Court," *Christianity and Crisis*, August 4, 1969, 211–12.
17. Ibid., 212.
18. Gibbs and Duffy, "President Obama Meets Billy Graham."

CHAPTER 9

Witnesses at Work

Being a witness for Jesus that involves *seeing something*, then *saying something* about what one has seen, and finally that may result in *suffering something* for the sake of what one has said is not limited to characters in the Bible. Many people in recent years have embraced the role of being a *marturia* for the cause of Jesus Christ.

Witnesses in History

Many preachers and laypeople in this country and around the world stood in the role of the prophet Amos during the same period of time that Billy Graham was playing the Amaziah role with US presidents. These people were willing to live out the full dimensions of what it meant to be a witness for Jesus Christ.

Oscar Romero

The first person I want to focus on as a witness, or *marturia*, is Oscar Romero. Pope Francis recently honored the ministry of this El Salvadoran Catholic bishop who was murdered on March 24, 1980, by a government-backed death squad while leading a mass in San Salvador. The motive for his death was "his open challenge of an oppressive US-backed regime in El Salvador."[1] His death was a direct result of his opposition to the policies and practices of the government of El Salvador, which included state-ordered torture and murder.[2]

Tom Gibb, writing in *The Guardian*, noted, "The motive was clear. He was the most outspoken voice against the death squad slaughter gathering steam in the US backyard. Romero was the voice of those without a voice, telling soldiers not to kill."[3] The shooting death of Archbishop Romero came not long after he spoke movingly about the death of four US nuns who were "stopped by the National Guard of El Salvador, kidnapped at gunpoint, raped and executed."[4] In commenting on their deaths, Romero said, "Those who work on the side of the poor suffer the same fate as the poor."[5] Romero was drawn into the ongoing El Salvadoran civil war by a group of a hundred government soldiers asking him to intervene regarding orders they had received to kill guerillas who were fighting against the government. In response to their pleas, Romero preached a sermon in which he said, "No soldier is obliged to obey an order contrary to the law of God. No one has to obey an immoral law. It is high time you recovered your consciences and obeyed your consciences rather than a sinful order. In the name of God, in the name of this suffering people whose cries rise to heaven more loudly each day, I implore you, I beg you, I order you in the name of God: stop the repression."[6] Romero was assassinated the day after he delivered that sermon.

In writing about the honor bestowed by Pope Francis, Elisabetta Pique, an expert on the papacy, wrote, "Romero is an icon of the church that Francis is seeking to build. . . . It is a church with pastors that are close to the people and especially to the marginalized and those who suffer."[7] Pope Francis himself said, "In times of difficult coexistence, Archbishop Romero knew how to lead, defend and protect his flock, remaining faithful to the Gospel and in communion with the whole Church. His ministry was distinguished by a particular attention to the poor and marginalized."[8] Romero was a witness, a *marturia* who saw something, said something, and then suffered something as a result of his preaching.

Dietrich Bonhoeffer

In addition to the honor bestowed on him by Pope Francis, Oscar Romero is also one of the ten martyrs of the twentieth century depicted in statues in Westminster Abbey in London. He joins such well-known martyrs of the church as Dietrich Bonhoeffer and Martin

Luther King Jr. Dietrich Bonhoeffer was a German Lutheran pastor and theologian who was arrested, imprisoned, tortured, and finally executed by the Nazis under Adolf Hitler because he refused to adapt his theology to the anti-Jewish and pro-Aryan propaganda being put forth as an alternative to the truths of Scripture.[9]

Author and ethics professor Reggie L. Williams has made the point that part of what equipped Bonhoeffer to be a *marturia* for the Lord in Germany in 1945 was his exposure to black churches and black preachers in the United States when he was a student in New York City in 1939. Bonhoeffer wrote specifically about a black classmate at Union Theological Seminary named Albert Fisher who was a third-generation preacher from the Sixteenth Street Baptist Church in Birmingham, Alabama. That church would be bombed by the KKK in 1963 because of its support of the civil rights movement and Martin Luther King Jr. Williams said that Bonhoeffer learned from Fisher the importance of "preaching the gospel as a means of resistance and survival."[10]

Dietrich Bonhoeffer was a signatory to the Barmen Declaration, which essentially declared that if Jesus Christ is Lord then Hitler is not. That seemingly self-evident observation by twenty-first-century standards was enough to get a person imprisoned and executed during the Nazi era in Germany from 1933 to 1945. Charles Marsh, a Bonhoeffer biographer, referred to the Barmen Declaration as "an inspiring example of radical Christian conviction and courageous dissent, a ray of light in those darkest of times."[11] Even more central to this book, church historian John Leith, in his book *Creeds of the Churches*, written about the Barmen Declaration, called it "a witness, a battle cry."[12] Clearly Bonhoeffer embraced all three aspects of what this book argues for in terms of being a witness for Jesus Christ.

Martin Luther King Jr.

There can be no list of those who were faithful witnesses for Jesus Christ that does not include Martin Luther King Jr. The witness of this preacher is magnified when people consider the options available to him in life. Born into a solid middle-class family in Atlanta, Georgia, in 1956, by the age of twenty-six, he had earned a PhD in systematic theology from Boston University. He could have entered an academic career at any of the colleges and universities that were clamoring for his services. He could have enjoyed the comforts of a secure pastoral assignment anywhere in the country. Instead, he *saw something* as black people throughout the country were confronted by racism and segregation in one form or another. Then he began to *say something* about racism, poverty, and militarism as the great evils preventing our nation from fulfilling its promise of liberty and justice for all. From 1956 to 1968 he was willing to *suffer something* for what he was saying. Long before he was struck down by an assassin's bullet, he had endured ridicule and scorn in the media, threats and intimidation from white society, phone taps by the FBI, and even the loss of support from many black people when his witness led him to oppose the war in Vietnam. He was popular enough to help Carl Stokes win the office of mayor of Cleveland, Ohio, but controversial enough not to be invited onto the stage to stand with Stokes on election night.[13]

There is no more courageous or prophetic moment of *parrhesia* (bold speech) than the sermon delivered by Martin Luther King Jr. at Riverside Church in New York City on April 4, 1967, titled "A Time to Break Silence." He began that speech by saying, "A time comes when silence is betrayal. That time has come for us in relation to Vietnam."[14] King seemed aware of the dangers associated with speaking publicly against the policies of his own country. King said, "Even when pressed by the demands of inner truth, men do not easily assume the task of opposing their government's policies, especially in times of war. . . . Some of us who have already begun to break the silence of the night have found that the calling to speak is often a vocation of agony, but we must speak."[15]

Undoubtedly, it is the "vocation of agony" that so many preachers are unwilling to embrace. How much easier it is to speak of promises of material prosperity than it is to speak against the evils of racial injustice, economic disadvantage and wealth disparity, and the costs of war in terms of the loss of more than fifty-eight thousand US military lives, not to mention the billions of dollars diverted from the War on Poverty to the war in Vietnam. Martin Luther King Jr. was a witness for Jesus Christ who *saw something*, *said something*, and then *suffered something* as a result of what he said.

Vernon Johns

Whenever I think about a preacher who has lived up to the challenge of being a witness for Jesus, I think not only about Martin Luther King Jr., but also about Vernon Johns, who was the predecessor of Dr. King serving as pastor of Dexter Avenue Baptist Church in Montgomery, Alabama, from 1947 to 1952. His life was the basis of an HBO film that now includes multiple YouTube segments as well. On the second Sunday of May in 1949, Johns posted this ironic sermon title on the bulletin board outside the church: "It's Safe to Murder Negroes."

The sermon was the result of Johns having observed the brutal way in which white police officers in Montgomery treated black residents in that city and throughout the state of Alabama. The sermon was his attempt to bring to public view this brutal pattern of police misconduct. Even before that Sunday rolled around, however, Johns was summoned to meet with the mayor of Montgomery, who had been informed of the sermon title and who cautioned Johns about preaching on such an inflammatory topic. That warning notwithstanding (which was echoed by members of his own congregation), Vernon Johns proceeded. Immediately after preaching the sermon, he was escorted out of the church by two white Montgomery police officers and accused of disturbing the peace.[16]

After a ministry of preaching persistent and relentless challenges to his congregation for their timidity in the face of white racism and especially of police brutality, Vernon Johns eventually resigned from that church. He attempted to remain in the church parsonage but was forced to leave when the church had the gas and electricity turned off.[17]

Vernon Johns had *seen something*. He was willing to *say something* about it, and he was willing to *suffer something* for daring to speak about what he had seen.

Not All Witnesses Will Be Preachers

Remember that preachers are not and should not be the only people in society who are willing to embrace the role of being a witness for the Lord—of *seeing something*, *saying something*, and *suffering something* for the gospel ministry. One of the most desirable outcomes of the witness of the preacher is when a similar passion to be a witness arises from the people in the pews who are responding in kind to what they heard in a sermon. In addition, preachers should be prepared to lift up in their sermons the stories and experiences of those faithful and courageous men and women who have been witnesses for the values of the gospel without ever setting foot near a pulpit.

Ida B. Wells Barnett

Preachers should consider persons like Ida B. Wells Barnett. Born into slavery in Mississippi in 1862, this African American woman would become the editor of the *Memphis Free Speech and Headlight* newspaper in Memphis, Tennessee, in 1889. She used her position to attack the brutal practice of lynch mobs after she became aware of three black men who had been lynched in Memphis by white mobs in 1892. The men owned a grocery store that was competing for business with a white-owned store directly across the street. In a gun battle that ensued when a white mob tried to close down the black-owned store, the three black owners were arrested. Within days a mob took them from the jail and lynched them without trial.

Barnett used her weekly column in the newspaper to urge black residents of Memphis to boycott the city buses and, if possible, to migrate out of Memphis altogether as a way of protesting those lynchings. In one of her columns, she attacked what she called "the thread-bare lie that lynching occurs as a result of black men raping white women."[18]

Her columns enraged the white population of Memphis. One of the white-owned newspapers in town wrote its own editorial in which they said that Barnett herself should be lynched. The paper said, "There are some things that the Southern white man will not tolerate. . . . We hope we have said enough."[19] Not long after that a group of white citizens broke into her office, destroyed her printing presses, and burned the building. She was in New York City when all of this occurred, but she knew her life would be in danger if she tried to return to Memphis. The threat of death was not without basis. In response to Barnett's assaults against lynching and about the rape of black women by white men, the editor of a white-owned Nashville newspaper, the *Commercial Appeal*, published an editorial that raged: "The black wretch who had written that foul lie should be tied to a stake at the corner of Main and Madison streets, a pair of tailor's shears used on him, and he should then be burned at the stake."[20]

One thinks about the words of Donald Gowan in his commentary on Amos: "Speaking the truth by no means guarantees acceptance, for the truth will be uncomfortable to someone, and if it disturbs the comfort of those in power, it will produce serious opposition."[21] That was certainly true for Ida B. Wells. For safety's sake she relocated to New York City and in 1892 to Chicago, where she continued her outspoken assault on lynching in the United States.[22] While not a member of the clergy, she was an active member of the African Methodist Episcopal Church. From that position, Ida B. Wells Barnett was a witness for the Lord who *saw something*, *said something*, and *suffered something* in return.

Henry Wallace

One of the great untold stories of American political history, and one of the great demonstrations of what it looks like to be a witness for the Lord, involved Henry Wallace of Iowa, who served as vice president of the United States under Franklin D. Roosevelt from 1941 to 1945. In the summer of 1943, Wallace delivered a speech in Detroit, Michigan, in which he identified "racial justice and tolerance as major challenges facing America in a postwar world. . . . We cannot plead for equality of opportunity for people everywhere, and overlook the denial of the right to vote for millions of our own people."[23]

Henry Wallace spoke up in his official capacity for the voting rights of African Americans at a time when members of his own Democratic Party in every southern state in the country was doing everything in its power to prevent that from happening. His advocacy on that issue resulted in his being replaced on the 1944 Democratic ticket by the efforts of those southern Democrats who had amassed enormous political power precisely because they had prevented blacks from gaining the right to vote.[24]

Wallace was replaced on the ticket by Harry Truman of Missouri, who became president of the United States in 1945 following the death of President Roosevelt. One can only wonder how the issue of civil rights in this country might have been more rapidly advanced if Henry Wallace had been able to remain in his position and later become president. When Harry Truman proved to be too slow in responding to civil rights issues, Wallace ran against him in 1948 and continued his strong witness for racial justice. Daisy Bates, who became famous in 1957 for her leadership in integrating Central High School in Little Rock, Arkansas, was present to hear one of Wallace's civil rights speeches. She said, "I had waited all of my life to hear a white man say what he said."[25]

Henry Wallace saw racial injustice, he spoke out about it at the very highest levels of government, and he suffered a loss that few people could even comprehend—the opportunity to be next in line as president of the United States. Henry Wallace was a witness for the Lord!

Twenty-First-Century Witnesses

Persecution around the World

In some regions of the world, twenty-first-century Christians suffer to the extremes of torture and death for their gospel witness. In 2015, when given the option of converting to Islam or being beheaded at the hands of the terror group ISIS, dozens of Ethiopians were executed solely because of their faith and their faithfulness under pressure.[26] Christians living in Iraq and Nigeria in recent years faced similar suffering as they clung to their faith in the face of persecution.[27]

In each case, these Christians saw the attempts by radical groups to forcibly convert persons to Islam. Rather than abandon their faith in Jesus Christ, these Christians continued with their confession that Jesus Christ is Lord. As a result of that simple confession, these men, women, and children were put to death by the most brutal means imaginable. Like martyrs of the first-century church described in Hebrews 11:39, these twenty-first-century witnesses "were all commended for their faith."

Faith-Based Civil Disobedience

I am reminded of the words in Hebrews 12:4, "In your struggle against sin, you have not yet resisted to the point of shedding your blood." For most of us in the United States, our resistance may extend as far as *saying something* about what we have *seen*, but we are not called to *suffer something* as violent as death for our convictions. More common in North America are Christians who choose to suffer as a result of civil disobedience for the sake of their faith commitments.

Wanted: Witnesses for the Lord

What happens when the issue seems clearer and the cause seems morally correct? Will preachers and the laity be willing to *suffer something* under those circumstances? Sadly, I have seen too many instances where the risk of *saying something* and then *suffering something* as a result was intentionally avoided.

During the Reagan administration, I traveled to Washington, DC, with a group of clergy to address a matter of urban policy and federal spending for inner-city neighborhoods. Our group was offered one of two options: we could use our time to talk policy with a representative of the president, or we could all pose for a one-on-one photo with the president himself, who would only come into the meeting for that purpose (a photo op). I was amazed to discover how quickly righteous indignation cooled off when some preachers got the chance to rub elbows with the rich and powerful. People stood next to the president to get their picture taken, but only a few used the opportunity to present their agendas. The experience taught me that Esau was not the only person willing to sell something precious for a mess of pottage (Genesis 25:34).

I remember another trip to Washington, DC, also during the Reagan years, when the Cleveland NAACP organized a group of clergy and local activists to lobby members of the US Senate Judiciary Committee in the hope of persuading them not to support the nomination of Robert Bork to the US Supreme Court. The plan was for us to break up into groups of two and go door-to-door speaking with senators or their staff members. Otis Moss Jr. and I went to see Senator Dennis DeConcini of Arizona, who did subsequently vote against Bork's nomination.

When it was time to gather at our agreed-upon meeting place, several of our colleagues were not there. Those who were finished with their meetings with the senators simply assumed that the others were still working the halls and would soon be on their way. How surprised we were when several of them pulled up to the meeting spot in a taxi, patting their stomachs in satisfaction after spending the afternoon at a popular soul food restaurant in that city. They had not made one visit to a Senate office. They had not spoken to one person. They traveled all the way from Cleveland, Ohio, to Washington, DC, at a critical moment in the life of the nation with nothing to show for it but the barbecue sauce under their fingernails.

Not everybody is willing to be a *marturia* at the level of *saying something*, much less at the level of *suffering something* as a result of what they have said.

Being a Witness in a "Worship" Generation

This idea of being a witness for Jesus in ways that might result in some form of suffering or hardship may be hard for many contemporary preachers to comprehend, first of all because they have rarely if ever heard such preaching from their peers or even their mentors. So many of the great prophetic voices of the twentieth century—Martin Luther King Jr., William Sloane Coffin, William Augustus Jones Jr., Prathia Hall, Peter Gomes, and Gardner C. Taylor—have died. On any given Sunday, any of those preachers was likely to come before a congregation with a word that was blazing with righteous indignation over matters of unjust foreign policies, the cruelties of racism, the arrogance of male chauvinism, or the ugliness of homophobia.

The same is true for the late, great nonpreachers who were witnesses for righteousness and justice, people such as Fannie Lou Hamer, Ida B. Wells Barnett, Septima Clark, A. Philip Randolph, and Ella Baker. Their remarks flowed from a place outside of a pulpit, but their witness was powerfully prophetic all the same.

It is sad to say that today such voices rising with righteous indignation are harder and harder to find. You can listen to The WORD Network, the Trinity Broadcasting Network (TBN), or any other station that offers religious broadcasting and seldom hear anything that would threaten to undo the present power arrangements or public policies of this country. In the words of Shakespeare in *Macbeth*, many of those TV sermons are little more than "sound and fury signifying nothing."

Gardner Taylor said in his 1975 Lyman Beecher Lectures at Yale Divinity School, "The manner in which we preach should never become more important than the matter about which we preach."[28] *What we preach* will always be of the utmost importance and urgency. No matter how creatively the words are shaped and the phrases are turned, you cannot say "nothing" well. Or in the language of the 1970s R&B singer Billy Preston, "Nothing from nothing leaves nothing."

Thankfully, preachers who are willing to *see something*, *say something*, and *suffer something* for what they are bold enough to say are still among us today. Preachers like Jeremiah Wright, Gina Stewart, Renita Weems, and James Forbes remain as a reminder of what prophetic preaching sounds like in terms of content and fury. Sadly, their voices and their message are often drowned out by those whose preaching is more popular, more pleasing, and more promising of prosperity. It was for this very reason that I wrote the book *Where Have All the Prophets Gone?*[29]

Today we are faced with a generation of preachers groomed on the idea that every sermon ought to end in celebration, with the congregation rejoicing and the preacher being applauded. It is hard to imagine that every sermon by Amos, Micah, John the Baptist, Jesus, or Paul would end in a celebration. More often than not, the hearers of those sermons cried out "Woe is me" rather than "Amen" or "Hallelujah." *Marturia* is not something that most of these preachers are eager to embrace.

Twenty-first-century preachers need to ask themselves if they are as focused on work and witness as they are on praise and worship. We all need to ask ourselves if we are more interested in preaching that results in celebration than we are in preaching that might result in some form of controversy or criticism. In other words, is there any cause we have noticed in the world around us about which we feel compelled to speak no matter how negatively our message might be perceived by some?

Are we preachers paying attention to such matters as human rights, economic disparity, war and peace, public policy, political activity, mass incarceration of persons of color, intracommunal violence in the black community, terrorism, global conflicts, and the environmental/ecological challenges that confront this planet? Are we viewing these issues through the lens of Scripture and the teachings of the church? Do any of these things move us to a place of righteous indignation? If the answer to all of the above is yes, then are we prepared to speak about what we have seen even if our views bring us into conflict with people in our congregations, with our clergy peers, and with the political leaders and values of our region and our nation?

Bear in mind that a great many preachers deliver sermons on a regular basis and are always looking to find something on which to speak. Acts 1:6-8 asks us every week, *Are you taking time to see something?* Do we have the courage to say something about what we have seen? Would we say what needs to be said if we knew there was a possibility that we might have to suffer something as a consequence? That is what it means to be a *marturia*, and that is what God expects of those who preach the gospel of Jesus Christ.

What Does the Lord Require of Us?

Acts 1:6-8 was the charge given by Jesus to his first disciples, and it remains the charge for every generation of preachers. "Be my witnesses" was what Jesus was expecting from his first disciples, and that is exactly what Jesus expects from preachers today. When preachers try to decide what they are going to preach on next Sunday, they need to ask themselves how they can turn their sermon and themselves into a witness for the Lord.

If the only thing we focus on is prosperity, which is the primary emphasis of some, or personal salvation or some form of positive thinking, which is the main focus of others, it is not likely that any suffering or persecution will come our way. The truth is, little if anything is being said by the world's most popular preachers that is likely to generate any push-back or rebuke from the entrenched forces of power in government, Wall Street, media outlets, or those who benefit most from the status quo. That being said, Jesus still calls on preachers to be his *marturia* who *see something*, who are willing to *say something* about what they have seen, and who are prepared to *suffer something* as a consequence of what they were willing to say. What would that look like in your preaching ministry as you decide what texts and topics you will lift up from week to week?

The vast majority of preachers and church members may never be called on to serve or suffer to extremes. Likewise, based on my observation of church life and preachers for the last fifty years, most preachers are not predisposed to engage in anything that might result in suffering. In other words, not all preachers will be drawn into controversy, and if they are not drawn in by others, they are unlikely to move in on their own. Nevertheless, Jesus expects that we will be willing to suffer something for the sake of the gospel.

Is there any inconvenience, any loss of friendship or fellowship, any experience of rebuke or reprisal that we are willing to endure at the hands of those who take offense at what we faithfully and truthfully say in our sermons? Are there any sermon topics or doctrinal conflicts we are likely to avoid because we do not want to enter into any controversy that might cause us to lose favor with a denominational leader, a pastoral colleague, a public official, or even a member of our own family? Not every preacher is willing to be a witness. That being said, God is still in need of witnesses who will enter their pulpits on Sunday morning fresh from having *seen something*, ready and willing to *say something*, and fully aware of the possibility that they may end up having to *suffer something* for what they have said.

Will We Risk the Hostile Stare?

A Christian hymn by John Bell of the Iona Community in Scotland titled "The Summons" has become popular in recent years. One brief lyric in that song raises the question, "Will you risk the hostile stare should your life attract or scare?"[30] This question is appropriate for those who are determined to be witnesses for Jesus.

Disapproval often begins with a hostile stare before it escalates to a hostile act. A furrowed brow often precedes a balled-up fist or a verbal assault. The hymn suggests that the hostile stare could come for one of two possible reasons: because of disapproval over those whom the messages attracts or as a result of the message scaring some. As this hymn properly asserts, this is the work to which Jesus is summoning those who would be his witnesses. Sometimes we will have to *suffer something* as a consequence of what we have said.

If preachers are afraid to be criticized or questioned by others about what they have dared to say, then perhaps they should change professions. If they are inclined to withdraw what they have said in a moment of courage because someone in a moment of anger does not like what they have said, then the speech of those preachers will be halted and stuttered for as long as their ministries last; they will always be trying to find a way never to hurt, challenge, or confront. In short, preachers who are reluctant to or determined not to *suffer something* as a result of what they have said will likely say nothing of any great consequence in their sermons.

These words of Jesus should speak to every preacher when our sermons and our public proclamations earn the wrath and condemnation of persons who do not want to have their power and position challenged: "Woe to you when everyone speaks well of you, for that is how their ancestors treated the false prophets" (Luke 6:26). Preachers would do well to heed the advice of President John Adams concerning political leadership. Adams, who served as our nation's second president from 1796 to 1800, noted, "A statesman must risk the people's displeasure sometimes, or he will never do them any good in the long run."[31]

The same thing is true for preachers; we must risk people's displeasure if we are to be fully helpful to them and fully faithful to God. In the language of Paul to Timothy, people will welcome our words when we encourage them, but they may not be as pleased or happy with us when we feel the need to correct or rebuke (2 Timothy 4:2). So be it. Preachers should not shrink from those moments when they may have to *suffer something* as a result of what they have said. If and when that happens, preachers should take heart in these words of Jesus: "Blessed are you when people insult you, persecute you and falsely say all kinds of evil against you because of me. Rejoice and be glad, because great is your reward in heaven, for in the same way they persecuted the prophets who were before you" (Matthew 5:12).

NOTES

1. Inés San Martín, "Five Things You Don't Know about Archbishop Oscar Romero," *Crux*, May 23, 2015, http://www.cruxnow.com/church/2015/05/23/five-things-you-dont-know-about-archbishop-oscar-romero-2/.

2. Tracy Wilkinson and Tom Kington, "Romero Beatification Signals Pope Francis' Plan for Catholic Church," *Los Angeles Times*, May 28, 2015, http://www.latimes.com/world/mexico-americas/la-fg-pope-direction-20150528-story.html.

3. Tom Gibb, "The Killing of Archbishop Oscar Romero Was One of the Most Notorious Crimes of the Cold War. Was the CIA to Blame?," *Guardian*, March 22, 2000, http://www.theguardian.com/theguardian/2000/mar/23/features11.g21.

4. Brett Wilkins, "On This Day, 1980: American Nuns Kidnapped, Raped and Murdered by U.S.–Trained Salvadoran Death Squad," Morallowground.com, December 2, 2010, http://morallowground.com/2010 /12/02/on-this-day-1980-american-nuns-kidnapped-raped-murdered-by-american-trained-salvadoran-death-squad/.

5. Ibid.

6. Gustavo Valdes, Merlin Delcid, and Mariano Castillo, "Martyred Salvadoran Archbishop Oscar Romero Closer to Sainthood," CNN, May 23, 2015, http://www.cnn.com/2015/05/23/americas/el-salvador-archbishop-oscar-romero-beatification/index.html.

7. Wilkinson and Kington, "Romero Beatification."

8. Valdes, Delcid, and Castillo, "Martyred Salvadoran Archbishop."

9. Charles Marsh, *Strange Glory: A Life of Dietrich Bonhoeffer* (New York: Knopf, 2014), 390–91.

10. Reggie L. Williams, *Bonhoeffer's Black Jesus: Harlem Renaissance, Theology, and an Ethic of Resistance* (Waco, TX: Baylor University Press, 2014), 20.

11. Marsh, *Strange Glory*, 223.

12. John H. Leith, ed., *Creeds of the Churches: A Reader in Christian Doctrine from the Bible to the Present* (Garden City, NY: Doubleday Anchor, 1963), 517.

13. Cornel West, *The Radical King: Martin Luther King, Jr.* (Boston: Beacon, 2015), xiii.

14. Martin Luther King Jr., "A Time to Break Silence," in *A Testament of Hope: The Essential Writings of Martin Luther King, Jr.* (New York: Harper & Row, 1986), 231.

15. Ibid.

16. Mo Barnes, "Dr. Vernon Johns: 'It's Safe to Murder Negroes.' The NYPD and Eric Garner," rollingout, July 29, 2014, http://rollingout.com/2014/07/29/dr-vernon-johns-safe-murder-negroes-nypd-eric-garner/; cf. *The Vernon Johns Story*, 1994, https://www.youtube.com/watch?v= lscNugS3EXE.

17. Marvin A. McMickle, "Vernon Johns," in *An Encyclopedia of African American Christian Heritage* (Valley Forge, PA: Judson, 2002), 105.

18. Alfreda M. Duster, *Crusade for Justice: The Autobiography of Ida B. Wells* (Chicago: University of Chicago Press, 1970), 66.

19. Thomas C. Holt, "The Lonely Warrior: Ida B. Wells Barnett and the Struggle for Black Leadership," *Black Leaders of the Twentieth Century*, ed. John Hope Franklin and August Meier (Urbana: University of Illinois Press, 1982), 43.

20. Duster, *Crusade for Justice*, 66.

21. Donald Gowan, *Amos*, The New Interpreter's Bible, vol. 7 (Nashville: Abingdon, 1996), 412.

22. Marvin A. McMickle and Jean Alicia Elster, "Ida B. Wells Barnett," in *Profiles in Black: Phat Fact for Teens* (Valley Forge, PA: Judson, 2008), 76–77.

23. Patricia Sullivan, *Lift Every Voice: The NAACP and the Making of the Civil Rights Movement* (New York: New Press, 2009), 280.

24. Ibid., 284.

25. Ibid., 366–67.

26. David D. Kirkpatrick, "Isis Video Appears to Show Executions of Ethiopian Christians in Libya," *New York Times*, April 19, 2015, http://www.nytimes.com/2015/04/20/world/middleeast/isis-video-purports-to-show-killing-of-ethiopian-christians.html.

27. Tim Keesee, *Dispatches from the Front: Stories of Gospel Advance in the World's Difficult Places* (Wheaton, IL: Crossway, 2014); cf. "Christian Persecution," opendoorsusa.org; "Cloud of Witnesses," *Christianity Today* March 26, 2015, 10.

28. This was part of the audiotaped version of the Lyman Beecher Lectures by Gardner C. Taylor at Yale Divinity School in 1975.

29. Marvin A. McMickle, *Where Have All the Prophets Gone?* (Cleveland, OH: Pilgrim, 2006).

30. John Bell, "The Summons," Iona Community (Chicago: GIA, 1987).

31. Gary Scott Smith, *Religion in the Oval Office: The Religious Lives of American Presidents* (New York: Oxford, 2015), 41.

CHAPTER 10

Preaching with a Map and a Metaphor

This book now moves from *what* Jesus challenged the first-century disciples to do, to *where* Jesus directed them to go to perform their work as his witnesses. Thus, we in the twenty-first century shift from concerns about the content of our preaching to considerations about the contexts in which we are called to go and be witnesses for God.

Acts 1:6-8 takes us to another equally vital issue that has to do with how far and wide we are prepared to go to deliver our sermons. In this text Jesus invites his first disciples to enter upon a steadily widening sphere of ministry that began in *Jerusalem*, extended to *Judea*, included a surprising call to go to *Samaria*, and finally took them to *the ends of the earth*. The same principle applies with this part of the text as applied with the earlier portion; namely, that we can learn much about our work as preachers in the twenty-first century by listening to and embracing what Jesus said to his disciples in the first century.

A Map and a Metaphor

In this theology of preaching, the references to Jerusalem, Judea, Samaria, and the ends of the earth have a double meaning. Those four locations are, of course, historic geographic destinations where the disciples' preaching ministry might lead them. We can read the charge about going to Jerusalem, Judea, Samaria, and the ends of the earth as a charge for the first disciples of Jesus to literally and physically travel to those places to preach and make known the name of Jesus.

In truth, that is precisely what that first generation of preachers did; they extended their preaching ministries as far and wide as they possibly could, traveling throughout as much of the known world as they could reach in their lifetimes. This impulse to reach and preach in ever more distant locations can also be heard in Paul's aspiration to go beyond Rome to preach in Spain (Romans 15:24).

That impulse to extend the claims of the gospel into every corner of the world remains one of the great distinctives of Christian preaching. None of the other Abrahamic faith groups take global evangelism as seriously as do the followers of Jesus. So central is the work of evangelism to the core identity of the Christian church that Ephesians 4:11 says among the offices that God has established for the nurture and expansion of the church is that of the evangelist, characterized as a work separate and apart from the apostle, the prophet, the pastor, or the teacher.

Today the work of evangelism goes on through stadium crusades, TV broadcasts, and church-sponsored missionary efforts on every continent of the earth. The *Wall Street Journal* reported that in 2015 more than 127,000 Christian missionaries were sent to countries all over the world from church bodies in the United States. The International Mission Board of the Southern Baptist Convention alone has an annual budget of $300 million to support global missions and evangelism.[1]

There can be no doubt that the mandates in Matthew 28:19, Mark 16:15, and Luke 24:47-48 place the work of global evangelism at the center of God's intention for the church. The three missionary journeys of Paul to Asia Minor and Europe confirm how seriously those mandates were taken by the apostles of the first century. Those four locations referenced by Jesus remain a call for preaching that takes some preachers to geographic sites all over the world. That is what sparked the preaching of such Christian evangelists as Billy Graham, Tom Skinner, Dwight L. Moody, William Seymour, Morris Cerullo, and so many others.

On the other hand, the same biblical reference to Jerusalem, Judea, Samaria, and the ends of the earth can also be thought of as a willingness to include in one's regular preaching certain themes and topics that reflect an awareness of local, regional, national, and even global matters of concern. In other words, the issue is not solely a matter of preachers physically traveling across the country and around the world. Rather, it is also a matter of preachers viewing and analyzing and addressing issues occurring across cultures and around the world through the lens of the biblical message.

This approach is all the more theologically sound if we assume that preachers should bear witness to the claims and concerns of a sovereign God. The Bible repeatedly asserts that God is the creator of "the heavens and the earth" (Genesis 1:1). The psalmist proclaims, "The earth is the LORD'S, and everything in it" (Psalm 24:1). Nebuchadnezzar, king of Babylon, said about the God of Daniel that "his dominion is an eternal dominion; his kingdom endures from generation to generation" (Daniel 4:34). God's global reach is such that the prophet Amos begins his oracle against Israel by first condemning the sins of Israel's neighbors: Damascus, Gaza, Tyre, Edom, Moab, and Judah (Amos 1–2). If God's sovereignty extends to the ends of the earth and to the conduct of all the nations of the earth, it would be hard for preachers to justify their sermons never extending beyond themes and topics that are no broader than their own backyards!

So what is being suggested here is that Jerusalem, Judea, Samaria, and the ends of the earth are not simply places on a map, nor is the implication that every twenty-first-century preacher should personally aspire to travel in order to declare the gospel message. Being a witness for Jesus in Jerusalem, Judea, Samaria, and the ends of the earth is also a metaphor for being sensitive to, aware of, and prepared to address the gospel to the specific themes and challenges that arise when one thinks about those distinct cultural and geopolitical settings.

When the challenges of Acts 1:6-8 are considered together, this means that preachers should be willing and able to *see something*, *say something*, and *suffer something* as a result of addressing issues that extend far beyond the life of a local church or a particular neighborhood in their city. Sermons must address such concerns as racial and ethnic tensions in communities around the nation, the mass incarceration of persons of color across the United States, human rights violations occurring every day in places as far away as Nigeria, Ukraine, Iraq, and China, and the surge of refugees flooding into Europe from Syria and Libya.

From Jerusalem to the Ends of the Earth

The last part of the charge that Jesus gave to his disciples involved the ever-widening context in which he expected their preaching to take place. The challenge was to begin in the place where they were currently located, Jerusalem, and radiate out from there. We will consider each of those locations briefly here and then explore each in more depth in the subsequent chapters.

Jerusalem

While the call to preach in the holy city did not involve much in terms of travel or proximity (the disciples were already there when Jesus issued his charge), preaching was risky because Jerusalem was the place where Jesus had only recently been crucified. Jerusalem was the place where the disciples still lived in hiding for fear of those who might seek to kill them because of their association with Jesus. Jerusalem was the heart and soul of the Jewish nation, and it was a city that had become a dangerous place to be in a time when religious and political unrest in the Roman Empire was often violent and bloody.

It was in that location that the disciples were being sent to proclaim the message that Jesus Christ is Lord. These words must have evoked in the disciples a sense of dread and great anxiety: "Be my witnesses in Jerusalem."

Judea

As important as their ministry in Jerusalem would be, that was not the only context that should occupy their attention. Jesus instructed them to extend their ministry to Judea. They had to preach both *to* their country and *about* their country. They had to travel throughout the larger region telling people about Jesus. More importantly, they had to lift up the values and teachings of Jesus as a lens through which to consider and critique what they would see going on in their nation. If Jerusalem was their immediate local context, being sent to Judea was their challenge from Jesus to pay attention to everything going on from the northern edge of the Sea of Galilee to the southern tip of the Dead Sea and from the banks of the Mediterranean Sea to the shores of the Jordan River.

Ministry that remains local and never attempts to reach out to consider what is happening in the nation around it is not being faithful to the command from Jesus to be my witnesses in Judea. Preaching that focuses only on what is happening across the street or around the corner from the church but never addresses issues occurring in the broader national arena falls far short of the challenge that Jesus gave to his first generation of preachers and that Jesus expects from every generation of preachers.

As I suggested in my book *Where Have All the Prophets Gone?*, "prophetic preaching shifts the focus of a congregation from what is happening to them as a local church to what is happening to them as a part of society."[2] James and Christine Ward reinforce this distinction between Jerusalem and Judea in a somewhat different way:

> The natural inclination of the Christian community, like all religious communities, is to adapt its witness of faith to its most immediate human needs. In doing this the community always runs the risk of obscuring the wider dimensions of the gospel, particularly the wider implications of God's demand for righteousness and justice. What is needed, therefore, is preaching that recovers these wider dimensions and illuminates the ways in which the community obscures them.[3]

Samaria

As challenging as going throughout Judea must have seemed to the first disciples, that was nothing compared to the next destination mentioned by Jesus: "Be my witnesses in . . . Samaria." While much more will be said about this later (see chapter 13), suffice it to say for the moment that Samaria was a place where self-respecting Jews did not want to go, and Samaritans were people whom self-respecting Jews did not want to encounter. Yet here is Jesus challenging the disciples (who were all Jewish) to do exactly that: go where they do not want to go and interact with people they would rather avoid.

The Samaritans were "those people." Every culture has created its own version of "those people." They are the people we look down on or hold in open contempt. They are the people we can openly discriminate against without fear or shame because discriminating against "those people" is socially acceptable in our culture. It's bad enough that Jesus challenges them to face the hazards of preaching in Jerusalem or the rigors of witnessing in Judea, but now he challenges them to ignore centuries-old prejudices and extend the message of God's love to people they had likely hated or avoided all their lives. One could imagine thoughts of Jonah crossing their minds and the command God gave to that Old Testament prophet to go and preach in Nineveh!

There are probably some places that preachers do not want to go largely because they do not like the people they will encounter in those places. You cannot be a witness for the Lord if you are only willing to go to the places you prefer and to the people you approve. At some point every preacher has to answer the call to be my witnesses in Samaria.

The Ends of the Earth

The final challenge for our preaching is to be witnesses for Jesus "to the ends of the earth." This does not mean that every single preacher must travel throughout the world preaching the gospel, although some may have both the aspiration and the opportunity to do just that. Rather, it requires that every preacher remember that God claims sovereignty over the whole of creation. It means that God cares about the people in every part of the world.

This was a reminder to first-century Jews that the God who loved the people of Israel loved the people of Egypt or Ethiopia or Greece no less. It is a reminder to twenty-first-century American preachers that, while

"God Bless America" may be a familiar patriotic song, it is far more likely that our Creator's favorite song is "He's Got the Whole World in His Hands."

When Pope Francis visited people in the slums of Ecuador, Bolivia, and Paraguay in July of 2015, he was acting out this principle of being a witness to the ends of the earth.[4] The love of God is not centered in the United States, Western Europe, and among the other developed nations of the world. God expects the church to care about and preachers to talk about what is happening to the aborigines of Australia, the untouchables of India, the native people of the Amazon rain forest, and the Palestinian people living on the outside of the wall in Israel. When busy preachers get ready for next Sunday's sermon, they should ask themselves when the last time was that their preaching material extended to the people and problems in these places: Jerusalem, Judea, Samaria, and the ends of the earth.

NOTES

1. Tamara Audi, "Missionaries Face a Recall," *Wall Street Journal*, October 26, 2015, A3.

2. Marvin A. McMickle, *Where Have All the Prophets Gone?* (Cleveland: Pilgrim, 2006), 2.

3. James Ward and Christine Ward, *Preaching from the Prophets* (Nashville: Abingdon, 1995), 11.

4. Jim Yardley, "My Travels with Pope Francis in Latin America," *New York Times*, July 14, 2015, http://www.nytimes.com/interactive/projects/cp/reporters-notebook/pope-francis-ecuador-bolivia-paraguay.

CHAPTER 11

Preaching in Jerusalem

For the purposes of this book, Jerusalem represents the local church and the witness of faith by Christians in the community in which their church is located and the city in which they live. When preachers are informed by the lessons of Acts 1:6-8, they will understand that some of their sermons must be focused on what is happening within their own local church, and other sermons must address events unfolding within the local community that surrounds and often impacts their local church. Some sermons will be intended to address congregational challenges, while other sermons will speak to the problems and pressures confronting the lives of people in the neighborhood in which their church is located. This means that preachers' work is not complete when they say something to the people who are already members of their churches and who are already familiar with the rhythms and rituals of religion. Their sermons must also have relevance for those who live just beyond the doors of their church buildings.

Preaching in Jerusalem must involve what we as preachers are willing to say about what we see of human suffering or societal evils unfolding in the streets, the schools, the job market, the police departments, and the intergroup relations in the towns and cities where we live and where our church buildings are located. This must be the case whether our church members are directly impacted by those things or not. That is the challenge of being a witness in Jerusalem.

In my book *Caring Pastors, Caring People* I use three concentric circles to show how the local church can carry out the Great Commission.[1] The first circle involves the pastor of a local congregation caring for his or her members in all the traditional areas of pastoral ministry. The second circle involves members of the congregation being equipped to show care and concern for one another. This is based on the message of Ephesians 4:11, where one of the challenges of the pastor-teacher is to "equip [Christ's] people for works of service." The third circle challenges the church to extend its care and concern beyond themselves and other members of their congregation and to demonstrate God's love to the people and problems that reside in the surrounding community. This would be the case whether those persons are members of that local church or not. This three-circle approach to ministry is useful when thinking about preaching in Jerusalem.

Circle One: A Caring Pastor

As it relates to the first circle, "pastoral care should be understood as the umbrella term under which a wide variety of ministry tasks are grouped, all of them done for the nurture and support of the congregation."[2] Pastoral care in the first circle includes such tasks as weddings, funerals, hospital calls, counseling sessions, and leading in Bible studies, and it most certainly includes preaching as well.

It was Harry Emerson Fosdick, the noted preacher of the mid-twentieth century, who wrote about preaching and pastoral counseling as a two-way street.[3] To paraphrase him slightly: "All preachers who in their sermons speak to the real condition of their people, making evident that they know what questions the people are asking, and where their problems lie, those preachers are bound to be sought out by individuals wanting their intimate advice."[4]

Preaching in Jerusalem is informed by this first circle of pastoral care because it serves as a metaphor for preaching that is designed to speak to the immediate needs and concerns of the congregation. The better the pastor knows the people in the congregation, the more effective his or her sermons will be in knowing "what questions they are asking and where their problems lie."

Thomas Oden, in his book *Pastoral Theology*, wrote about "learning properly to shepherd the flock of God."[5] Oden argued that just as one would expect persons trained in law or medicine to approach their profession with an integral theory or overarching conception of their official duty, the same should be true for pastors. He said, "The importance of the office of pastor still quietly pleads with us to think with extraordinary care about the better and worse ways in which that office might be conceived and practiced."[6]

One of the ways by which we can positively think about the office of the pastor is to think about preaching that speaks directly to the hopes and fears, doubts and dilemmas, and aspirations and obstacles faced by the people in our local churches. This is a large part of what it means to be a witness for Jesus in Jerusalem. When preachers are informed by the lessons of Acts 1:6-8, they will understand that some of their sermons must be focused on what is happening within their own local churches.[7] The first circle involves the pastor of a local congregation caring for his or her members in all the traditional areas of pastoral ministry.

On the other hand, preaching in Jerusalem is not entirely about those forms of pastoral care designed to encourage and sustain people through the most challenging times of their lives. Being a witness in Jerusalem also involves finding the courage to say a word of rebuke and correction to those same people when the need arises.

As one who served as pastor of two local churches over a period of thirty-four years, I know only too well how challenging it was and is to embody the charge of Paul to Timothy and allow one's preaching to "correct and rebuke" as well as to "encourage" (2 Timothy 4:2). I fully understand the observation from Reinhold Niebuhr developed during his seventeen years as a pastor in Detroit as he sought to understand why so few pastors showed much willingness to engage in prophetic preaching. Niebuhr said, "I think the real clue to the tameness of a preacher is the difficulty one finds in telling unpleasant truths to people whom one has learned to love."[8]

Preaching in Jerusalem, in one's hometown and more precisely in one's home church, demands the same three aspects of being a witness: *see something*, *say something*, and *suffer something*. Jesus is calling on preachers to have a ministry that is faithful and attentive to the people and problems within their particular local churches and their surrounding local communities. The more intimately preachers are aware of the struggles and anxieties of individuals in their congregations, the more equipped they will be to say something that is pastoral or prophetic about what is going on. Visiting church members in the hospital, sitting with them in their homes after the death of loved ones, and listening to the content of their prayers and testimonies in worship services and Bible classes are all pathways into the lives of those to whom we preach.

Recall from chapter 5 Cleophus LaRue's five domains of experience: personal piety, care of the soul, social justice, corporate concerns, and maintenance of the institutional church.[9] These domains were observed in the sermons of black preachers, but in truth they are a useful guide for all preachers who seek to speak into the hearts and minds of their local congregations. Two of those domains, personal piety and care of the soul, apply directly to my first circle of pastoral care.

As preachers seeking to be witnesses for Jesus, we want to encourage people to develop the habits of personal piety: daily devotions, public and private times of prayer, regular Bible study, a personal spirit of humility, and a willingness to offer forgiveness to those who may have hurt or offended us. We need to challenge our listeners with the sentiment expressed in the hymn title "Take Time to Be Holy."[10]

As preachers we should also want to direct our sermons to those matters having to do with the care of the soul, such as those times when death, sickness, sudden tragedy, or another unexpected or overwhelming event has occurred in someone's life. The pastor-preacher's role is to employ steps that can encourage and sustain people as they pass through challenging times.

Circle Two: Church Members Caring for One Another

The second circle of pastoral care is also crucial to being a witness in Jerusalem because it focuses on the ways in which sermons are employed to encourage people in the church to care for one another.

One of the fundamental ways by which the early church was to distinguish itself from the rest of the world is captured in the challenge "Let us love one another" (1 John 4:7).

That recurring phrase is at the heart of what it means to be a Christian community. We "carry each other's burdens" (Galatians 6:2), and we "mourn with those who mourn" (Romans 12:15). Paul says, "As we have opportunity, let us do good to all people, especially to those who belong to the family of believers" (Galatians 6:10). By the end of the second century AD, the theologian and apologist Tertullian of Carthage in North Africa envisioned a Christian community about which the world would have to say, "Behold how they love one another."[11]

Preaching from Circle Two

On every first Sunday of the month during my thirty-four years as a pastor, I led those faithful Baptists in declaring aloud a church covenant that served as our pledge about the ways in which we would seek to love in community with one another. Some parts of that covenant were personal and family commitments to read and study the Bible and to engage in a life of prayer. Some parts of the covenant involved our willingness to affirm the doctrines and practices of the Baptist church and to support the church with our tithes and offerings. However, a few lines in the covenant pointed directly to the aspirations of this second circle in which people were encouraged to care for one another. That part of the covenant says, "We further engage to watch over one another in brotherly love; to remember each other in prayer; to aid each other in sickness and distress; to cultivate Christian sympathy in feeling and courtesy in speech; to be slow to take offense, but always ready for reconciliation and mindful of the rules of our Savior to secure it without delay."[12]

This characteristic of a community marked by its love, care, and concern for one another is at the heart of the second circle of pastoral care. Such a community must constantly be nurtured and encouraged, and preaching plays a major role in that process.

Lazarus, Martha, and Mary—One of the best texts for preaching about the second circle is found in John 11, which relates the story of the death of Lazarus. Most often, sermons based on this passage focus on the actions of Jesus, who did not arrive in Bethany until Lazarus had already been dead for four days, and who then raised Lazarus from the dead. This account includes one of the seven "I am" sayings of Jesus found in John's Gospel. In this instance it is "I am the resurrection and the life. The one who believes in me will live even though they die; and whoever lives by believing in me will never die" (John 11:25-26).

Other sermons on this text focus on the grief of Mary and Martha and on their chastising Jesus for not coming to heal Lazarus, whom Jesus loved. Still other sermons on this same passage have focused on the question raised by Jesus with Martha at the end of his "I am" saying: "Do you believe this?" (John 11:26), and on Martha's response in verse 27 where she says, "Yes, Lord. I believe that you are the Messiah, the Son of God, who is to come into the world." This is great preaching material for those delivering a eulogy or providing comfort for grieving families as part of a circle-one ministry.

However, there is another angle from which this text can be read that links it to a second-circle approach to ministry. Tucked away in John 11:18-19 is a wonderful example of a community of faith that is caring for one another. It says, "Now Bethany was less than two miles from Jerusalem, and many Jews had come to Martha and Mary to comfort them in the loss of their brother." Nobody needed to call them into action. They did not wait until the arrival of Jesus. They were a community of faith, and two members of their community had suffered the death of a beloved brother. The people of Bethany showed up to care for two members of their community.

Those people entered into the observance of the Jewish practice known as "sitting *shiva*," a period of seven days when the community assumed all household duties so the bereaved family could mourn the death of a loved one. When Jesus arrived at the sisters' house, he found that the community had already gathered. The rabbi did not have to be present for their work to begin. Nobody in that community was expected to say anything theological or pastoral. This was what we would now refer to as "the ministry of presence," in which simply being there is the gift that is offered. Preaching that invites and encourages believers in the twenty-first century to emulate the people of Bethany in the first century is always useful.

Four Good Friends—Something similar can be done with the story in Mark 2:1-12, in which four nameless men carried a paralytic who was hoping to be healed by Jesus. This text offers multiple avenues of approach for a sermon on how members of a congregation can care for one another.

The account depicts a house so crowded with people that it was not possible to open or close the door. Every square inch was occupied by people who had come to hear Jesus. When the paralyzed man was brought into his presence, Jesus made the pronouncement that his sins were forgiven (Mark 2:5), a controversial statement to which the teachers of the law took offense. That encounter finally prompted the miraculous healing when Jesus told the paralyzed man, "Get up, take your mat and go home" (v. 11).

What we have considered so far points only to a circle-one ministry, where a caring person (Jesus) shows pastoral concern for a needy soul (the paralytic). Up to this point, we have referenced only one actor: Jesus. In truth, however, nothing would have ever happened to that paralyzed man if four unnamed men had not engaged in a circle-two act of caring for one another.

Jesus did not go out of the house to heal this man. The man was carried to the house by four men seeking nothing for themselves; they were simply coming to the aid of a member of their community. When they arrived at the house carrying this paralyzed man on his pallet, they could not enter because of the standing-room-only crowd. Instead of allowing their ministry to be thwarted by the crowd, those men climbed up on the roof of the house, tore open a hole (to the dismay of the homeowner, I'm sure!), and lowered their friend down by ropes into Jesus' presence.

Whatever Jesus did to and for that man occurred only after what those four nameless friends had already done for him. The text says Jesus acknowledged their efforts: "When Jesus saw their faith, he said to the paralyzed man, 'Son, your sins are forgiven'" (Mark 2:5).

Two Exodus Stories—Numerous other texts can be used for sermons that help people bear witness to their faith by joining in second-circle ministries in which they show care and concern for one another. Preach about Aaron and Hur in Exodus 17:8-13, who held up the hands of Moses during the battle with the Amalekites. Joshua had been sent to lead the army in the actual battle. Moses went up on a hilltop where he was to hold up the staff of God. As long as the staff was raised, Israel prevailed, but whenever his hands were lowered due to fatigue, the Amalekites prevailed. Aaron and Hur did not attempt to assert themselves in any way. All they did was provide support to Moses as he carried out his assignment. Theirs was a second-circle act of ministry.

The same is true about the advice of Jethro to Moses in Exodus 18:14-23 to delegate much of his work to others in the community who can care for the needs of the people. Like many pastors in the twenty-first century, Moses was burning himself out by not delegating any work to others who could help him. He was attempting to handle the pressures of conflict resolution in the community by himself. Jethro's advice was to identify reliable persons who could handle the majority of the cases that were presently being entirely handled by Moses. Jethro said, "That will make your load lighter, because they will share it with you" (Exodus 18:22).

The First Diaconate—Acts 6:1-6 is another text that yields itself to preaching on some second-circle ministry themes. Peter was urged to intercede in a dispute within the Jerusalem church community involving an early form of racial or ethnic discrimination. The widows of Greek-speaking or Hellenistic Christians were complaining that they were not receiving the same level of benevolence from the commonly held money (see Acts 4:34-35) that was being offered to the widows of

Palestinian or Hebrew-speaking Christians. Peter decided not to allow the apostles to take on any more work (first circle). He said that they must focus on the ministry of the Word and on prayer. So he directed the community to identify seven persons from among themselves who could be assigned to the task of overseeing the commonly held property in a fair manner (second circle).[13]

Peter's decision was not a choice to ignore or set aside the complaint of the Hellenistic Christians. It was a decision to create a community in which members help take care of one another whether the leaders (e.g., clergy) are present and involved or not! Sermons that challenge members to display love to one another and to bear one another's burdens are absolutely essential if the church is to fully embrace the ministry of being witnesses for Jesus in Jerusalem.

Circle Three: A Congregation Caring for the Community

Preachers cannot, however, remain solely focused on the limited context of the people and issues inside the local church. Preachers who accept the challenge of being witnesses must also invite and encourage their local congregations to pay attention to what is going on outside their doors in the community in which the church is located and the city or town in which the members live.

Preaching must travel beyond the confines of a Sunday morning sermon that is heard only by the members of the congregation. Sermons must also address the problems and pressures confronting the lives of people who may not be members of that local church but whose conditions may have been described by Jesus in Matthew 25:31-44 when he said: "I was hungry and you gave me something to eat, I was thirsty and you gave me something to drink, I was a stranger and you invited me in, I needed clothes and you clothed me, I was sick and you looked after me, I was in prison and you came to visit me" (vv. 35-36).

What I refer to as the third circle of care, in which the focus of a congregation is moved beyond its own life to the life of the surrounding community, matches what Cleophus LaRue has referred to as the preaching domains of social justice and corporate (community) concerns. For LaRue, social justice involves "matters pertaining to racism, sexism, ageism, and other forms of discrimination. . . . Social justice is a basic value and desired goal in democratic societies and includes equitable and fair access to institutions, laws, resources, and opportunities without arbitrary limitations based on age, gender, national origin, religion, or sexual orientation."[14] Preaching on social justice focuses on all of the major areas in which our entire society stands in need of reform, believing that "God is the source of social justice and that God's power is on their side in their quest for social reform."[15]

On the other hand, preaching on corporate concerns involves faith communities focusing on the problems and challenges that are exclusive to them and their unique historical experiences. LaRue says, "Inasmuch as this domain has as its center matters that pertain specifically to blacks, it tends more toward exhortations of self-help, uplift, and racial solidarity."[16] One could make the case that social justice preaching is our response to what the broader society does to us, while corporate concerns are our response to the things we are doing to ourselves.

A Glimpse into Urban America

Preaching in Jerusalem involves what we as preachers are willing to say about the human suffering and societal evils we see unfolding in the streets around us. Sermons must reflect our concerns about the growing problem of homelessness and people sleeping on the streets. Communities large and small, rural and urban, wealthy and impoverished are struggling with increased levels of alcoholism and drug addiction. Many residents are struggling with undiagnosed or untreated mental illnesses, while others are returning citizens who have been released from prison only to find out that they must serve what feels like a life sentence because they cannot find a job, cannot qualify for some social services, and in some states cannot vote.

The challenges in Jerusalem that exist just outside the door of our churches also include failing public schools marked by low attendance and high dropout rates, and rising unemployment rates at a time when the jobs that are being created are located outside the city in places that are inaccessible by public transportation. The challenges include high rates of teen pregnancy and children born out of wedlock, often into families marked by generational poverty so that the newborn children are disadvantaged at birth. Police-community relations are poisoned, decent housing for people with low incomes is limited, and such housing is usually concentrated in a few locations rather than spread out over a wider region within the county-wide structure. The fact that so many suburban towns will not allow affordable or low-income housing to be erected in their communities results in the concentration of poverty in a few inner-city neighborhoods where the consequences of extreme poverty are magnified many times over.

A sense of "ghettoization" exists just outside the door of many urban congregations. Some churches are in neighborhoods with no high-quality grocery stores, no full-service banks, no pharmacies, and no restaurants beyond fast-food franchises. On the other hand, there are taverns, liquor stores, and small grocery stores that sell beer and liquor on almost every corner. Other churches are surrounded by a sea of urban violence marked by drive-by shootings and gang wars over turf and territory. Sermons must address these concerns if they are to have relevance for a twenty-first-century audience.

Nowhere is this truer than for the black church in urban America. In his "I Have a Dream" speech at the March on Washington on August 28, 1963, Martin Luther King Jr. described the black communities of America as "a lonely island of poverty in the midst of a vast sea of material prosperity."[17] Today, however, if one were to set foot inside of most black churches on a Sunday morning, especially in urban communities, one would see "an island of material prosperity surrounded by a vast ocean of poverty." The fashions in the pews and the luxury automobiles sitting in the parking lot of the church belie the socioeconomic conditions that grip the surrounding community. The fact that in many churches armed security guards are employed to protect both people and property whenever the doors are open is itself an indicator of the dissonance between local churches and the communities that surround them. The task of preachers is to bridge that gap by challenging their congregations to open their hearts, doors, and financial resources for the benefit of their immediate neighbors.

This list of challenges is set forth because they help to describe and define the scope of the problems faced by people who are not members of our churches but who just happen to live across the street or around the corner or down the block from where we preach every Sunday. The third circle of care that informs how to be a witness in Jerusalem challenges us to be sure that preachers care about, and also that preachers challenge their congregation to care about those people and their problems—whether those people ever join the church or not! This is the challenge of being a witness in Jerusalem; it is very much a matter of local context driven both inside and outside the doors of the local church.

If You See Something, Say Something

In the airports and transportation centers around this country, one can see signs that declare, "If you see something, say something." This statement is a response to the elevated concerns about security following the terrible events of September 11, 2001. The point is clear: if you happen to see something that looks suspicious, dangerous, threatening, or out of place, you should report that to a law enforcement official.

The phrase "If you see something, say something" is a perfect way to think about preaching within this third circle of pastoral care in which we are paying attention to the cares and concerns of our surrounding community. Our sermons as preachers and our mission as local churches cannot be limited to what is going on within the life of our local churches. If we see poverty, prejudice, and petty politicians who value politics over the people they were elected to serve, we should say something about it in various formats including the content of our sermons. This is what third-circle preaching is all about.

Can a Congregation Go to Hell?

In thinking about being a witness in Jerusalem and about how this third circle of care can shed light on that challenge, I have found it useful to draw a link between Christian congregations and the parable of the rich man (traditionally called Dives, from the Latin word for "rich") and Lazarus in Luke 16:19-31. It is a story of great prosperity and extreme poverty living side by side. One man ate sumptuously every day, while the other man would have eaten "what fell from the rich man's table." One man was dressed in purple and fine linen, while the other man was covered in sores. One man lived in luxury every day, while the other man was left every day at the gate of the rich man's home to beg from those who went in or out or simply passed by. In time both men died and awoke in two different locations. Lazarus was found in heaven in the bosom of Abraham, while the rich man found himself in hell.

Earlier in my life I took great comfort in using this story as a racial paradigm in which the rich man was the embodiment of white society and poor Lazarus represented all oppressed black people. It seemed convenient to point the finger away from myself and to blame someone else for the sins of the world and the sufferings in my own life. That reading of the text changed when I went to seminary and studied the Bible with James A. Sanders, who cautioned me, "Anytime you read a biblical text and come away feeling better about yourself, you can be sure that you just misread that text." As a result of that lesson, I was forced to reconsider the message in this story.

Today I understand this text as having nothing to do with racial or ethnic relations; it is about two men of the same culture who are divided by wealth on the one hand and want on the other. However, the wealth gap is not at the heart of the story, nor is the issue of being rich. Abraham would certainly have been considered a rich man, and yet he was the one in heaven in whose arms Lazarus was being cradled. Thus, the rich man did not go to hell simply because he was rich. The rich man went to hell because he never lifted a finger to assist poor Lazarus, who sat outside the rich man's door every day. He never invited Lazarus to come in, and he is never described as extending anything that might be a benefit to the man sitting just outside his door.

It is not possible that Dives did not know about Lazarus. There was almost no geographic distance between them. The poor man did not live on the other side of town far removed from the sight of Dives. The text clearly says that Lazarus was placed just outside his gate every day. The story hints at something else as well when it says, "Lazarus . . . longing to eat what fell from the rich man's table"—if even those crumbs had been offered. Dives did not go to hell because he did not fund the needs of starving children in Africa or China as so many TV commercials appeal to us to do these days. Dives went to hell because he practiced self-indulgence and gluttony in the face of the hunger, sickness, and poverty that resided just outside his front door!

There are a great many congregations where the majority of the membership—beginning with the pastor—is in danger of going to hell because that church does absolutely nothing to help or empower the community in which it is located or to address the needs of the people who, like Lazarus, are just outside the door. As I wrote in my book *Where Have All the Prophets Gone?*:

> Many Christians worship in immaculately maintained churches that are situated in neighborhoods that look like bombed-out war zones. Many Christians drive from the suburbs to churches located within a community that has been ravaged by poverty, drug trafficking, the loss of industry through outsourcing and factory closings, and underfunded and overwhelmed public schools. Of course, many Christians never have to see these sights or confront the people and the problems in these inner-city communities. They have elected to move out of the inner-city to pristine outer-ring suburbs and have also moved their churches to those upscale areas.[18]

And as Gustavo Gutiérrez, the Peruvian liberation theologian, observed, "It is no longer possible for someone to say, 'Well, I did not know about the suffering of the poor.' Poverty has a visibility today that it did not have in the past."[19]

Introverted and Externally Focused Congregations

James Henry Harris of Virginia Union University has very helpfully reflected on the values and practices of those congregations that are, in the language of Harry Emerson Fosdick, "rich in things and poor in soul."[20] Harris referred to them as introverted churches: "Introverted churches act like an independent entity, divorced from the suffering of the external world . . . failing miserably to understand the need to abandon its neutrality on issues of social and political justice . . . basking in the beauty of its bricks and mortar and the melodious syncretizing of its chancel choirs, pipe organs, and grand pianos."[21]

Harris's critique continues as he suggests the course of action that such introverted churches should take. What he suggests is precisely what I am defining as third-circle pastoral care. He says that such churches "must move beyond personal conversion to community transformation. The concept of community needs to be expanded to include the whole community—the church and the world."[22]

Harris's use of the term "introverted church" is creatively offset by the term "externally focused congregation," as used by Rick Rusaw and Eric Swanson. They contend, "It's not really church if it's not engaged in the life of the community through ministry and service."[23]

Making this shift in the mind and practice of a local church will never be easy. This is where the work of preaching becomes important as someone takes the time to *see something* in the community outside the walls of the local church, finds the courage to *say something* about how and why that local congregation should respond to the needs of the community, and then be prepared to *suffer something* from that same congregation who does not want to be challenged, critiqued, or called out for their lack of involvement beyond the walls of their church building.

Preachers must offer sermons that encourage and then equip their congregations to embrace this third circle of care—a congregation caring for the community in which their church is located. This is what the third circle of pastoral care is all about: moving the focus and energy of a local church outside of its doors to engage the people and issues in the neighborhood and city in which their church is located.

The Lord's reference to being a witness in Jerusalem is a challenge to preachers to recognize that the gospel does have something to say that is meaningful, relevant, encouraging, transformative, and redemptive concerning the people and problems residing just outside the doors of our churches. The question is whether preachers can end their fascination with prosperity theology and church-growth strategies long enough to speak a word of life and renewal into the crumbling neighborhoods that can be seen in every town and city in this country. The Lord needs preachers to be witnesses in their own particular Jerusalem! Only then can the church truly be witnesses for Jesus in Jerusalem.

Failure to respond to the challenges that await us just outside the doors of our churches may well leave us vulnerable to the critique found in a variation of Matthew 25:31-44 that was used as a litany at a poor people's rally in Albuquerque, New Mexico.

I was hungry
and you formed a humanities club
and you discussed my hunger.
Thank you.

I was imprisoned
and you crept off quietly
to your chapel in the cellar
and prayed for my release.

I was naked
and in your mind
you debated the morality of my appearance.

Preaching in Jerusalem

I was sick
and you knelt and thanked God
for your health.

I was homeless
and you preached to me
of the spiritual shelter of the love of God.

I was lonely
and you left me alone
to pray for me.
You seem so holy;
so close to God.

But I'm still very hungry
and lonely
and cold.

So where have your prayers gone?
What have they done?
What does it profit a man
to page through his book of prayers
when the rest of the world is crying for his help?[24]

NOTES

1. Marvin A. McMickle, *Caring Pastors, Caring People* (Valley Forge, PA: Judson, 2011), 6.

2. Ibid., 3–4.

3. Paraphrased from Robert Moats Miller, *Harry Emerson Fosdick: Preacher, Pastor, Prophet* (New York: Oxford University Press, 1985), 339–41; and Harry Emerson Fosdick, "Preaching as Personal Counseling," in *The Company of Preachers*, ed. Richard Lischer (Grand Rapids: Eerdmans, 2002), 396–400.

4. Lischer, *Company of Preachers*, 396.

5. Thomas Oden, *Pastoral Theology* (New York: Harper & Row, 1983), 13.

6. Ibid.

7. McMickle, *Caring Pastors*, 6.

8. Reinhold Niebuhr, *Leaves from the Notebook of a Tamed Cynic* (Louisville: Westminster John Knox, 1980), 47.

9. Cleophus LaRue, *The Heart of Black Preaching* (Louisville: Westminster John Knox, 2000), 21.

10. William Longstaff, "Take Time to Be Holy," *The United Methodist Hymnal*, Nashville, TN, p. 395.

11. "Apology," chap. 39, in *The Ante-Nicene Fathers, Volume 3: Latin Christianity: Its Founder, Tertullian*, ed. Alexander Roberts and James Donaldson (Grand Rapids: Eerdmans, 1976), 46.

12. This church covenant language is typically found pasted to the inside front cover or printed on the first page of hymnals used in black Baptist churches.

13. See Marvin A. McMickle, *Deacons in Today's Black Baptist Church* (Valley Forge, PA: Judson, 2010).

14. LaRue, *Heart of Black Preaching*, 22–23.

15. Ibid., 23.

16. Ibid.

17. Martin Luther King Jr., "I Have a Dream," in *A Testament of Hope: The Essential Writings of Martin Luther King, Jr.*, ed. James M. Washington (New York: Harper & Row, 1986), 217.

18. Marvin A. McMickle, *Where Have All the Prophets Gone?* (Cleveland: Pilgrim, 2006), 3–4.

19. Daniel Hartnett, "An Interview with Gustavo Gutirrez [sic]," *America*, February 3, 2003, http://americamagazine.org/issue/420/article/remembering-poor-interview-gustavo-gutirrez. (Note: The misspelling of Gutiérrez's name is found in the actual URL.)

20. Harry Emerson Fosdick, "God of Grace and God of Glory," in *Total Praise* (Chicago: GIA, 2011), 135.

21. James Henry Harris, *Pastoral Theology: A Black Church Perspective* (Minneapolis: Fortress Press, 1991), 34.

22. Ibid., 336.

23. Rick Rusaw and Eric Swanson, *The Externally Focused Church* (Loveland, CO: Group, 2004), 25.

24. James H. Cone, "The Servant Church," in *The Pastor as Servant*, ed. Earl E. Shelp and Ronald H. Sunderland (New York: Pilgrim, 1986), 63–64.

CHAPTER 12

Preaching in Judea

The next challenge for today's preachers is to find ways to include in our preaching rotation some sermons that respond to Jesus' mandate to be his witnesses in Judea. With this mandate, Jesus shifted the focus of his witnesses in the first century, as he does in the twenty-first, from preaching in our local church and the immediate community that surrounds it, to a broader range of issues going on within the region and nation in which we live.

Preachers have to lift our eyes to see what is happening at the national level. The US Congress, Supreme Court, or White House may be taking action on matters of environmental safety, gun control, minimum sentencing regulations, nuclear arms proliferation, voting rights changes, immigration reform, and minimum wage increases—just to name a few issues. Not only should preachers be well informed about the impact that these policies can have on the lives of people all across the country, but some may have to assume the prophetic role of a Nathan, Deborah, Isaiah, Jeremiah, Huldah, John the Baptist, Jesus, or Paul and speak God's truth to people in power. God needs preachers to be witnesses in the context of the country in which we live. This means that our preaching will be informed by the things occurring not only right around us, but also by events unfolding on the national scene as well.

Paying Attention to the Headlines

Every night television and radio broadcasts, from local sources to the twenty-four-hour national news outlets, not to mention the alerts and newsfeeds we can access via smartphone, tablet, or other Internet connections, offer a deluge of information and headlines about events occurring across the country as well as around the corner. One can be sitting where I am in Rochester, New York, and hear about events in Ferguson, Missouri; Staten Island, New York; Cleveland, Ohio; and Baltimore, Maryland. One can sit at home in the Midwest or in New England and hear about the drought in California, about horrific storms in Oklahoma and Kansas, about the terrible murder and burning of an entire family in Washington, DC, or about the challenges of border security in Texas versus the desperate struggle of people risking their lives to immigrate to the United States.

The question for us as preachers is what we are willing to say about these events, and also what we are prepared to urge congregants to do in the face of these realities.

MLK Jr. as a Model for Preaching in Judea

This shift from Jerusalem to Judea, from the local community to locations throughout the country, was at the heart of the dispute between Martin Luther King Jr. and the eight white clergymen in Birmingham, Alabama, who challenged his presence in that city in 1963. They questioned why Dr. King was getting involved in affairs in their community, which was many miles removed from King's church on Auburn Avenue in Atlanta, Georgia. Dr. King's answer points us once again to the prophet Amos, who traveled from his home in the town of Tekoa in the southern kingdom of Judah to preach his message in the northern kingdom of Israel.

In his "Letter from the Birmingham Jail," Dr. King wrote:

> Just as the prophets of the eighth century BC left their villages and carried their "thus saith the Lord" far beyond the boundaries of their home towns, and just as the Apostle Paul left his village of Tarsus and carried the gospel of Jesus Christ to the far corners of the Greco-Roman world, so am I compelled to carry

> the gospel of freedom beyond my own home town. Like Paul, I must constantly respond to the Macedonian call for aid.[1]

Dr. King was keeping alive a practice that was at work in the Old and New Testaments—bearing witness to truths gleaned from Scripture in places far removed from one's own community. Whether he was going to Albany, Georgia, in 1962, or Birmingham, Alabama, in 1963, or Montgomery, Alabama, in 1965, or my hometown of Chicago in 1966, or Memphis, Tennessee, in 1968, Dr. King was demonstrating what it looks like to be "be my witness in Judea."

Whether the issue was racism in the cities mentioned above; poverty, as dramatized by the Poor People's Campaign; or militarism, as evidenced in his public opposition to the Vietnam War, Dr. King and those who followed his lead were witnesses for Jesus in Judea. Today's preachers need to examine the breadth and width of our ministries and find ways to expand our influence and involvement beyond the safe confines of our local churches and familiar places in our surrounding communities.

When we take seriously the challenge to be God's witnesses in Judea, our sermons suddenly become peppered with references to the struggle for justice, freedom, equal opportunity, and human dignity as those stories are played out every day in this country. Here in the United States, preachers who are aware of the call to be witnesses in Judea would necessarily want to find out what the gospel has to say to the church about race relations, wealth disparity, police-community relationships, the steep decline in persons who self-identify as Christians, and the broad denominational and religious diversity that often serves to divide those people who still cling to religious faith.

Why should preachers of the gospel be interested in and vocal about what is happening in our modern-day Judea? Because Judea is where a national budget is formed and funded that invests more on defense spending than it does on decent housing, affordable and accessible health care, and quality public education. Judea is the increasingly polarized social and political climate that presently engulfs this country and prevents political and social reform from taking place. Judea is where 70 percent of all Americans and more than half of all Cuban Americans favor an end to the embargo against Cuba, but after more than fifty years progress on ending that embargo remains blocked by a handful of conservative politicians.[2]

Preaching in Judea means that our sermons must occasionally refer to all of these matters of national importance and urge our hearers to seek those things that can bring justice, peace, and reconciliation to the world wherever possible. To be a witness in Judea is to *see something*, *say something*, and be prepared to *suffer something* as we speak the truth of God to the powers and about the problems currently facing not just the communities where we reside and where our churches are located, but also the pressing and urgent issues that confront us as a nation.

Public Policy vs. Personal Piety

I understand that some preachers are loathe to address such issues, believing them to be political in nature and therefore not a part of their job description. Many preachers are far more inclined to believe that their job is to focus on matters of personal conversion and spiritual formation. During the days of the civil rights movement, there were many pastors and preachers, especially but not exclusively within the Holiness and Pentecostal church traditions, who never got involved in the protests, the marches, the sit-ins, or the acts of civil disobedience at either the local or national level. They believed such activities were not in keeping with the holiness mandate; thus they remained aloof from those activities that did not directly contribute to an individual's godly life.

I watched this dynamic play itself out in my hometown of Chicago in the summer of 1966 when Martin Luther King Jr. came to head an open-housing campaign. He came there to dramatize the fact that racial segregation was not a problem unique to the southern United States. At that time several northern cities, such as Chicago, Detroit, Cleveland, and Gary, Indiana, were among the most segregated cities in the nation. Some preachers stayed away from the marches and demonstrations.

Some were personally opposed to Dr. King for reasons of jealousy or resentment that he was moving into their "turf" without their endorsement, and some simply believed that involvement with such things was not a part of what they felt called as preachers to address.[3]

The issues of neighborhoods being segregated based on race could not have been more apparent. The fact could not be denied that members of almost every faith community in the city, black and white, Protestant, Catholic, and Jewish, lived in largely segregated communities and gathered in segregated houses of worship. Yet most clergy never got involved in that struggle in my hometown in the summer of 1966. They preferred preaching about personal piety over focusing on those public policies that resulted in social inequality and lack of opportunity. They were not prepared to *see something*, *say something*, and *suffer something* over what was clearly going on in that city. In a strange way, the black clergy in Chicago were behaving like the white clergy in Birmingham in 1963 in terms of refusing to speak out about the evils going on around them, and also in their resistance to the presence of King and the Southern Christian Leadership Conference in their city.

I say again that in 1963 it was eight white preachers in Birmingham, Alabama, who wrote to Martin Luther King Jr., urging him not to come to their city to tackle the problem of racial segregation.[4] They had undoubtedly seen the injustices heaped on black people in that city, but they were not willing to tell the truth about what they had seen. They were far more upset by the protests of those seeking civil rights in US society than they were by the behavior of the white power structure of Birmingham that did everything in its power to lock the black citizens of Birmingham out of the American dream.

Like Amaziah's response to Amos (Amos 7:10-12) and like Hananiah's response to Jeremiah (Jeremiah 28), those eight white Protestant, Catholic, and Jewish clergymen preferred to assure the political establishment that everything in Birmingham was fine from God's perspective, rather than speak God's truth to persons in power. In his "Letter from the Birmingham Jail," King said he had come to Birmingham because "Injustice anywhere is a threat to justice everywhere."[5]

However, King also raised another question about the silence of so many Christians in the face of conspicuous oppression and injustice. He reflected on the beautiful churches of white Christians throughout the South whose members and clergy did and said nothing about the struggles going on around them or about the reasons for those struggles.

> What kind of people worship here? Who is their God? Where were their voices when the lips of Governor Barnett dripped with words of interposition and nullification? Where were they when Governor Wallace gave a clarion call for defiance and hatred? . . . I see the church as the Body of Christ. But, oh! How we have blemished and scarred that body through social neglect and through fear of being nonconformists.[6]

White Christians and their clergy have not been the only group whose voices have remained silent when it comes to the great social ills that afflict our society. One hears far more about prosperity theology and personal salvation in most black churches than one hears of righteous indignation over the ills of our society. More energy and attention are given to the parochial matters of the local Baptist association, the state and national conventions, and the pursuit of positions within various denominational structures than to the alleviation of the effects of systemic racism, gender discrimination, environmental hazards, and economic injustice.

Surrounded by a Cloud of Witnesses

We are not the first generation of Christian preachers who have been called to be witnesses within the context of events in our nation. There is no clearer example of this fact in recent history than the confessing church in Germany that saw the dangers of Nazi rule and said something about it, resulting in great suffering and even death. Dietrich Bonhoeffer, Martin Niemoller, Karl Barth, Rudolf Bultmann, and others whose sermons have been collected by Dean Stroud in *Preaching in*

Hitler's Shadow give clear evidence of a willingness to say something about the injustice and atrocities they had seen in Judea, their home country.[7] More importantly (and perhaps this is the real issue that prevents so many preachers from assuming this role), those preachers in the confessing church of Germany in the 1930s gave real meaning to what it might mean when one chooses to "be my *marturia*." Many of them also *suffered something* for their witness.

These bold preachers stood in sharp contrast to the majority of German Christians and German pastors who remained silent in the face of the growing terror in Germany marked by the implementation of Kristallnacht when Jewish synagogues and businesses were vandalized and ransacked, the imposition of laws that stripped away the civil liberties of Jews, and the near deification of Adolf Hitler.[8] It is often at the point of becoming a *marturia* that many preachers decide that what they have seen may deserve some bold comment from pulpits and preachers, but they are not prepared to do so themselves because they are not prepared to run the risk of suffering as a result of their comments. The fear of consequences in one form or another pushes them into silent compliance with the evils all around them.

I am reminded of the statement by Martin Niemoller, who was arrested in Germany in 1937 for the crime of "misusing the pulpit"[9] because he spoke out against what was being done by the Nazis. He responded, "First they came for the Socialists, and I did not speak out because I was not a socialist. Then they came for the Trade Unionists, and I did not speak out because I was not a Trade Unionist. Then they came for the Jews, and I did not speak out because I was not a Jew. Then they came for me, and there was no one left to speak for me."[10]

Little Has Changed over Fifty Years

I think back on historical events here in the United States and abroad in Nazi Germany, I realize with some disappointment that not much has changed when it comes to preachers being prepared to be witnesses for Jesus in Judea at any level beyond matters of personal salvation and congregational life. In this age of televangelism, I am amazed by how many sermons I hear from TV preachers who speak to congregations of thirty thousand to forty thousand members but have absolutely nothing to say about what is happening in our country today. Many of them live in major cities like Dallas, Atlanta, New Orleans, New York City, and Chicago—cities that are riddled by poverty, racial tension, failing public schools, political corruption, and gang-related gun violence and homicides. Their churches are located in cities and states where attempts are constantly being made to deny voting rights to more and more people. They observe the struggle for the extension of civil rights to persons in the lesbian, gay, bisexual, transgender, queer, intersex (LGBTQI) community. They hear reports about the ever-widening wealth gap between the richest and poorest persons in the country. Yet when you listen to them preach, whether in person or on TV, you would have no idea, based on the focus and content of their sermons, that any of these things are going on in the world around them.

Worse, you would have no reason to believe that any of these things are of the least interest to them. They seem to be informed by a theology of preaching that allows them to preach about personal salvation and personal prosperity and happiness, while never shining the light of the gospel on the people who were so important to Jesus—"the least of these," as defined by Matthew 25:31-44.

How can you not speak about prison overcrowding and mass incarceration of people of color, as author and civil rights advocate Michelle Alexander has so powerfully demonstrated in her book *The New Jim Crow*,[11] when Jesus commands us to be concerned about the fate of those who are in prison? How do you have a preaching ministry that never says a word about poverty or hunger, immigration or access to affordable health care, when Jesus has commanded us to pay attention to those who are hungry, thirsty, and sick, and to the strangers or foreign-born among us?

I am haunted by the prediction made by the black theologian Joseph Washington more than fifty years ago, who said, "Negro ministers have forgotten that black religion is a tradition interested not in pseudo-Protestantism, but in freedom with equality."[12] When that focus is lost, Washington warned, "folk religion becomes dissipated into entertainment and the church is relegated to the status of an amusement center."[13]

Preachers who are wondering what to focus on from week to week should pay close attention to what is happening in Judea and preach sermons that bring clarity to the problems and highlight God's call for righteousness and justice to prevail.

Preaching Prophetically

There is little wonder that our society is so devoid of mercy and compassion for the neediest among us. Those whose job it is to keep those matters ever before the minds and hearts of the church are focused instead on buying $65 million jets, driving Bentleys, competing for speaking slots at megafests, and generally reducing the church to a carnival atmosphere where everything is for sale including the pulpit! Custom-made clothing and luxury living have become of greater importance than the broken lives scattered across the American landscape and our government's many broken promises about "liberty and justice for all." One can almost hear Amos declaring:

> Woe to you who are complacent in Zion, and to you who feel secure on Mount Samaria. . . .You lie on beds adorned with ivory and lounge on your couches. You dine on choice lambs and fattened calves. . . . You drink wine by the bowlful and use the finest lotions, but you do not grieve over the ruin of Joseph. Therefore you will be among the first to go into exile; your feasting and lounging will end. (Amos 6:1, 4-7)

The prosperity gospel continues to attract people in the pulpit and the pew, offering what Luke Powery, dean of chapel at Duke Divinity School, calls "candy theology."[14] He references a well-known interview with Gardner Taylor, who observed that his daughter would have eaten candy at every meal if it would have been allowed. Powery then points out that prosperity preaching is a "candy homiletical theology that is sweet and pleasant, but cannot sustain people's lives."[15]

Being sustained through the ups and downs of life is precisely what people need these days, and that need will only be met through the faithful preaching of the message of Jesus. However, when faithful preaching ceases and ear-teasing promises of health and wealth become the sole diet being fed to the church, then the devil need not worry, because the church will wither into irrelevance.

Missions Doesn't Replace Social Justice

A great many churches have a deep commitment to what they refer to as "foreign missions." As mentioned earlier, there were 127,000 US church-sponsored missionaries scattered around the world in 2015.[16] Congregations are eager to send missionaries to remote locations throughout the nations of Africa, Asia, and the Caribbean. They are deeply moved by the images of people in Haiti suffering the lingering effects of earthquakes that have all but shattered the infrastructure of that tiny island nation. They are moved by the impact of cultural and ethnic tensions between Haitians and their island-sharing neighbors of the Dominican Republic, who recently began a move to expel all Haitians from the Dominican side of the island initially named Hispaniola by Christopher Columbus.[17]

However, what is disconcerting is to see US churches focus on foreign or overseas missions while neighborhoods all across this country are ravaged with equally serious problems. Cities and towns across the United States are struggling with extreme poverty, gang-related violence, racial strife, drug addiction, and crumbling and inadequate housing stock. Our twenty-first-century Judeas are impacted by failing schools with staggeringly high dropout rates and stunningly low graduation rates. Are those "mission-minded churches" saying anything about what is going on right here in the United States?

Preaching in Judea

Jesus challenged his first disciples, just as he challenges the church today, to be his witnesses beginning in our own local Jerusalem but extending to Judea as well.

Preaching beyond Evangelism

Some preachers travel throughout the nation to evangelize or preach revivals that are geared toward personal salvation. I have no opposition to or criticism of such activities. However, I do become concerned when preachers and the churches in which they preach never make the shift from evangelism to activism, from spiritual formation to social reform, and from repentance of sin at an individual level to direct involvement with any of the social and economic issues mentioned above for which our whole society needs to repent.

Those who hold to the approach to preaching that favors evangelism over activism typically do so based on their reading of Scripture and their own theological perspective about the work of the preacher and about the ministry of the church in the world. At the very least, a better understanding of Jesus' charge in Acts 1:6-8 should challenge the inadequacy of preaching that takes this approach.

Preaching that prefers evangelism over activism or actively engaging in addressing the social ills in our society falls woefully short of Jesus' challenge to his disciples in the first and the twenty-first centuries to "be my witnesses in Jerusalem, and in all Judea and Samaria, and to the ends of the earth." Essential to that task is *seeing something*, *saying something* about what one has seen in Judea—in one's own country, and then being prepared to *suffer something* as a result of what one has dared to say.

NOTES

1. Martin Luther King Jr., *Why We Can't Wait* (New York: Signet, 1964), 77.

2. CBS News Poll: Resuming Relations with Cuba," CBS News, July 20, 2015, http://www.cbsnews.com/news/cbs-news-poll-resuming-relations-with-cuba/; and Michelle Caruso-Cabrera, "Cuban Americans Support Ending Embargo against

Cuba," CNBC, April 1, 2015, http://www.cnbc.com/2015/03/31/cuban-americans-support-ending-embargo-against-cuba.html.

3. Taylor Branch, *At Canaan's Edge: America in the King Years 1965–1968* (New York: Simon and Schuster, 2006), 262–63, 355, 429, 504.

4. King, *Why We Can't Wait*, 76.

5. Ibid., 77.

6. Ibid., 91.

7. Dean Stroud, *Preaching in Hitler's Shadow* (Grand Rapids: Eerdmans, 2013).

8. See Charles Marsh, *Strange Glory: A Life of Dietrich Bonhoeffer* (New York: Knopf, 2014); J. Deotis Roberts, *Bonhoeffer and King: Speaking Truth to Power* (Louisville: Westminster John Knox, 2005); Reggie L. Williams, *Bonhoeffer's Black Jesus* (Waco, TX: Baylor University Press, 2014).

9. Marsh, *Strange Glory*, 259.

10. Stroud, *Preaching in Hitler's Shadow*, 87; Wolfgang Gerlach, *And the Witnesses Were Silent* (Lincoln: University of Nebraska Press, 2000).

11. Michelle Alexander, *The New Jim Crow: Mass Incarceration in the Age of Colorblindness* (New York: New Press, 2012).

12. Joseph R. Washington Jr., *Black Religion: The Negro and Christianity in the United States* (Boston: Beacon, 1964), 38.

13. Ibid., 44.

14. Luke Powery, *Dem Dry Bones* (Minneapolis: Fortress, 2012), 5.

15. Ibid.

16. Tamara Audi, "Missionaries Face a Recall," *Wall Street Journal*, October 26, 2015, A3.

17. Yamiche Alcindor, "Haitian Deportation Crisis Brews in Dominican Republic," *USA Today*, July 12, 2015, http://www.usatoday.com/story/news/world/2015/07/11/haitian-deportation-fears—oas-mission-begins—dominican-republic/30003307/.

CHAPTER 13

Preaching in Samaria and to the Ends of the Earth

As challenging as the first two steps of preaching in Jerusalem and Judea might have been for those first disciples of Jesus, the challenge inherent in the third location to which they were being directed—Samaria—was almost unimaginable.

For all first-century Jews, Samaria was a place to be avoided, and Samaritans were a people to be scorned. Just as the Old Testament prophet Jonah did not want to accept God's assignment to go and preach to "those people" in the city of Nineveh (Jonah 1:1-3), it was almost certainly the case that Jesus' disciples did not want to witness for him to the people of Samaria. Samaria was where "those people" lived. What does it say about Jesus being concerned about "the comfort zone" of preachers when he directs his disciples to preach and do ministry in Samaria?

Samaria was home to people whom the Jews viewed as a racially mixed population and whose religious rituals they viewed as being corrupted and even blasphemous. Great hostility had existed between Jews and Samaritans for more than four hundred years. We get a sense of that when we read in John 4:7-9 of how Jesus stopped in a Samaritan village and asked a Samaritan woman for a drink of water. She responded to his request by saying, "You are a Jew and I am a Samaritan woman. How can you ask me for a drink?" The text explains, "For Jews do not associate with Samaritans" (v. 9).

Samaria, which was a region in Palestine between Judea in the south and Galilee in the north, was less about the geographic location and more about the people who lived in that location. Today the State of Israel refers to its ancestral roots as being "Judea and Samaria," so there seems to be no objection now to the location itself. The objection in the first century was with the Samaritans as an ethnic and religious community.

The Samaritans were ethnically defined as descendants of those Jews in the northern kingdom of Israel who were not exiled in 722 BC, and who intermarried with the persons sent by successive Assyrian monarchs to colonize what had become part of the Assyrian Empire. Thus, as a result of many generations of such intermarriage, the people in Samaria were not viewed as full-blooded Jews.

The ethnic difference between Jews and Samaritans was further exasperated by three monumental differences in religious practice. First, as a result of the long-standing sacredness of Mount Gerizim as noted in Deuteronomy 11:29 and Joshua 8:33, the Samaritans erected their own distinctive temple on Mount Gerizim in the northern part of Israel and claimed that they no longer had to worship God in the temple of Solomon or on any of the subsequent replacements on Mount Zion in Jerusalem. The second major distinction involved the fact that Samaritans viewed the Torah—Pentateuch—the five books of Moses, as the only authoritative texts for their religion, thus dismissing the history, Prophets, Psalms, and wisdom books. The third distinction involved their dismissing of the need to wear prayer shawls and phylacteries, which Jews wore in obedience to Deuteronomy 6:8. Thus not even all of the Torah was being observed.[1]

The disciples would have had good reason to be surprised that Jesus was putting Samaria on their preaching itinerary. There was a time in his life when Jesus himself seemed to hold a very different view about extending his ministry to the Samaritans. In Matthew 10:5 Jesus was about to send his disciples out two by two on their first preaching mission. His message to them at that time was, "Do not go among the Gentiles or enter any town of the Samaritans. Go rather to the lost sheep of Israel" (vv. 5-6). However, here in Acts 1:8 those instructions seem no longer to be in force. Jesus makes it clear that the ministry of his disciples was to include the region of Samaria.

Simply stated, metaphorically Samaria is the location, the setting, the context where preachers might never go voluntarily. Samaria can also serve as a metaphor for a variety of themes and topics that very few preachers would voluntarily choose to address. Jesus directs us to preach to people and preach about issues that we might otherwise prefer to avoid.

The question that must be raised here is who are "those people" for the twenty-first-century church at both the local and national level? For some people Samaria is lesbian, gay, bisexual, transgender, queer, intersex (LGBTQI) people and issues. For other people Samaria is convicted criminals or returning citizens. For some people in middle-class, suburban churches, Samaria is ministry among the homeless in the urban areas that are only a few miles away in distance but are light-years away in terms of lifestyle and living conditions. For others Samaria may be the Muslims who are now living in the community or worshiping down the street. And especially in a polarized nation in a presidential election year, Samaria could be those of the *other* political party or even Christians of a more liberal or conservative persuasion.

Samaria is not necessarily a region of the country or a community within a city. Samaria can simply be associating and caring for people you may have been previously taught to hate, to scorn, or simply to avoid. Whoever and wherever Samaria is in your life and mine, that is where Jesus is sending us to do ministry and to preach the gospel. With that in mind, consider the parable of the good Samaritan and the care and concern shown toward a distressed Jewish traveler by someone from that hated and scorned group. What Jesus was challenging his disciples to do was just as unexpected as what the Samaritan did in that parable—love beyond the expected boundaries and limits.

In a sense, our national discussion about immigration policy and building a wall that divides this country off from people coming from Mexico is a discussion about a modern Samaria—those people. The same is true about suggestions regarding banning Muslims from entering the country as espoused by one presidential candidate.[2] One can add to that "us" and "them" feeling the suggestion by another candidate of having the police patrolling Muslim neighborhoods.[3]

What is the role of the church and the preacher when it comes to the issues of the people and places that fall under the rubric of being our modern-day Samaria?

Preaching That Reaches the Ends of the Earth

The final challenge Jesus placed before his disciples was witnessing that would extend to the ends of the earth. Does God care and should we care when more than two hundred schoolgirls are kidnapped in Nigeria, never to be heard from again? Does God care and should we care when a kosher grocery store in Paris becomes the site of a horrific terrorist attack? Does God care and should we care when Buddhist priests in Myanmar burn themselves alive to protest the denial of human rights in their country? Does God care and should we care when environmental practices by multinational corporations threaten to permanently damage the earth's air and water?

The answer to all of these questions is an unequivocal yes! God does care about the whole of God's creation, about all nations and about all people. Furthermore, God expects those who preach the gospel of Jesus Christ to care about these matters as well.

Pope Francis set us an example of that when he quickly spoke up about the beheading of twenty-one Coptic Christians in Libya at the hands of ISIS. He wanted the world to know that he was concerned, and he hoped that those who look to him for spiritual direction would be concerned, about matters going on all over the world.[4]

Other Professions Are Reaching Out to the World

This willingness to extend our preaching to the ends of the earth is not only mandated by Jesus, but it allows us to keep up with other sectors of American society that have long since sought to operate within a global arena.

Consider the new book by US Supreme Court Justice Stephen Breyer, *The Court and the World*,[5] in which he writes that "an increasing number of high court cases require understanding of international developments before they can be decided."[6] "International security, commerce, the environment and human rights often require a keen understanding of other nations' laws and customs."[7] Breyer says that "only by solving problems beyond our shores collectively can American values be protected."[8]

The legal and judicial communities are not alone in reaching to the ends of the earth. Almost all American corporations, including those in banking, retail, technology, transportation, education, the military, manufacturing, entertainment, and the arts, are seeking new markets and establishing new centers of operation. International sporting events are now commonplace. United States performing artists, from orchestras to jazz musicians to pop singers, hold concerts in countries all over the world. The National Basketball Association has attracted players from Europe, Africa, Asia, and South America. As a result, the game of basketball is an international phenomenon, and the biggest stars in that game, like Lebron James, are global superstars whose jerseys are worn by children in India as well as in Indiana.

Can it really be possible in this world that is increasingly a global village that the commercial and cultural sectors of society will be more aggressive than the church in trying to reach and influence the nations of the world? One of the reasons why people may be showing their declining interest in the church is because the church seems to have little interest in anything going on outside of their doors or outside of their narrow theological ideology. In honor of those first-century disciples who carried the gospel and both encountered and overcame Greco-Roman culture in the process, we need to find ways to embrace the language of Acts 1:6-8 and be witnesses for Jesus to the ends of the earth.

A Sovereign God Deserves Our Global Vision

The fundamental theological reason why preachers should embrace this command from Jesus and be his witnesses to the ends of the earth is because God is creator of the universe and, as such, has sovereignty over the whole of creation. God's sovereignty does not stop at the city line where we live or at the national borders that divide nations. The fact that some nations claim to be Marxist and atheistic is irrelevant to a sovereign God who seeks to make godly values present everywhere. When Pope Francis visited with Cuban president Raul Castro in Rome in May of 2015, Castro, who is an avowed atheist, said publicly, "If the pope keeps talking like this, sooner or later I will start praying again and I will return to the Catholic Church."[9]

The purpose of that meeting in May was to lay the groundwork for a papal visit to Cuba in September 2015 and also to continue work on the normalization of diplomatic relations between Cuba and the United States. The pope visited both Cuba and the United States in September 2015 to talk about ending the US embargo and about easing political restrictions in Cuba.

It is clear that the Roman Catholic Church is well positioned to have a global impact, given that it has 1.5 billion members scattered in every corner of the world. It is exciting that Francis is from Argentina and is the first person in history elected to be pope from outside of Europe. That fact alone has awakened an interest in the Roman Catholic Church and in Francis. The Catholic Church has not always used its global presence to address global problems, but they face the same mandate as their Orthodox and Protestant brothers and sisters: to be witnesses for Jesus to the ends of the earth.

The church in the United States needs to resist the tendency to believe that their country is the only place on earth that matters. Our national preoccupation with what we believe to be "American exceptionalism"[10] can sometimes result in a form of ministry in which the church is more concerned about exporting American values than it is in exalting Jesus Christ. Take our attachment to the song "God Bless America" by Irving Berlin. That song is a wonderful patriotic tune. It is what you might expect to be written by someone like Berlin, who came to this country from Russia in 1893 to escape oppression in the form of pogroms, or forced removals of Jews, and who found liberty and opportunity in the United States.

However, patriotic hymns do not always reflect correct theology. It may well be that the hymn we preachers should be singing if we are truly witnesses for Jesus says:

He's got the whole world in His hands,
He's got you and me brother in His hands,
He's got you and me sister in His hands,
He's got everybody here in His hands,
He's got the whole world in His hands.

That is why we must pay attention to what is happening around the world; it is because people around the world are children of God just as much as those who sing "God Bless America." It is because God is concerned about what is happening in the most remote location on earth as much as God is concerned about what is happening anywhere in the United States. That is the message in the hymn written by the African American songwriter and singer Harry T. Burleigh that says:

In Christ there is no east or west,
In him no south or north;
But one great fellowship of love,
Throughout the whole wide earth.[11]

Gifts from the Liturgical Calendar

Two major observances in the Christian calendar point directly to the global nature of the gospel and the global focus that preachers must always maintain; those two observances are Epiphany and the day of Pentecost.

Epiphany involves an observance immediately after the Christmas season—January 6, often referred to as the twelfth day of Christmas. It is when the focus is given not to the birth of Jesus, but rather to the magi who had traveled "from the east" to Bethlehem to pay homage to the newborn king and then returned to their homeland (possibly Persia or Iran), carrying with them the message about what they had seen (Matthew 2:1-12). In that story the news about the birth of Jesus is carried beyond Palestine by these individuals, often referred to as the "wise men."

In Scripture the day of Pentecost was the occasion when Peter preached the gospel message to a congregation gathered in Jerusalem for the Jewish celebration of Pentecost. That congregation represented nations stretching from parts of Europe, Asia, and North Africa (Acts 2:8-9). The day of Pentecost, which is observed fifty days, or seven weeks, after Easter, is most noted as a time to preach about the birth of the church or the outpouring of the Holy Spirit and the practice of speaking in tongues (*glossolalia*). However, it is also an opportunity for preachers to point out the international, multicultural, multilingual nature of the first congregation to hear the gospel. In addition, it is an occasion to consider how the gospel was carried to all of those nations when those persons left Jerusalem and returned to their homes around the Mediterranean Sea, the Fertile Crescent, and the Nile Valley.

A more careful reading of the Bible will quickly reveal that within thirty years of the death of Jesus, the gospel was already being spread and church leaders were already being drawn from places such as Cyrene and Ethiopia, Greece and Rome, and places in modern-day Turkey, such as Galatia, Ephesus, Sardis, and Smyrna. Paul wrote to the church in Rome telling them that he had preached the gospel "from Jerusalem all the way around to Illyricum" (Romans 15:19), which sits on the northwest coast of Greece very near to Italy. This is easily a distance of more than a thousand miles.[12] Paul then went on to say that he planned to visit the church in Rome when he went to Spain (Romans 15:24). The first generation of preachers did an excellent job of taking the gospel to the ends of the earth.

The African Presence in the Bible

One of the important but largely overlooked results of the spread of the gospel to the ends of the earth involves the realization of how early and how often one encounters the African presence in the Bible. Consider the events recorded in Acts 13:1-3. The ordination and commissioning board that sent Paul and Barnabas forth on their mission to the Gentiles included two men who are described as well as named—Simeon called Niger (black) and Lucius of Cyrene (in North Africa).

The presence of persons with a connection to the African continent may come as a surprise to many readers of this book or any readers of the Bible. The biblical story has become so westernized and Anglicized that any association with the people who actually lived in the regions of Palestine and North Africa has been lost.[13]

While Rome emerged early as the center of Roman Catholicism, the Coptic Orthodox Church in both Egypt and Ethiopia represent Christian communities from exactly the same historical era. We may even preach about Philip, who tutored and then baptized the Ethiopian eunuch who was in the service of the Kandake (queen of the Ethiopians). However, the fact that a convert to Christianity was an Ethiopian who would undoubtedly carry the story of Jesus with him to that location, not in the Nile Valley, but at the horn of Africa situated along the Red Sea, often goes unnoticed.

You could watch a dozen movies about the Bible made in Hollywood over the last sixty years, and few of them would give any hint of the presence of black or African people in the biblical story. Think about *The Ten Commandments*, with Moses played by Charlton Heston and Ramses played by Yul Brenner. Neither were accurate representations of Egyptians in the twelfth century BC. With the exception of Sidney Poitier in *The Greatest Story Ever Told*, who had a nonspeaking role as Simon of Cyrene, and black actor Woody Strode, who had two nonspeaking appearances in *The Ten Commandments,* all of the actors in the classic movies based on the Bible were white.

Even more recently, Mel Gibson's *Passion of the Christ* in 2004 featured a white American actor (Jim Caviezel) as Jesus, and other characters were played by predominantly white European actors. The blockbuster films of 2014, *Noah* and *The Exodus,* both featured white actors in all the leading roles, with no blacks among the supporting actors and few even among the extras! The same was true for *Exodus: Gods and Kings* in 2015 with Christian Bale in the role of Moses. In 2016, the remake of *Ben-Hur* and the new movies *Risen* and *The Young Messiah* also had overwhelmingly white casts.

It is worth noting, however, that an attempt to reflect the actual racial and ethnic diversity of the lands of the Bible in ancient times is in evidence in the made-for-TV series *A.D. The Bible Continues* and also in the miniseries *Tut* about Pharaoh Tutankhamen, both released in 2015. And while ABC's *Kings and Prophets* 2016 television series featured white actors in the lead roles of King Saul and David, other leading players reflected greater cultural diversity, including a Lebanese actor as Saul's son Jonathan. The 2016 live television musical production of *The Passion* strove for greater contemporary diversity in its casting, with a Latino Jesus, a multicultural cast of disciples, Seal playing Pilate, and Tyler Perry hosting.

Preaching in the Age of a Global Economy

The challenge to be witnesses to the ends of the earth is not limited to noticing how quickly the gospel spread throughout vast regions of the known world in the first century AD. This is not an issue merely of evangelism or of geography. As Harry Emerson Fosdick once said, "Only the preacher proceeds still upon the idea that folks come to church desperately anxious to discover what happened to the Jebusites."[14] In other words, focusing on the ancient past while ignoring current events rapidly unfolding in the world today is a wasted opportunity in preaching about God's global concerns.

Being a witness for Jesus has important implications for our preaching in the twenty-first century as well. Let us begin by considering how a once vast global population has suddenly become a global community.

As president of a school in Rochester, New York, I was directly affected by the recent stock market troubles of China. Although the physical soil of China is eight thousand miles away from Rochester, the interconnectedness of global financial markets made it easy for the endowment funds of our divinity school to be negatively impacted by financial conditions in another country. Decreased demand in China for consumer goods such as cell phones, automobiles, and a host of retail products has an immediate impact on US manufacturers who risk losing once-steady profits from that enormous Chinese market.

Increased demand in China for more and more natural resources like oil and gas puts an added strain on the already fragile ecosystem in which we live together on this planet.[15]

Writers such as Fareed Zakaria and Thomas Friedman have spent the last ten years talking about and warning about massive shifts in global economic activity.[16] They highlight the emergence of personal computers and access to the Internet, cellular communication, the capacity of e-commerce, blogging, and social media, all of which have worked together to make the world more of a global village. Such technology has had a major impact on India, for example, a country that is home to a third of the world's poor. The mobile app known as Uber, which connects individual passengers with independent drivers, has spawned hundreds of thousands of entrepreneurs operating in eighteen cities in India, making that country the biggest market for Uber outside of the United States.[17]

Ideas flow much faster. Commercial markets can be tapped more quickly. Persons with goods or service who were once cut off from society because of physical distance or geographical or topographically barriers, like mountains or deserts or oceans, can now compete in the marketplace. What happens with oil prices in Venezuela or Canada, with political instability in Ukraine or Libya, or with environmental hazards in the Amazon rain forests or the Gulf of Mexico all have the capacity to have an immediate and lasting effect on persons living in the United States and in countries around the world. The drivers of the global economy are already at work imagining and shaping the future.

What is lagging behind are the moral values, the human rights concerns, the environmental and ecological safeguards, the trade policies, and the worker and workplace safety issues that should be in place while all of this change is occurring. Here is an opportunity for some important preaching, as well as some much-needed resolutions from clergy groups and denominational bodies to speak with one voice about the sovereign God who instructed us to have dominion over the earth.

Hispanic Immigration to the United States—Immigration is a pressing problem all over the world. In particular, civil wars, drug-related violence, and economic hardships in Honduras, Guatemala, and other Central American nations have resulted in increased immigration into this country. That puts an added strain on our social service networks and creates more competition for jobs, housing, social mobility, and political influence. These factors have also contributed to the war of words among many political leaders around the issues of legal and illegal immigration.

The very character of our nation is at stake in this debate. It must never be forgotten that the only persons who did not immigrate to the United States (whether as free colonists, as indentured servants, or as slaves) are the Native Americans, indigenous tribes who fully occupied this hemisphere from Canada to the southern tip of Chile. This is a country built by immigrants from every corner of the world.

Bear in mind that throughout the Bible, special focus is given to how God's people treat and view three categories of persons who were especially vulnerable to persecution at that time: the widow, the orphan, and the stranger or foreigner. One could easily insert the words so common to our twenty-first-century dialogue: *refugee*, *immigrant*, *alien*, or *undocumented worker*.

Exodus 22:21 says, "Do not mistreat or oppress a foreigner, for you were foreigners in Egypt." Deuteronomy 10:19 says, "You are to love those who are foreigners, for you yourselves were foreigners in Egypt." Both Exodus 20:10 and Deuteronomy 5:14 declare that strangers or resident aliens should be included in the rest period that comes on the Sabbath Day. Jeremiah 7:6 and 22:3 both warn Judah not to oppress the foreigner, the fatherless, or the widow. Add to that the fact that in Matthew 25:35 Jesus includes treatment of strangers as a consideration on the day of Judgment: "I was a stranger and you invited me in."

Immigration in Europe—From a global perspective, immigration issues are by no means an American issue. A recent headline in *USA Today* read, "Europe's Migrant Crisis Spins Out of Control."[18] This is a reminder that people all over the world are being driven from their homes as a result of religious, political, or ethnic persecution. Civil wars and religious persecution in places such as Syria and Iraq have created an even larger and more desperate immigration crisis for countries such as Hungary, Austria, Croatia, and Germany. This is evidenced in the *USA Today* article:

> As many as 50 bodies believed to be those of migrants were found in an abandoned truck near the Austria-Hungary border Thursday, highlighting anew the crisis Europe faces in dealing with the greatest deluge of displaced persons since World War II. . . . The tired, yearning masses that this summer have swelled to as many as 3,000 a day in parts of the continent are fleeing war, persecution and economic hardship in the Middle East and Africa.[19]

Mass migrations are under way in Serbia and Bosnia, in Syria and Iraq, and in Sudan and Nigeria. In other words, immigration and the social and economic pressures it produces are occurring on every continent of the earth. Rhetoric about border security and building walls to keep out foreigners is not unique to Donald Trump and a certain conservative brand of American politics. A wall is being built in Hungary to keep out Serbians, and border security has been increased around the tunnel that links Britain and France so that migrants cannot enter either country by that route.[20]

Immigration involves two numbers that should concern preachers who have a global perspective for their ministry. The first number has to do with the number of persons who are migrating into Europe and the United States every year, and the second number has to do with the number of persons who die every year in the process of attempting to migrate from one country to another. A recent *TIMES* article revealed that 219,000 persons migrated to Europe from the Middle East and Africa in 2014. The number at the midyear point of 2015 had already reached 310,000. In one weekend in 2015, 4,000 persons attempted to enter Austria through Hungary, having migrated from nations in the Baltic area—Bosnia, Serbia, Estonia, and Latvia among others.[21]

At the same time, 2,500 people drowned at sea in 2014 in an attempt to reach Italy or Greece by sailing across the Mediterranean Sea on makeshift, overcrowded rafts. By mid-2015 that number had already reached 3,500. On August 27, 2015, at least 150 people drowned in one day when an overloaded ship capsized in the waters between Libya and Crete.[22] This does not take into consideration the number of migrants (refugees?) who die in overcrowded trucks or while traveling on foot from Central America in an attempt to get into the United States. What are the issues of immigration policy about which witnesses for Jesus must *see something*, *say something*, and then be willing to *suffer something* as a result of their testimony? Our God has an interest in all the nations on earth, not just the United States. The preaching of the gospel should extend to matters that are inclusive of wherever the sovereignty of God extends.

It was in response to this global crisis that Pope Francis challenged every Roman Catholic parish in Europe (a number in excess of 150,000) to take in and host a migrant family until they can get on their feet in a new country.[23] The last time so many migrants were on the move in Europe was during World War II, and the response of the Christian church at that time was abysmal. That was most especially true for Jews attempting to escape death at the hands of the Nazis. The church has another chance to speak to this global crisis. Preachers need to challenge churches to respond in any way they can. That is what it looks like to be a witness on a global scale.

Israel and Palestine—There are other places and problems in the world that demand the attention of preachers and those to whom they preach. One of the most complicated global issues for Christian preachers to navigate involves the role played by the United States in the Middle East in general, and the relationship between the United States and Israel/Palestine in particular. Here is an instance in which foreign policy has a direct impact on our domestic agenda as a nation. There is an enormous debate going on within American society about how Christians should line up when it comes to the Israeli-Palestinian dispute. The policy of the federal government has been clear since President Kennedy assured Golda Meir, who was then the foreign minister of Israel, that "the United States has a special relationship with Israel in the Middle East, really only comparable to that which it has with Britain over a wide range of world affairs."[24]

The question for preachers who are witnesses for Jesus in Judea, Samaria, and to the ends of the earth is whether the will of God and the foreign-policy agenda of the United States are synonymous. Should Christians line up on the side of Israel under any and all circumstances? Should we all embrace the views of Christian Zionists who link the second coming of Christ to a stable Jewish state? Should the witness of the church on this issue take on eschatological or end-of-time urgency as we prepare the way for the Lord's return? Should Christians in the United States embrace the argument that the modern State of Israel is a direct continuation of the ancient biblical lands of Judea and Samaria, as is the argument for many advocates for the legitimacy of the Jewish state that was created in 1947? Shall we embrace the views of Ron Domina, a local pastor here in Rochester who is the head of a group called Christians United for Israel, who speaks glowingly of the Israeli Defense Forces? He describes them as "the boys I met on Israel's border who guard their borders from the enemies at the gates . . . and who keep safe the land of the Bible for us all."[25]

Or is there something to be said for Christians aligning themselves with the Palestinian people and speaking forcefully about the conditions under which they are being forced to live in what is most certainly the Palestinian ancestral homeland as well? When Christians travel to Israel on Holy Land tours, what will they say about the enormous wall that divides parts of Israel from various Palestinian communities? What will they say about the border crossings and the checkpoints manned by heavily armed members of the Israeli Defense Force? Are they in fact guarding their borders from the enemies at the gate, as Pastor Domina suggested above, or is it possible that in their attempts to maintain security for themselves within the State of Israel that the Jewish people are doing to the Palestinians precisely what had been done to Jews all over the world in earlier times—a form of racial profiling and the ghettoization of part of the national population in Gaza along the Mediterranean Sea and along the West Bank of the Jordan River?

That concern is raised by Marc Ellis, of Baylor University, who is an expert on Israeli/Palestinian issues. In his book *Judaism Does Not Equal Israel*, Ellis writes:

> Coterminous with the Holocaust and the founding of Israel have been the conquest and destruction of much of Palestine. The creation of Israel forced an ethnic cleansing of more than seven hundred thousand Palestinians to create room for the Jewish state. . . . These policies continue today in the Jewish "settlements"—really expansive towns and small cities—that mark the future of Israel's dominant and permanent presence in Jerusalem and the West Bank. . . . It appears our empowerment is tainted with the same abuse of power others have used against us, an abuse we have condemned.[26]

The issue of the security of Israel is at the heart of US political discussions revolving around the nuclear weapons deal between Iran and the P5+1 group that consists of the five permanent members of the UN Security Council, which includes Britain, France, Russia, China, the United States, plus Germany and the European Union. Should Western nations be concerned about Iran developing the technology to create a nuclear bomb? Has Iran threatened to "wipe Israel off the face of the earth"? Should Israel be concerned about its security if Iran does possess a nuclear bomb? The answer to all of those questions is a resounding yes!

Should US presidential candidates be allowed to give the impression that if elected they could or would scrap the deal entirely "on their first day in office," given the fact that it is a multinational document? Should the prime minister of Israel be allowed to address a joint session of the US Congress to attack a plan on which the secretary of state of this country was still at work?[27] Should we be concerned that a political action group spent $30 million in an attempt to influence members of the US Congress and their constituents? Should that group be concerned that the Iran nuclear was not defeated after all the lobbying that went on?[28]

Should we be concerned that every single member of the Republican Party in both houses of Congress voted against the multinational deal limiting Iran's nuclear program, and promised to do so before they had even read the language of the document on which they would be voting? Should forty-seven United States senators, all members of the Republican Party, write a letter directly to the leader of Iran, warning the Iranians not to sign any deal made with the Obama administration based on internal political differences?[29]

Preachers may use a variety of platforms to extend their witness beyond the confines of their local church and their Sunday sermon. Consider submitting letters to the editor of your local and regional newspapers, posting on your personal social media sites or responding to the posts of others, and writing online article on a blog site—your own or as guest writer for others' blogs.

Ethiopian Israelis—While all eyes are on the multinational nuclear weapons deal with Iran, what is being said about the complaints raised by many within the Ethiopian Jewish community in Israel? They were brought to Israel in a much-celebrated airlift in 1991 called Operation Solomon, but they are now facing well-documented instances of racial discrimination.[30] These Ethiopian Jews are a telling reminder of at least two significant biblical narratives.

The first is the encounter between King Solomon of Israel and the queen of Sheba as recorded in 1 Kings 10 and 2 Chronicles 9. Modern-day Ethiopian Christians (Coptics) traditionally trace their descent from a union between Solomon and the queen of Sheba that resulted in a son named Menelek who established Judaism in that country.[31] Almost all of the black Jewish sects in the United States also embrace this link with

Solomon, the queen of Sheba, and the Ethiopian Jews that resulted from that union.[32] Right here in Rochester, New York, there is a black Jewish community called the Church of God and Saints of Christ who observe worship on the Sabbath Day, maintain a kosher diet, and wear prayer shawls and yarmulkes in the sanctuary.

The other biblical text that links Christians in the United States to Jews in Ethiopia is Acts 8:27-39, which describes the encounter between Philip and an Ethiopian eunuch in the service of the Kandake. He very likely came to Jerusalem to observe one of the Jewish festivals (8:27), a sign of his membership within the Jewish community. However, he was baptized by Philip (8:38) and returned to his home a Christian. Here is another instance of an early follower of Jesus being a witness (Philip), resulting in the conversion of a highly influential person from Ethiopia who may have returned there to spread the news about Jesus. These two biblical narratives link our preaching to people and places all over the Middle East and Africa.

ISIS and Global Terrorism—Preachers who are witnesses for Jesus to the ends of the earth must be prepared to address the scourge of terrorism that has been active throughout the world for more than forty years and has been front-page news in this country since the horrific attacks in the United States on September 11, 2001. What should we say about al-Qaeda, the Taliban, ISIS (Islamic State in Syria), or ISIL (Islamic State of Iraq and the Levant)? What response by our government should Christians support in response to beheadings, train bombings, ethnic cleansing, and the persecution and even mass murder of Christians in Syria and Iraq? What should we say about the mass killings in France involving *Charlie Hebdo*? What should we say about the bombing of a monastery in Syria that dated back to the fifth century AD?[33]

Surely we cannot enter our pulpits acting as if none of these things have occurred and are still occurring. Members of our churches or their loved ones are deployed to various regions of the world to combat global terrorism. Young people from the United States and many nations in Europe are either going to Syria to fight with ISIS, or they are becoming self-radicalized and are looking for opportunities to stage a terrorist attack here in the United States.

Every gruesome deed performed by ISIS is matched by the brutality of the Nigerian-based terror group known as Boko Haram, which has now sworn allegiance to ISIS. More than 1.5 million people have fled Nigeria, Chad, and Niger in response to the unimaginable acts of brutality employed by this terrorist group. While that group is most notorious because of its kidnapping of approximately 250 Nigerian school girls in 2014, the group killed an additional 17,000 people in acts of religious persecution in 2014.[32] It had expressed a desire to kill an additional 200,000 Christians in Nigeria in 2015. According to the New York Times, by November 2015 Boko Haram had actually caused more deaths through terrorist attacks than ISIS.[35]

What lies behind most of these mass migrations is the fear of the mass murder of Christians by persons in other religious groups. Surely preachers in the United States should be willing to *see something*, *say something*, and *suffer something* for what we say about global terrorism.

Not a Multiple Choice Exam

Preachers should understand that the emphasis on Jerusalem, Judea, Samaria, and the ends of the earth in Acts 1:6-8 does not reflect a multiple-choice option in which preachers are free to select the context or location that most suits their liking. Jesus did not say that they could go to Jerusalem *or* Judea, and he did not say that they could go to Samaria *or* to the ends of the earth. What he said was that they must be willing to engage in a preaching ministry that allows for an ever-widening sphere of focus and concern. Acts 1:6-8 makes it clear that their sphere of preaching must extend as far as the sovereignty of God extends.

Jerusalem was where the disciples were when Jesus gave them this challenge. However, Jerusalem was not where he expected them to remain for very long. God is sovereign over the whole of the creation, and as such God is neither pleased nor well served by preachers who are unwilling to bear witness to Jesus Christ in places beyond our local community, our cultural enclave, or our native shores. As preachers, we need to understand that just as our sermons may on occasion "afflict the comfortable," so too does God reserve the right to afflict overly comfortable preachers by challenging us to venture beyond our parochial places and views, and go into those places we might otherwise choose to ignore or avoid. Acts 1:6-8 challenges every preacher to embrace the spirit of the Christian hymn that says: "Where he leads me I will follow. I'll go with him all the way."[36]

NOTES

1. S.v., "Samaritans," in George Arthur Buttrick and John Knox, *The Interpreter's Dictionary of the Bible: An Illustrated Encyclopedia*, 4 vols. (Nashville: Abingdon, 1962), 4:190–95.

2. Jeremy Diamond, "Donald Trump: Ban All Muslim travel to U.S.," cnn.com, December 8, 2015.

3. Eugene Scott, "Ted Cruz: Program patrolling Muslim neighborhoods was a Success," cnn.com, March 30, 2016.

4. Tony Gentile, "Pope Condemns Killings of Ethiopian Christians in Libya," Reuters, April 20, 2015, http://www.reuters.com/article/us-mideast-crisis-islamicstate-ethiopia-idUSKBN0NC00T20150421; and Sarah Pulliam Bailey, "Pope Francis Denounces ISIS Beheadings," *Washington Post*, February 16, 2015, https://www.washingtonpost.com/news/local/wp/2015/02/16/pope-francis-denounces-isis-beheadings-their-blood-confesses-christ/.

5. Stephen Breyer, *The Court and the World: American Law and the New Global Realities* (New York: Knopf, 2015).

6. Stephen Breyer, quoted in Richard Wolf, "Breyer: Court Must Take World View," *USA Today*, September 20, 2015, 3B.

7. Ibid.

8. Ibid.

9. Elliott C. McLaughlin, "Raul Castro May Join Catholic Church, He Says after Pope Francis Meeting," CNN, May 14, 2015, http://www.cnn.com/2015/05/10/europe/italy-raul-castro-pope-francis-meeting/index.html.

10. Ian Tyrell, "What Is American Exceptionalism?," Iantyrell.wordpress.com, https://iantyrrell.wordpress.com/ papers-and-comments/.

11. Harry T. Burleigh, "In Christ There Is No East or West," quoted in Craig von Buseck, *Nobody Knows: The Harry T. Burleigh Story* (Grand Rapids: Baker, 2014), 231–32.

12. Herbert G. May, *Oxford Bible Atlas* (New York: Oxford University Press, 1978), 88–89.

13. Marvin A. McMickle, "African Americans and the Bible," in *An Encyclopedia of African American Christian Heritage* (Valley Forge, PA: Judson, 2002), 221–23.

14. Richard Lischer, *The Company of Preachers* (Grand Rapids: Eerdmans, 2002), 398.

15. Keith Bradsher, "China Falters, and the Global Economy Is Forced to Adapt," *New York Times*, August 26, 2015, http://www.nytimes.com/2015/08/27/business/international/china-falters-and-the-global-economy-is-forced-to-adapt.html.

16. Thomas Friedman, *The World Is Flat: A Brief History of the Twenty-First Century* (New York: Farrar, Straus and Giroux, 2005); Fareed Zakaria, *The Post-American World* (New York: Norton, 2008).

17. Trisha Thadani, "Watch Out, China! Another Nation Is On the Rise," *USA Today*, August 30, 2015, 6B.

18. Kim Hjelmgaard, "Europe's Migrant Crisis Spins Out of Control," *USA Today*, August 28, 2015, 3B.

19. Ibid.

20. Ibid.

21. Massimo Calabresi, "A Wave of the World's Displaced Crashes on Europe's Shores," *TIME*, September 15, 2015, 15.

22. Alison Smale, Melissa Eddy, and Kareem Fahim, "Europe Reels from Migrant Deaths on Land and Sea," *New York Times*, August 28, 2015, http://www.nytimes.com/2015/08/29/world/europe/migrants-bodies-austria-truck.html.

23. Rick Lyman and Alison Smale, "As Europe Grasps for Answers More Migrants Flood Its Borders," *New York Times*, September 6, 2015, http://www.nytimes.com/2015/09/07/world/europe/pope-calls-on-europeans-to-house-refugees.html.

24. Keith P. Feldman, *A Shadow over Palestine: The Imperial Life of Race in America* (Minneapolis: University of Minnesota Press, 2015), 1.

25. Ron Domina, "A Moving Trip to Israel," *Democrat and Chronicle*, April 5, 2014, 12A.

26. Marc Ellis, *Judaism Does Not Equal Israel* (New York: New Press, 2009), xiv.

27. "The Complete transcript of Netanyahu's address to Congress," Washington Post.com, March 3, 2015.

28. Julie Hirschfield Davis, "Influential Pro-Israel Group Suffers Stinging Political Defeat", NewYorkTimes.com, September 10, 2015, p. 1.

29. Peter Baker, "G.O.P. Senators' Letter to Iran about Nuclear Deal Angers White House," *New York Times*, March 9, 2015, http://www.nytimes.com/2015/03/10/world/asia/white-house-faults-gop-senators-letter-to-irans-leaders.html.

30. Oz Rosenberg, "Thousands in Jerusalem Protest Racism against Ethiopian Israelis," HAARETZ.com, January 18, 2015, http://www.haaretz.com/israel-news/thousands-in-jerusalem-protest-racism-against-ethiopian-israelis-1.407998.

31. S.v. "Saba" in *Harper's Bible Dictionary*, ed. Madeline Miller and J. Lane Miller (New York: Harper and Row, 1961), 630–31.

32. Marvin A. McMickle, "Wentworth Arthur Matthew" in *An Encyclopedia of African American Christian Heritage* (Valley Forge, PA: Judson, 2002), 197–98.

33. "Dastardly Deeds," *Christian Century*, September 16, 2015, p. 8.

34. Dionne Searcey and Marc Santora, "Boko Haram Ranked Ahead of ISIS for Deadliest Terror Group", NewYorkTimes.com, November 18, 2015.

35. Mark Anderson, "Nigeria Suffers Highest Number of Civilian Deaths in African War Zones," *Guardian*, January 23, 2015, http://www.theguardian.com/global-development/2015/jan/23/boko-haram-nigeria-civilian-death-toll-highest-acled-african-war-zones.

36. E. W. Blandy, "Where He Leads Me I Will Follow," *African American Heritage Hymnal* (Chicago: GIA, 2001), 550.

CHAPTER 14

The Role of the Holy Spirit in Preaching

"You will receive power when the Holy Spirit comes on you; and you will be my witnesses in Jerusalem, and in all Judea and Samaria, and to the ends of the earth."—Acts 1:8

One last aspect of the challenge that Jesus gave to his first disciples must now be considered: the role and power of the Holy Spirit. In order of appearance in the text, the Holy Spirit actually appears in the center of the Acts 1:6-8 passage. It bridges the gap between the question raised by the disciples about what Jesus was going to do next (v. 6) and the directive he gave them concerning the mission he was directing them to undertake (v. 8b). In this study I have chosen to keep this discussion until the end, because the role and importance of the Holy Spirit in preaching is the theme that I hope the reader will take away from this book.

To be sure, the work of being a witness is central to the work of the preacher in the twenty-first century. In addition, the challenge to find ways to extend the message to the ends of the earth, in partnership with other agencies and groups, remains our primary distinctive as Christians in relation to the other Abrahamic faith traditions, Islam and Judaism (not to mention the other great religions of the world). The question that remains is whether preachers can accomplish their mission by their own natural skills and resources alone. The answer to that question is a resounding no insofar as Acts 1:8 is concerned. Jesus explicitly told his disciples, "You will receive power when the Holy

Spirit comes on you; and you will be my witnesses." In short, nothing should be attempted and nothing will likely be accomplished unless and until the disciples are operating with the power of the Holy Spirit.

Writing about Acts 1:6-8, biblical scholar Robert Wall links the work of being a witness for Jesus with the act of being empowered by the Holy Spirit. Wall begins by pointing out that by receiving the Holy Spirit "there is continuity between the prophetic ministry of Jesus and his apostolic successors because each is baptized into the realm of this same Spirit of prophecy who empowers an effective ministry of word and witness."[1]

Recall that Jesus himself was anointed with the power of the Holy Spirit following his baptism by John the Baptist in the Jordan River in Luke 3:22. The role of the Holy Spirit continued in the life of Jesus in Luke 4:1, which says, "Jesus, full of the Holy Spirit, left the Jordan and was led by the Spirit into the wilderness, where for forty days he was tempted by the devil."

Notice that Jesus did not begin his public ministry until he had been anointed with and empowered by the Holy Spirit. Indeed, he began his inaugural sermon in the synagogue in Nazareth by reading from the scroll of the prophet Isaiah: "The Spirit of the Lord is on me, because he has anointed me to proclaim good news to the poor. He has sent me to proclaim freedom for the prisoners and recovery of sight for the blind, to set the oppressed free, to proclaim the year of the Lord's favor" (Luke 4:18-19; cf. Isaiah 61:1-3).

Thus any attempt to explain or understand the ministry of Jesus apart from the working of the Holy Spirit would be both unfaithful to God and unproductive in terms of any meaningful outcomes. Like the Old Testament prophets before him, great attention must be paid to the phrase spoken by Jesus, "The Spirit of the Lord is on me."

If Jesus was reliant on the power of the Holy Spirit, it is not surprising that he urges a similar reliance on the Holy Spirit by those who will be his witnesses to the world. Robert Wall continues his analysis of Acts 1:8 by observing, "The Holy Spirit in Acts is more functional than soteriological." In other words, the book of Acts is more focused on what the Spirit does in the lives of believers than on who the Spirit is in relation to personal salvation through Christ. Wall goes on to say, "Initiation into the realm of the Spirit enables the believers to bring an effective witness of the risen Jesus to the world. Unlike the Pauline emphasis on the Spirit's mediation of God's salvation-creating grace, for Luke the images and ideas of the Spirit's role are almost always tied to the apostle's mission or to the authority of their leadership."[2]

A Consistent Message

It is interesting to note that all three aspects of the challenge given by Jesus to his first disciples in Acts 1:6-8 (be my witnesses—in Jerusalem and beyond; rely on the power of the Holy Spirit) are also captured in the last words spoken by Jesus to his disciples in Luke 24:46-49. There Jesus says, "The Messiah will suffer and rise from the dead on the third day, and repentance for the forgiveness of sins will be preached in his name *to all nations, beginning at Jerusalem*. You are *witnesses of these things*. I am going to send you what my Father has promised; but stay in the city until you have been *clothed with power from on high*" (emphasis added).

Notice that in both Luke 24 and Acts 1, Jesus commissioned his disciples to be witnesses. In both texts, Jesus also spoke to the ever-widening context for the disciples' ministry, beginning in Jerusalem. And in both passages, Jesus also promised power from outside the disciples' own resources—power from on high in Luke 24, and power from the Holy Spirit in Acts 1.

Both Acts 1 and Luke 24 make it clear that the work of being witnesses in any location was to be preceded by being clothed with or receiving the power of the Holy Spirit. Nothing was to be said and nothing was to be done until after the power of the Holy Spirit had been imparted to them. They were not to make any moves to preach in the city or beyond until the power of the Holy Spirit had been received.

The conclusion we must draw is that the work the disciples were being sent out to do could not be done solely by their own energies, talents, experiences, and testimonies. The time was soon coming when resistance and persecution from those to whom they would preach would be matched with weariness and exhaustion from the sheer magnitude of the undertaking—from the physical, emotional, and spiritual strain of carrying the message to distant locations. Jesus knew they would need strength and a power that could undergird and sustain them in their work long after their own strength and imagination had waned. They would need the Holy Spirit!

In his book *The Christian Imagination: Theology and the Origins of Race*, Willie Jennings points out that several times in quick succession, actions by the Holy Spirit resulted in major developments in the life and work of the first-century Christian community. Jennings recounts: "It was the Spirit of God who was driving Israel toward the Gentiles in the space constituted by Jesus' body. It was the Spirit who drove the Gentiles toward Israel and into languages of other people. In Acts 8, it was the Spirit who drove the Jewish believer Philip to join himself to the chariot of an Ethiopian eunuch who was trying to understand Torah."[3]

I may have disagreed with Jennings's assessment of the disciples' question in Acts 1:6 (see chapter 3), but I believe he is right on the mark here. Throughout the Scriptures, God demonstrates a passion and compassion, not only for the chosen people of Israel, but also for the nations of the world. At Pentecost itself, the Holy Spirit's first action in the midst of the disciples was to bestow a gift of tongues—of multiple languages—so that the multicultural, multinational crowd could all hear the gospel message. And the Spirit didn't just prompt Philip to approach the Ethiopian stranger; it was the Holy Spirit who had "beamed" Philip there in the first place!

Education Is Incomplete Preparation

As a person who has spent the better part of his life first acquiring and then helping to deliver theological education, I know better at age sixty-seven than I did at age twenty-seven or even fifty-seven that theological education alone is not enough to sustain a preaching ministry over the years. After thirty-four years as a pastor, thirty years as a professor at five different seminaries, and now after five years as president of Colgate Rochester Crozer Divinity School, I am by no means suggesting that there is no value in formal theological training for those aspiring to careers in ministry. Quite the contrary, the years I spent as a seminary student at Union Theological Seminary in New York City learning from such persons as James Cone and James Sanders were absolutely essential for both my intellectual and faith development. I remain in touch with both of them to this day, and I continue to send them drafts of documents I am working on in hopes of their giving me a good grade! Now, much to my surprise and occasional delight, students I have worked with over the years stay in touch with me and seek my continued involvement in their lives and ministries.

In short, theological education at its best is not solely about courses in the curriculum nor the awarding of academic degrees. Theological education is also about mentoring, about modeling, and most important, about relationships that often last long after students have left the classroom. This is the path I pursued in preparation for my own ministry as well as in aiding those who have chosen to follow a similar approach. As the nineteenth-century spiritual declares, "I wouldn't take nothing for my journey now."

Benefits and Challenges of Theological Education

I fully recognize that not every person presently or previously involved in the preaching ministry has done so only after attending seminary or divinity school. Many persons may have desired such an experience, but factors ranging from finances to family obligations to no previous formal training prevented them from enrolling. Others I have encountered consciously chose not to attend seminary, believing that formal theological education would have a negative impact on both their faith and their preaching. I have heard people both playfully and intentionally refer to the seminary as a cemetery where people go to have their faith killed and buried. I have heard people say that "too much learning will affect your burning." That is, they think a historical-critical approach to the study of Scripture might cause them to lose their Spirit-fueled zeal and enthusiasm for preaching.

Let me pause to acknowledge this reality: I know a great many preachers and pastors who served their churches and their communities without having spent one single day in a graduate-level classroom. But an absence of formal theological education in no way prevented many of those preachers from engaging in various forms of lifelong learning and serious theological reflection.

Consider, for example, the late Caesar A. W. Clark of Good Street Baptist Church in Dallas, Texas, who never attended seminary. He was, nevertheless, one of the most widely heard and greatly honored black preachers of the twentieth century. The secret to his success, at least in part, was that he carried two suitcases with him when he left Dallas to do weeklong revivals across the country. In one suitcase he carried his clothing and personal items, and the other one was stuffed with books that he would read voraciously in his hotel room. Rather than spending his days in fellowship with local pastors, he remained in fellowship with God and in intense hours of reading and reflecting.

I observed a similar trait in my uncle, James B. Alford. He never finished college, but he spent forty-four years as pastor of Progressive Church of God in Christ (COGIC) in Maywood, Illinois. Like most COGIC pastors of his generation, he was neither required nor encouraged to seek formal training. However, two things were true in his case, one of which is central in this chapter. First, he maintained an enviable personal library far larger than that of many seminary graduates that included biblical commentaries, books on theology, pastoral care, church history, and Christian ethics, as well as a wide range of other kinds of literature and journals. Second, he maintained a disciplined life of study that made his preaching vivid and informative. He was a well-read, self-taught, highly effective pastor.

Education and Inspiration

Whether a preacher's theological education comes through formal training at an accredited seminary or school of theology or through the self-discipline of lifelong learning and avid study, Acts 1:8 (and Luke 24) reminds us that education must always be supplemented, supported, and inspired by the power and presence of the Holy Spirit.

I saw this truth vividly displayed in the life of my uncle. In addition to his relentless pursuit for self-guided theological education, you see, James B. Alford was a Pentecostal in the Azusa Street Revival sense of that word.[4] He embraced speaking in tongues as a sign of salvation, and he affirmed the holiness aspects of that tradition in keeping with the constant call of Romans 12:2, which says, "Do not conform to the pattern of this world." That resulted in a long list of dos and don'ts, but mostly (it seemed to me) it was don'ts. Don't dance, don't go to the movies, don't wear facial makeup, and don't even play Monopoly, since it involves throwing dice. Not having been raised in a household with those rules, my brother and I never looked forward to spending two weeks every summer at our uncle's home. Neither of us ever aspired to that degree of holiness.

Most importantly, however, my uncle also believed in the work and power of the Holy Spirit in other areas of life. I remember as if it were yesterday that one of his sons became ill during a family holiday gathering in Chicago. While his two younger sisters were rushing to the phone to call an ambulance to rush the child off to the nearest hospital, my uncle was completely engrossed in a James 5:13 act of ministry involving anointing with oil and the effectual, fervent prayer of the righteous on behalf of the sick.

By the time the ambulance arrived at our house, there was nothing for the medics to do. Uncle James told them that while their ambulance was on the way, the Holy Spirit had come and gone! He did not learn that level of faith in a seminary classroom, for such a level of faith is not generally taught by or demonstrated by the vast majority of those who teach at seminaries. He believed in, trusted in, and called upon the power of the Holy Spirit as much in his preaching as he did in his parenting.

Balancing Head and Heart

For those who have pursued formal theological training, it is important to have an appreciation for the role of the Holy Spirit in our ministry in general and in our preaching in particular. It was the search for this balance between mind and spirit, between intellectual rigor and religious exuberance that was at the heart of the emergence of the Full Gospel Baptist Church Fellowship under the direction of Paul Morton Sr.

Morton was immersed in the Pentecostal movement early in his life. His grandfather was one of the founders of the Church of God in Christ (COGIC), and his father became one of the bishops of that church. He, however, left the church of his upbringing and became the assistant pastor and later the pastor of Greater St. Stephens Baptist Church in New Orleans.

That church enjoyed tremendous growth, and along the way Morton realized why that was the case. He said:

> We believed the basics of the Bible that you needed to be saved. We believed in the death, burial and resurrection of Jesus Christ. But growing up in the Pentecostal church, I knew that God had another level for us as it related to the fullness of the Holy Spirit, as it related to casting out demons, laying hands on the sick, speaking in a heavenly language. So what God did, He said to transition the traditional Baptist church I had into the fullness of the Holy Spirit. . . . And God began to bless Greater St. Stephens in such a mighty way.[5]

Today the Full Gospel Baptist Church Fellowship and the Church of God in Christ are the two fastest-growing denominations within the African American community. In fact, the Pew Research Study on Religion in American Life noted that Pentecostalism is the fastest-growing segment of all Christian denominations worldwide, accounting for 25 percent of the world's 2 billion Christians. While mainline denominations are either in a slow decline or in free fall in terms of membership and viable congregations, Pentecostal movements are growing rapidly all over the world.[6] In addition to the above-named black denominations, the largely white Pentecostal movements, including the Assemblies of God and the Church of God (Cleveland, Tennessee), can be added to this discussion. In every case, their sustained growth has been attributed to their belief in and openness to the power of the Holy Spirit.

It is worth asking whether the decline in mainline churches is in some way related to their lack of focus on the work of the Holy Spirit. Can it be that the primary focus on the largely academic, critical, rational, and cerebral approach to teaching and preaching by so many scholars and pastors in the last one hundred years may account for the loss of power and lack of results in their preaching and in the life of their churches? While keeping pace with the scientific focus on data, facts, reason, and the belief that the human mind is the ultimate judge of truth, twenty-first-century preachers in the mainline Christian traditions may have locked themselves away from the very thing Jesus instructed them to rely on most as far back as Luke 24:46-49 and Acts 1:6-8.

The increased secularization of Western society and the rise of the so-called postmodern world has no doubt greatly contributed to the gradual decline of religious identity and enthusiasm on the part of an increasing number of persons. What may also have contributed to the decline of religious faith was a conscious move away from religious zeal and enthusiasm by those charged to preach the gospel. How strange that the level of enthusiasm that was once the mark of many white preachers during the First and Second Great Awakenings (1720–40 and 1792–1820) gradually gave way to the forms of delivery that were almost entirely academic and instructional, rather than uplifting and inspiring.

Henry Mitchell has pointed out that the fervor of the Great Awakening was its most distinctive characteristic. He notes, "The Methodist church, known in the Awakenings as 'The Shouting Methodists,' was growing at a phenomenal rate. Starting from zero, Methodists became the largest denomination in the United States by

1820. Today, Methodism and all the other mainline denominations are losing ground rapidly."[7]

John Wesley, one of the main voices of the First Great Awakening, raised in and ordained by the Church of England with all of its formality and restraint, spoke one of the most memorable lines in church history. While hearing a moving sermon by a preacher at a church on Aldersgate Street in London, he said, "I felt my heart strangely warmed."[8] Persons coming to hear our sermons may be hoping for and expecting that their hearts will be strangely warmed as well.

When sermons became more about facts than about faith and more about the head than the heart, people may have concluded that there was nothing being offered by the church that could not be just as easily found in a college classroom or a Chautauqua lecture platform. It is not information alone that makes for an effective sermon; it is also the work of the Holy Spirit energizing the preacher and awakening the souls of the people who hear our sermons.

Like John Wesley, James Forbes, one of the great preachers of the last one hundred years, also spoke of a reliance on the role of the Holy Spirit in his preaching ministry. He was raised in the United Holy Church which was a Pentecostal movement started even before Azusa Street. He pursued higher education against the wishes of the leaders in that church movement, who feared that formal theological training would negatively impact his zeal. What happened instead was the emergence of a preaching style that perfectly balanced head and heart, faith and fervor, the authority of Scripture and the free movement of the Holy Spirit.[9]

Forbes went on to enjoy a stellar career that included becoming the professor of preaching at his alma mater, Union Theological Seminary in New York City, and pastor of Riverside Church, also in New York City, and delivering the Lyman Beecher Lectures at Yale Divinity School in 1986. Out of those lectures came his book *The Holy Spirit and Preaching*, in which he wrote, "It is the Spirit who has inspired the scripture lessons of the day. It is the Spirit who has shepherded the word through complicated translations, and transmissions to the present time. It is the Spirit who convenes a congregation to hear the word of God. And it is the Spirit who opens our hearts and minds to receive anew God's self-disclosure in the living word."[10]

NOTES

1. Robert W. Wall, "The Acts of the Apostles," *The New Interpreter's Bible: A Commentary in Twelve Volumes* (Nashville: Abingdon, 2002), 10:41.

2. Ibid.

3. Willie James Jennings, *The Christian Imagination: Theology and the Origins of Race* (New Haven, CT: Yale University Press, 2010), 270.

4. Marvin A. McMickle, *An Encyclopedia of African American Christian Heritage*, cf. articles on Charles Harrison Mason, Church of God in Christ, and William Joseph Seymour (Valley Forge, PA: Judson, 2002).

5. Ibid., 38.

6. "Spirit and Power: A 10-Country Survey of Pentecostals," Pew Research Center, October 5, 2006, http://www.pewforum.org/2006/10/05/spirit-and-power/.

7. Henry H. Mitchell, "African American Preaching: The Future of a Rich Tradition," *Interpretation*, October 1999, 381.

8. John Wesley, quoted in Mark A. Noll, *The Rise of Evangelicalism: The Age of Edwards, Whitefield and the Wesleys* (Downers Grove, IL: InterVarsity, 2003), 97.

9. McMickle, "Forbes, James Alexander, Jr.," in *Encyclopedia of African American Christian Heritage*.

10. James A. Forbes, *The Holy Spirit and Preaching* (Nashville: Abingdon, 1989), 19.

CHAPTER 15

The Holy Spirit at Work in Preaching

"You will receive power when the Holy Spirit has come upon you; and you will be my witnesses."—Acts 1:8

Taking seriously the work and power of the Holy Spirit is vital for preachers, because that focus was an essential part of what Jesus told his disciples in Acts 1:6-8. He said, "You will receive power when the Holy Spirit comes on you; and you will be my witnesses in Jerusalem, and in all Judea and Samaria, and to the ends of the earth." They were not to undertake the work of being witnesses until the anointing power of the Holy Spirit had been imparted to them.

The need for that power is no less today, and weak and impotent preaching may be the direct result of preachers who are working with their heads but not with their hearts, and who are more open to the instruction of biblical commentaries and theological journals than they are to the unpredictable and often uncontrollable movement of the Holy Spirit.

William C. Turner, professor of preaching at Duke University Divinity School and an active pastor in Durham, North Carolina, reinforces the central role that the Holy Spirit plays in preaching. He writes, "Preaching relies on the Spirit in every aspect. Only by the Spirit is the word present within the scriptures. The Spirit communicates that living word to the preacher and fashions it as a vital address to the hearer. The Spirit works in sermon preparation and delivery to discern the heart and the situation of those who hear preaching and to guide their spiritual walk."[1]

Thus it is no more possible to understand preaching without reference to the Holy Spirit than it is to understand air travel without reference to lift, thrust, and gravity. You cannot have one without the other. In fact, it is the Holy Spirit who works to give preaching its lift, its thrust, and its ability to break through the gravity of the soul and allow the sermon to take flight.

The work that Jesus assigned to his disciples in the first century, a work that also falls to his disciples in the twenty-first century, cannot be accomplished solely by natural giftedness or even the most rigorous prayerful preparation. As James Forbes observed, "Jesus said to his disciples, 'Without me you can do nothing.' It is understandable then why many burn out so soon. They have sought to do a spiritual task without the aid of the Spirit."[2] Preachers, we need the Holy Spirit if our preaching is to have power and purpose. Every sermon should begin with a whispered prayer that captures the lyrics of this hymn:

> Spirit of the living God, fall afresh on me…
> Melt me, mold me, fill me, use me.
> Spirit of the living God, fall afresh on me.[3]

A First-Century Lesson for Twenty-First-Century Disciples

Another way to think about the important role of the Holy Spirit in preaching is to think about the disciples after they had spent three years with Jesus but before they had received the Holy Spirit. If instruction and theological training alone were sufficient for a career in ministry, then Jesus' first disciples should have been successful from the start. We can safely say that there has never been a better context for theological education than that provided to those twelve disciples of Jesus who spent three years in his presence on a daily basis. They heard him preach. They observed his miracles. They saw the response of people whose lives were touched by encounters with

Jesus. Surely, if anyone was thoroughly trained for ministry, it was those first disciples.

Nevertheless, even for them, three years of theological education in Jesus' company was not sufficient for the work that awaited them. That was made obvious by their actions that began in the Garden of Gethsemane and extended to the days after Jesus' crucifixion. Judas committed suicide, and the remaining eleven disciples concluded that their mission had been stopped and went into hiding (John 20:19). During that brief period of time, Judas betrayed Jesus, three times Peter denied even knowing Jesus, and the others simply ran away and left Jesus alone in the hands of those who would eventually put him to death. Whatever they had learned from Jesus was not enough to hold them firm in their faith when the attacks against Jesus began in Gethsemane.

Those disciples needed something more than a theological education if they were to become those men described in Acts 17:6 who were turning the world upside down (see KJV)! What they needed was the power of the Holy Spirit. That is why, before issuing his charge, Jesus first said to them in Acts 1:8, "You will receive power."

Jesus' promise in Acts 1:8 reiterated what he had told his disciples earlier: "Do not leave Jerusalem, but wait for the gift my Father promised, which you have heard me speak about. For John baptized with water, but in a few days you will be baptized with the Holy Spirit" (Acts 1:4-5). Prior to his crucifixion, Jesus had also mentioned this need for and reliance on the Holy Spirit: "But the Advocate, the Holy Spirit, whom the Father will send in my name, will teach you all things and will remind you of everything I have said to you" (John 14:26). Of course, the dramatic experience of the day of Pentecost described in Acts 2:1-4 was what fully and finally equipped the disciples for the work that lay ahead of them.

Consider Peter in the hours and days after Pentecost. Before Pentecost he was the man who had denied knowing Jesus and who was afraid to show his face in the streets of Jerusalem, much less to preach in public in the name of Jesus. After Pentecost Peter was prepared to go out and preach to the very people who had earlier conspired to have

Jesus crucified. He went out to preach to those from whom he had been hiding only days before. He went out to preach, perhaps encountering one of those to whom he had earlier denied even knowing Jesus.

What was the reason for this dramatic transformation in Peter? One factor must surely have been his face-to-face encounter with the risen Jesus. The other factor was the empowerment that came over him on Pentecost when he was anointed by the Holy Spirit.

In Acts 4:8 Peter and John were brought before the Sanhedrin following the healing of a lame man whom they had encountered as he sat outside the temple. The text begins, "Then Peter, filled with the Holy Spirit, said to them. . . ." Then after he spoke to the Sanhedrin, the text says, "When they saw the courage of Peter and John and realized that they were unschooled, ordinary men. . ." (v. 13). The Greek word for "courage" is another use of the word *parrhesia* as discussed in chapter 5, which means bold or fearless speech. It seems that the source of the *parrhesia* by these unschooled men was not a natural expression by Peter and John, but was the result of the outpouring of the Holy Spirit that had occurred on the day of Pentecost.

The Holy Spirit and Paul

It is not possible to understand the transformation in the life of Saul of Tarsus into the apostle Paul without reference to the transformational work of the Holy Spirit. At the beginning of Acts 9, Saul was "breathing out murderous threats against the Lord's disciples." By verse 28, Saul was "speaking boldly (*parrhesia*) in the name of the Lord." What could account for the sudden and dramatic change in the life of this man and in his attitude and actions toward the followers of Jesus?

Without doubt his encounter with the risen Christ on the Damascus road was a decisive moment in Saul's life. But that was not the moment when he was prepared for the work that lay ahead of him. That moment of readiness did not come until Acts 9:17 when Ananias visited Saul as he sat in a house in Damascus with his eyes blinded by scales. "Then Ananias went to the house and entered it. Placing his hands on

Saul, he said, 'Brother Saul, the Lord—Jesus, who appeared to you on the road as you were coming here—has sent me to you that you may see again and be filled with the Holy Spirit."

For all of Paul's other gifts and attributes, it was not his heritage as a member of the tribe of Benjamin, nor his status as a Pharisee, a student of Gamaliel, nor his Roman citizenship that sustained him through the terrors and travails of his ministry so graphically described in 2 Corinthians 11:23-27. Paul spoke of floggings, shipwrecks, hunger, nakedness, and constant danger wherever he went. The power of the Holy Spirit that worked within him sustained him through all of it. Paul referred to that power in Romans 15:13 when he said, "May the God of hope fill you with all joy and peace as you trust in him, so that you may overflow with hope by the power of the Holy Spirit."

Not Just for Pentecostals

Talking about the power and work of the Holy Spirit may sound strange coming from a Baptist, at least in the ears of some readers. The assumption might be that references to the Holy Spirit are more in the domain of Pentecostal communities of faith. We Baptists talk a lot about the ministries of Word and ordinances, about the authority of Scripture and the separation of church and state. That being said, we must also pay attention to the power and work of the Holy Spirit. Acts 1:8 clearly points out that the power of the Holy Spirit is not the sole prerogative of Pentecostal and charismatic Christians, any more than talking about baptism is the sole prerogative of Baptists.

As William C. Turner also notes, "The work of the Holy Spirit in preaching does not refer to any particular understanding that serves to distinguish some Christians from others."[4] The power of the Holy Spirit is God's gift to the whole church universal and not just to one segment or denominational grouping. Thus this challenge to wait for and rely on the power of the Holy Spirit stands at the very beginning of the call to ministry for the first generation of disciples. The claim of this book is that those words remain in force as a caution to all subsequent generations of preachers no matter what their denominational affiliation might be: "You will receive power when the Holy Spirit comes on you; and you will be my witnesses."

As a seminary graduate, a seminary professor, and now as a seminary president, I can attest to the fact that acquiring a graduate theological degree was not enough to equip and sustain me over the forty-five years of my preaching and teaching ministry. Over and over again, I, too, have had to wait until I "received power."

By the power of the Holy Spirit, we will find the boldness to preach what the world often does not want to hear. By the power of the Holy Spirit, we are sustained in ministry when our attempts to be witnesses are met with scorn or rejected by those to whom we preach in Jerusalem, Judea, Samaria, or to the ends of the earth. By the power of the Holy Spirit, we will find the courage to risk being a *marturia* who dares to engage in *parrhesia*.

Sustained by the Spirit

One could easily make the case that the name of the biblical book in which these words from Jesus appear could be the Acts of the Holy Spirit rather than the Acts of the Apostles. In truth, the Holy Spirit far more than any single human character, including Peter and Paul, is the primary actor in the movement of the church from Jerusalem to Antioch, from Antioch to Ephesus, from Ephesus on to Corinth, and finally from Corinth to Rome. Just as important, it is by the power of the Holy Spirit and not simply by human efforts that the church has continued to exist and the gospel continues to be proclaimed.

Indeed, I would argue that the first role of the Holy Spirit at work in the world is related to the life of the church, Christ's body on earth. Jesus' promise to Peter concerning the future of the church was that "the gates of Hades will not overcome it" (Matthew 16:18). That promise was not based on any assessment of what Peter was going to do in the coming years. That promise was not rooted in how effective Jesus expected the disciples to be when they began their ministry. That promise was rooted in the power and presence of the Holy Spirit that had just revealed to Peter the true identity of Jesus.

In Matthew 16:16, Peter declared to Jesus, "You are the Messiah, the Son of the living God." In response to that, Jesus said, "Blessed are you, Simon son of Jonah, for this was not revealed to you by flesh and blood, but by my Father in heaven. And I tell you that you are Peter, and on this rock I will build my church" (vv. 17-18).

Was the future of the church being entrusted to Peter and thus to those who follow after him as preachers and disciples based solely on individual giftedness? No! The future of the church is guaranteed by the presence of the Holy Spirit so that no matter how badly human beings may mismanage church affairs, misrepresent the gospel message, or misuse and abuse other Christians based on differences in race, gender, sexual orientation, or denominational focus, the Holy Spirit will continue to sustain and direct the church.

Considering how the church has been used and abused over the last two thousand years, it is a miracle that the church, locally and globally, still exists. From the horrific persecution of Christians by the Romans during the first three hundred years of its existence, to the schisms resulting from the Reformation in the sixteenth century, to the impact of steadily increasing secularism in countries that once were solidly identified with Christianity, the church has persisted. To that one could add not only the things done to the church, but also the horrific things done by or with the sanction or silence of the church. That would include the church's role in the Inquisition of the fifteenth and sixteenth centuries in Spain where Jews and Muslims were forced to convert to Christianity or face torture and death.[5] It would include the ruling by Pope Alexander VI in 1497 that essentially allowed for European nations to launch the transatlantic slave trade that resulted in millions of Africans being kidnapped, transported, auctioned off in slave ports throughout the Americas, and then forced into lifelong chattel slavery.[6] It would include the so-called German Church that sought to bring about a synthesis between Nazism and Christianity in the 1930s.[7] It would also include the Dutch Reformed Church in

South Africa, known as the National Party at Prayer, that "formed a close working relationship in the racist design of apartheid."[8]

How is it and why is it that despite the dramatic decline in church attendance in most Western nations including the United States, somehow the name of Jesus continues to be exalted? Despite outward persecution of Christians in places around the world, how is it and why is it that those who believe in the name of Jesus continue to gather in places ranging from storefront churches to great cathedrals and from the inner cities of the United States to the villages and towns of nations in Africa, Asia, and the Caribbean?

The answer is not related solely to the skill and force of our preaching. It has everything to do with the faithfulness of God who continues to keep faith with the church even when so much of our preaching turns from faithfulness to foolishness. That is why Jesus told those first disciples that they should not attempt to begin their ministry until they had received the Holy Spirit.

A Balm in Gilead

So the first role of the Holy Spirit involves the power by which the church remains vital and by which preaching remains effective in a global sense. A second role, however, is just as important as the first. It has to do with our times of discouragement and disappointment as pastors and preachers over the course of our ministries. The Holy Spirit not only empowers and illuminates us in times of action and engagement, but he also supports, sustains, and soothes us when our ministries seem to turn to drudgery and we wonder whether we will be able to carry on.

Not every day in the service of the church will be uplifting and gratifying. Sometimes our sermons will fall on deaf ears of those we were intending to help. We will have church meetings when we will wonder if our congregation members have ever heard or understood a single word we have said to them about the purpose of the church and the expected lifestyle of true Christians. At those times we will need the power of the Holy Spirit to act as a balm to our weary and worn human spirits.

I can remember one evening when I was sitting in a trustee meeting at one of the churches I had served as senior pastor. The manner in which the work of the church was being conducted was marked by the sheer meanness of some toward others in the room and by a general disregard for the sacred duty that had been entrusted to those who had gathered that evening. In a fit of desperation, I asked the chairperson of those proceedings, "What do you think the Lord would say about what you all are saying and doing here tonight?" Far from being troubled by my question, this person responded, "He's not here, so I don't know."

The Lord of the church was not there? The one who promised never to leave us alone was not there? Jesus' promise was that "where two or three gather in my name, there am I with them" (Matthew 18:20). We were gathered in the church building. We were attending to the business of the church. Yet the spirit that prevailed in that room throughout that meeting and many more just like that one was captured in the comments of that church leader: "He's not here."

Those words were entirely appropriate outside the empty tomb of Jesus on the day he was resurrected when the women had gone to the tomb to anoint his body. "He is not here" said the angel. "He has risen, just as he said" (Matthew 28:6). However, when those same words were spoken that night, I discovered that there was no course I had taken in seminary and no lesson I had yet learned in life that was able to keep me from leaving that meeting deeply discouraged.

In that same church I had a conversation with a member of the deacon board, a prominent leadership role in a black Baptist church. I inquired of him why I never saw him in attendance at the midweek prayer service. The deacon board was in charge of that service, and all the other deacons attended on a fairly regular basis. His response to me was as disheartening as the one described above. He said that he no longer attended because "I have paid my dues."

He was not suggesting anything having to do with paying his tithes and offering, which are referred to as "dues" in some churches. Instead, he was suggesting that he had attended the prayer service often enough and long enough in the past that he was now exempting himself from the need for any further participation. Thus one major lay leader in that church assured me that Jesus was not present in the church, and the other one was assuring me that he, a deacon, would not be present there either. "I have paid my dues."

Many ministry encounters over the course of my thirty-five years as a senior pastor were as disheartening as the two just described. Such encounters left me wondering what difference I was making and how I could possibly carry on among people who possessed such feelings about the church. Thanks be to God for the lyrics of "There Is a Balm in Gilead," an anonymous spiritual from the slave era that I turned to on more than a few occasions:

> Sometimes I feel discouraged and think my
> work's in vain,
> But then the Holy Spirit revives my soul again.
> There is a balm in Gilead to make the
> wounded whole,
> There is a balm in Gilead to heal the sin sick soul.

One Moment in Montgomery, Alabama

On an even more serious note, I am mindful of the experience related by Dr. Martin Luther King Jr. during the Montgomery bus boycott of 1955–56 when he acknowledged how the presence of the Holy Spirit revived his spirit late one evening, just days after his home had been fire bombed. He said that it was the assurance of the presence of God with him in that struggle that gave him the courage and faith to carry on.

> I am here taking a stand for what I believe is right. But now I am afraid. The people are looking to me for leadership, and if I stand before them without strength and courage they will falter too. I am at the end of my powers. I have nothing left. I've come to the point where I can't face it alone. At that moment

> I experienced the presence of the Divine as I had never experienced Him before. . . . Almost at once my fears began to go. My uncertainty disappeared. I was ready to face anything.[9]

That experience of "God with us" is crucial for all preachers as we undertake the task of being God's witnesses. Not only does his presence empower us for the work we undertake, but it also sustains us when it seems that the load is more than we can bear. It was the assurance of "God with us" that emboldened Moses when God directed him to go to Pharaoh and lead the people of Israel out of slavery. "Moses said to God, 'Who am I that I should go to Pharaoh and bring the Israelites out of Egypt?' And God said, 'I will be with you'" (Exodus 3:11-12).

This assurance of "God with us" gave courage to Joshua when he was called on to lead the people of Israel across the Jordan River into Canaan after the death of Moses. We read God's encouraging words to Joshua in Joshua 1:6-9: "As I was with Moses, so I will be with you; I will never leave you nor forsake you. Be strong and courageous. . . . Have I not commanded you? Be strong and courageous. Do not be afraid; do not be discouraged, for the LORD your God will be with you wherever you go."

That same assurance of "God with us" extended into the New Testament with the Great Commission found in Matthew 28:19-20: "Go and make disciples of all nations, baptizing them in the name of the Father and of the Son and of the Holy Spirit, and teaching them to obey everything I have commanded you. And surely I am with you always, to the very end of the age."

This is the good news for those who are called to be witnesses for Jesus in Jerusalem, Judea, Samaria, and to the ends of the earth. God will be with you! The Great Commission is not only an assignment to go forth and preach the gospel to the ends of the earth. It is also a promise, a "blessed assurance" that the God who has called us into ministry and Jesus who has given us our marching orders will be with us, with the whole church universal, not only until the end of our lives, but also until the very end of time.

I remember the Sunday morning in 1973 when I was first called on to perform a baptism, which in the Baptist church is done by immersion. I had no idea how to do this, and no course on baptism was offered at my seminary. I was working at Abyssinian Baptist Church in New York City, which was a congregation with about twenty-five hundred persons in attendance each week. The baptismal pool was sunken in the floor just behind the lectern on the pulpit. I was terrified over the prospect of taking someone's life into my hands as I tried to execute the tricky maneuver of first lowering them into the water and then bringing them back up "alive."

I expressed my anxiety to the pastor, Rev. Dr. Samuel Proctor, who had given me this assignment. He smiled at me, placed his hand on my shoulder, and said, "McMickle, I am not sending you out there by yourself. I am going in the pool with you. Together, we will get this job done."

That is what God says to every preacher: "I am not sending you out there by yourself. I am going with you, and together we will get this job done." Go forth as witnesses for Jesus Christ, and the peace, the power, and the presence of the Lord Jesus will be with you. Amen!

NOTES

1. William C. Turner, "Holy Spirit and Preaching," in *Concise Encyclopedia of Preaching*, ed. William H. Willimon and Richard Lischer (Louisville: Westminster John Knox, 1995), 229.

2. James A. Forbes, *The Holy Spirit and Preaching* (Nashville: Abingdon, 1989), 50.

3. Daniel Iverson, "Spirit of the Living God," in *African American Heritage Hymnal* (Chicago: GIA, 2001), 320.

4. Turner, "Holy Spirit and Preaching," 227.

5. F. L. Cross, "Inquisition," in *The Oxford Dictionary of the Christian Church* (New York: Oxford University Press, 1990), 706.

6. James Climent, *Atlas of African American History* (New York: Checkmark, 2001), 15.

7. Cross, "Inquisition," 560.

8. David Chidester, *Christianity: A Global History* (San Francisco: Harper, 2000), 532.

9. Martin Luther King Jr., *Stride toward Freedom: The Montgomery Story* (New York: Harper & Row, 1958), 114–15.

Recommended Resources

Bond, Adam L. *The Imposing Preacher: Samuel DeWitt Proctor and Black Public Faith*. Minneapolis: Fortress Press, 2013.

Brown, Teresa L. Fry. *Can a Sistah Get a Little Help? Encouragement for Black Women in Ministry.* Cleveland: The Pilgrim Press, 2008.

———. *Weary Throats and New Songs: Black Women Proclaiming God's Word.* Nashville: Abingdon Press, 2003.

Brueggemann, Walter. *The Prophetic Imagination.* (2nd ed.) Philadelphia: Fortress Press, 2001.

Cone, James H. *The Cross and the Lynching Tree*. Maryknoll, NY: Orbis Books, 2013.

Dorrien, Gary. *The New Abolition: W. E. B. Du Bois and the Black Social Gospel.* New Haven, CT: Yale University Press, 2015.

Forbes, James A., Jr. *The Holy Spirit and Preaching*. Nashville: Abingdon Press, 1989.

Gilbert, Kenyatta R. *The Journey and Promise of African American Preaching.* Minneapolis: Fortress Press, 2011.

Gutierrez, Gustavo. *A Theology of Liberation: History, Politics, and Salvation.* Maryknoll, NY: Orbis Books, 1988.

Harris, James H. *Preaching Liberation.* Minneapolis: Fortress Press, 1995.

———. *The Word Made Plain: The Power and Promise of Preaching*. Minneapolis: Fortress Press, 2004.

Jennings, Willie James. *The Christian Imagination: Theology and the Origins of Race.* New Haven, CT: Yale University Press, 2011.

King, Martin Luther, Jr. *Stride toward Freedom: The Montgomery Story.* Boston: Beacon Press, 2010. Reprint edition.

Recommended Resources

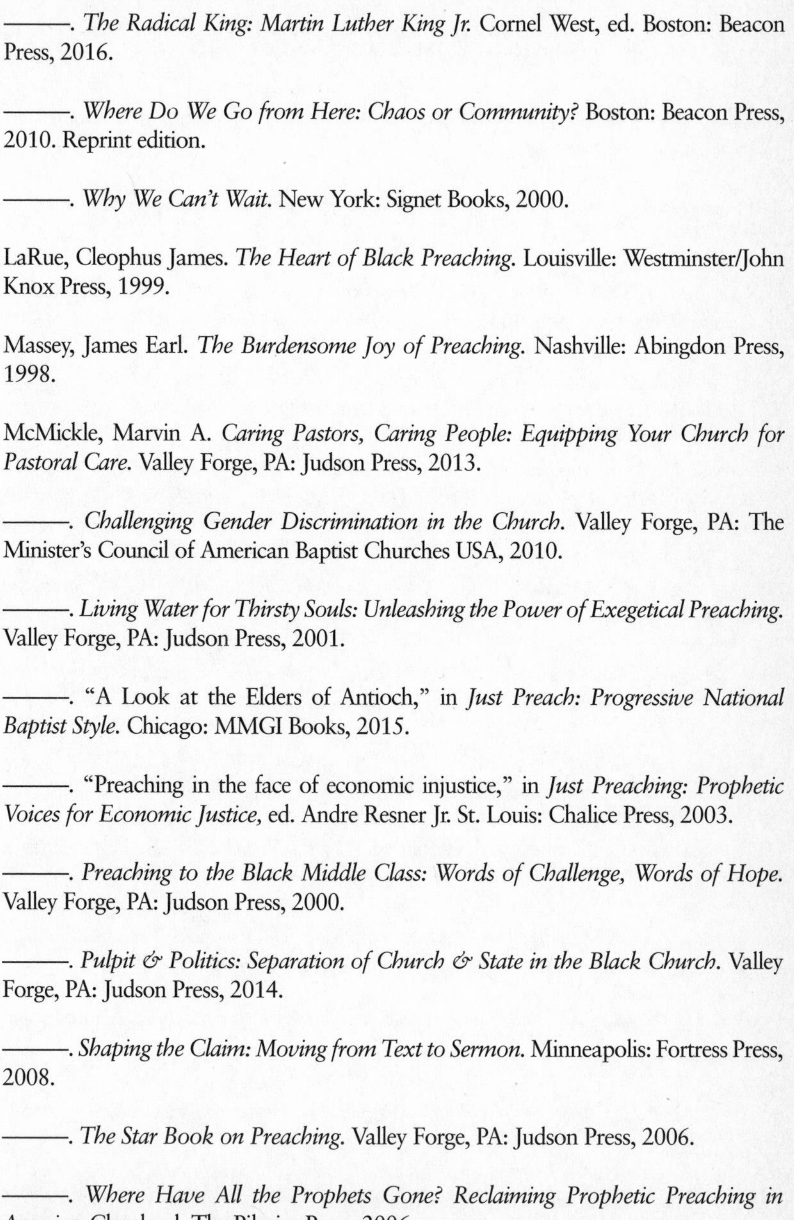

———. *The Radical King: Martin Luther King Jr.* Cornel West, ed. Boston: Beacon Press, 2016.

———. *Where Do We Go from Here: Chaos or Community?* Boston: Beacon Press, 2010. Reprint edition.

———. *Why We Can't Wait.* New York: Signet Books, 2000.

LaRue, Cleophus James. *The Heart of Black Preaching.* Louisville: Westminster/John Knox Press, 1999.

Massey, James Earl. *The Burdensome Joy of Preaching.* Nashville: Abingdon Press, 1998.

McMickle, Marvin A. *Caring Pastors, Caring People: Equipping Your Church for Pastoral Care.* Valley Forge, PA: Judson Press, 2013.

———. *Challenging Gender Discrimination in the Church.* Valley Forge, PA: The Minister's Council of American Baptist Churches USA, 2010.

———. *Living Water for Thirsty Souls: Unleashing the Power of Exegetical Preaching.* Valley Forge, PA: Judson Press, 2001.

———. "A Look at the Elders of Antioch," in *Just Preach: Progressive National Baptist Style.* Chicago: MMGI Books, 2015.

———. "Preaching in the face of economic injustice," in *Just Preaching: Prophetic Voices for Economic Justice,* ed. Andre Resner Jr. St. Louis: Chalice Press, 2003.

———. *Preaching to the Black Middle Class: Words of Challenge, Words of Hope.* Valley Forge, PA: Judson Press, 2000.

———. *Pulpit & Politics: Separation of Church & State in the Black Church.* Valley Forge, PA: Judson Press, 2014.

———. *Shaping the Claim: Moving from Text to Sermon.* Minneapolis: Fortress Press, 2008.

———. *The Star Book on Preaching.* Valley Forge, PA: Judson Press, 2006.

———. *Where Have All the Prophets Gone? Reclaiming Prophetic Preaching in America.* Cleveland: The Pilgrim Press, 2006.

Moss, Otis, III. *Blue Note Preaching in a Post-Soul World: Finding Hope in an Age of Despair.* Louisville: Westminster/John Knox Press, 2015.

Niebuhr, Reinhold. *Leaves from the Notebook of a Tamed Cynic.* Louisville: Westminster/John Knox Press, 1990.

Powery, Luke A. *Dem Dry Bones: Preaching, Death, and Hope.* Minneapolis: Fortress Press, 2012.

Proctor, Samuel DeWitt. *The Certain Sound of the Trumpet: Crafting a Sermon of Authority.* Valley Forge, PA: Judson Press, 1994.

Riggs, Marcia Y., ed. *Can I Get a Witness? Prophetic Religious Voices of African American Women.* Maryknoll, NY: Orbis Books, 1997.

Simmons, Martha, and Frank A. Thomas, eds. *Preaching with Sacred Fire: An Anthology of African American Sermons, 1750 to the Present.* New York: Norton, 2010.

Smith, Gary Scott. *Religion in the Oval Office: The Religious Lives of American Presidents.* New York: Oxford Press, 2015.

Stroud, Dean G., ed. *Preaching in Hitler's Shadow: Sermons of Resistance in the Third Reich.* Grand Rapids: Eerdmans Press, 2013.

Taylor, Gardner C. *The Words of Gardner Taylor, Vols. 1–6.* Edward L. Taylor, compiler. Valley Forge, PA: Judson Press, 2002.

Ward, James, and Christine Ward, *Preaching from the Prophets.* Nashville: Abingdon Press, 1995.

Washington, James Melvin, ed. *A Testament of Hope: The Essential Writings of Martin Luther King Jr.* New York: HarperOne, 2003. Reprint edition.

West, Cornel. *Democracy Matters: Winning the Fight against Imperialism.* New York: Penguin Press, 2005.

——— and Christa Buschendorf. *Black Prophetic Fire.* Boston: Beacon Press, 2015.

Williams, Reggie L. *Bonhoeffer's Black Jesus: Harlem Renaissance Theology, and an Ethic of Resistance.* Waco, TX: Baylor University Press, 2014.

Index

Index